Drug Legalization

Karen F. Balkin, *Book Editor*

Bruce Glassman, *Vice President*
Bonnie Szumski, *Publisher*
Helen Cothran, *Managing Editor*

CURRENT CONTROVERSIES

GREENHAVEN PRESS
An imprint of Thomson Gale, a part of The Thomson Corporation

THOMSON
——★——™
GALE

Detroit • New York • San Francisco • San Diego • New Haven, Conn.
Waterville, Maine • London • Munich

THOMSON

GALE

™

LIBRARY OF CONGRESS CATALOGING-IN-PUBLICATION DATA

Drug legalization / Karen F. Balkin, book editor.
   p. cm. — (Current controversies)
Includes bibliographical references and index.
ISBN 0-7377-2202-9 (lib. : alk. paper) — ISBN 0-7377-2203-7 (pbk. : alk. paper)
   1. Drug legalization—United States. 2. Narcotics, Control of—United States.
I. Balkin, Karen, 1949– . II. Series.
HV5825.D77663 2005
364.1'77—dc22   2004059684

Printed in the United States of America

Contents

Chapter 2: Should U.S. Drug Policies Be Liberalized?

Yes: U.S. Drug Policies Should Be Liberalized

decline, and police will no longer badger citizens living in poor communities.

No: U.S. Drug Policies Should Not Be Liberalized

deterred from crime if they are certain to receive severe punishment regardless of the judge who hears their case.

Drug Policies Should Be Not Based on Harm Reduction

Chapter 3: Should Marijuana Laws Be Relaxed?

Yes: Marijuana Laws Should Be Relaxed

No: Marijuana Laws Should Not Be Relaxed

Foreword

By definition, controversies are "discussions of questions in which opposing opinions clash" (Webster's Twentieth Century Dictionary Unabridged). Few would deny that controversies are a pervasive part of the human condition and exist on virtually every level of human enterprise. Controversies transpire between individuals and among groups, within nations and between nations. Controversies supply the grist necessary for progress by providing challenges and challengers to the status quo. They also create atmospheres where strife and warfare can flourish. A world without controversies would be a peaceful world; but it also would be, by and large, static and prosaic.

The Series' Purpose

The purpose of the Current Controversies series is to explore many of the social, political, and economic controversies dominating the national and international scenes today. Titles selected for inclusion in the series are highly focused and specific. For example, from the larger category of criminal justice, Current Controversies deals with specific topics such as police brutality, gun control, white collar crime, and others. The debates in Current Controversies also are presented in a useful, timeless fashion. Articles and book excerpts included in each title are selected if they contribute valuable, long-range ideas to the overall debate. And wherever possible, current information is enhanced with historical documents and other relevant materials. Thus, while individual titles are current in focus, every effort is made to ensure that they will not become quickly outdated. Books in the Current Controversies series will remain important resources for librarians, teachers, and students for many years.

In addition to keeping the titles focused and specific, great care is taken in the editorial format of each book in the series. Book introductions and chapter prefaces are offered to provide background material for readers. Chapters are organized around several key questions that are answered with diverse opinions representing all points on the political spectrum. Materials in each chapter include opinions in which authors clearly disagree as well as alternative opinions in which authors may agree on a broader issue but disagree on the possible solutions. In this way, the content of each volume in Current Controversies mirrors the mosaic of opinions encountered in society. Readers will quickly realize that there are many viable answers to these complex issues. By questioning each author's conclusions, students and casual readers can begin to develop the critical thinking skills so important to evaluating opinionated material.

Current Controversies is also ideal for controlled research. Each anthology in the series is composed of primary sources taken from a wide gamut of informational categories including periodicals, newspapers, books, United States and foreign government documents, and the publications of private and public organizations. Readers will find factual support for reports, debates, and research papers covering all areas of important issues. In addition, an annotated table of contents, an index, a book and periodical bibliography, and a list of organizations to contact are included in each book to expedite further research.

Perhaps more than ever before in history, people are confronted with diverse and contradictory information. During the Persian Gulf War, for example, the public was not only treated to minute-to-minute coverage of the war, it was also inundated with critiques of the coverage and countless analyses of the factors motivating U.S. involvement. Being able to sort through the plethora of opinions accompanying today's major issues, and to draw one's own conclusions, can be a complicated and frustrating struggle. It is the editors' hope that Current Controversies will help readers with this struggle.

Greenhaven Press anthologies primarily consist of previously published material taken from a variety of sources, including periodicals, books, scholarly journals, newspapers, government documents, and position papers from private and public organizations. These original sources are often edited for length and to ensure their accessibility for a young adult audience. The anthology editors also change the original titles of these works in order to clearly present the main thesis of each viewpoint and to explicitly indicate the opinion presented in the viewpoint. These alterations are made in consideration of both the reading and comprehension levels of a young adult audience. Every effort is made to ensure that Greenhaven Press accurately reflects the original intent of the authors included in this anthology.

"Rather than protecting the public from potential harm, criminalizing a drug may instead prohibit doctors and other medical professionals from prescribing the drug for legitimate medical use or from doing necessary research."

Introduction

The Drug Enforcement Administration (DEA) maintains that the purpose of declaring a drug illegal is to deter recreational use of that drug and thus protect the public from the harmful effects of its use. However, rather than protecting the public from potential harm, criminalizing a drug may instead prohibit doctors and other medical professionals from prescribing the drug for legitimate medical use or from doing necessary research. Ecstasy (MDMA) became illegal when the Federal Controlled Substances Analog Act of 1986—sometimes called the Designer Drug Act—was passed. This broadly written law criminalized many of the club drugs popular in the 1970s and 1980s. DEA administrators who were committed to vigorously waging the war on drugs initially claimed to be ignorant of any therapeutic uses for MDMA in the treatment of Post-Traumatic Stress Disorder (PTSD) although such uses were well documented in scientific literature beginning in 1973. According to drug researcher Marsha Rosenbaum and head of the Multidisciplinary Association for Psychedelic Studies (MAPS) Rick Doblin, the DEA's criminalization of Ecstasy did little to deter its recreational use. In fact, criminalization of Ecstasy had the opposite effect—it increased the demand and raised the drug's street price. However, almost all physicians and therapists, wary of prosecution and professional censure, abandoned their therapeutic use of Ecstasy. Rosenbaum and Doblin note in *The Drug Legalization Debate*, "Ultimately, criminalization had little deterrent effect on the recreational [Ecstasy] user population while substantially reducing its therapeutic use. Perhaps the most profound effect of MDMA's illegality has been the curtailment of scientific research and experimentation with a drug that held therapeutic potential."

Although Ecstasy was first synthesized in Germany in 1912 by Merck Pharmaceuticals, the drug was virtually unknown in the United States and Europe for several decades. It was not until 1973, when literature mentioning the Army's Chemical Center toxicology research done in the early 1950s was published, that researchers became interested in Ecstasy. A small group of doctors began using the drug therapeutically because they found that it reduced their patients' fears and allowed suffering individuals to experience emotions without feeling threatened. These early researchers noticed no harmful physical effects of the drug in this controlled setting. Scientists estimate that about five hundred thousand doses of Ecstasy were consumed between the early 1970s and early 1980s, most of them in therapeutic settings. However, by 1983 a Los Angeles distributor seeking to enlarge his market beyond the therapeutic community coined the street name "Ecstasy" for the not-yet-illegal MDMA. The distributor is said to have commented, "'Empathy' would be more appropriate, but how many people know what it means?" About the same time, distributors in Texas started openly selling the drug as Ecstasy in clubs and bars in Dallas. Ecstasy use became recreational rather than therapeutic, but still was not widespread.

The DEA's Drug Control Section began to investigate Ecstasy sales and use in 1982. By 1984 Texas senator Lloyd Bentsen, disturbed by open sales of the drug in upscale bars and clubs, requested that the DEA determine the potential for abuse and harmfulness or acceptable medical use of the drug. The DEA immediately filed a formal notice in the Federal Register of its intent to make Ecstasy a Schedule I drug. According to the Controlled Substances Act of 1970, drugs placed in the Schedule I category must have a high potential for abuse, no accepted medical use, and no accepted safety levels for use under medical supervision. The only legal uses of a Schedule I drug are for limited medical or scientific purposes specifically—and very rarely—authorized by federal authorities. Psychiatrists and therapists all over the country formally requested that the DEA hold hearings before classifying MDMA as a Schedule I drug. Media interest in Ecstasy grew as respected professionals came forward to mount a legal defense for medical use of the drug.

Advocates of Ecstasy argued that it should be made a Schedule III drug so that it could still be used for medical treatment and research (all recreational use would be criminalized). Their attorney asserted that, based on the minimal number of mentions of Ecstasy in the National Institute on Drug Abuse's Drug Warning Network at the time of the hearings (1984), the drug did not have a high potential for abuse but rather a medium or low potential. Moreover, many psychiatrists testified that the drug did have acceptable medical uses and that three separate studies supported the claim that the drug had accepted safety levels for use under medical supervision. As further evidence of the safety of Ecstasy under medical supervision, the attorney cited the absence of alleged harm to any patient who used the drug. The DEA's chief attorney countered these arguments with three basic allegations. He claimed that a drug did not actually have to cause harm to anyone before being placed in the Schedule I category, it simply needed to have a high potential for abuse. Further, he insisted that since only the Food and Drug Administration (FDA) could accept a drug for medical use, a drug that did not have FDA approval could not have accepted safety levels under medical supervision. In May 1986—after two years of hearings— DEA administrative judge Francis L. Young recommended that Ecstasy be placed in Schedule III. Judge Young's ruling notwithstanding, the DEA placed the drug in Schedule I. Advocates for Ecstasy argue that the DEA's insistence on Schedule I status for the drug reflects the war on drugs' message that all illegal drugs are inherently harmful and should be prohibited. Judge Young called the DEA's refusal to accept the potential medical use of Schedule I drugs "disingenuous, arbitrary, and capricious."

The Ecstasy scheduling hearings received extensive media attention. The press had been fascinated with the drug since its prescheduling days. The name Ecstasy; the idea that it was used by young, affluent, white patrons of the trendy bar and club scene; and the fact that some of its most ardent supporters were medical professionals made Ecstasy stories irresistible. The free publicity helped build recreational interest in the drug among nontherapeutically oriented professionals, students, and yuppies. Researchers maintain that demand for Ecstasy increased due to media attention, and the price increased due to criminalization. The average price per dose went from ten dollars to fifteen dollars after Ecstasy was placed in Schedule I; consumption increased from 200,000 to 400,000 doses per month. A recreational, post-1985 Ecstasy user indicated that criminalization made MDMA more exciting. He said, "If it's illegal, it's probably good." While scheduling did not deter recreational users, its effect on the therapeutic community was devastating. Almost all therapists in the United States stopped using Ecstasy rather than risk losing their licenses and their careers. However, therapeutic Ecstasy use and research continued in other parts of the world. For example, psychiatrists and researchers in Israel are currently studying the use of the drug to help sufferers of PTSD due to terrorist attacks.

Doblin at MAPS and other scientists continued to pressure the government to reschedule Ecstasy and allow further research into the therapeutic potential—as well as the dangers—of this drug. The FDA, an agency made up of scientists whose mission is to help develop medicine, not eradicate illegal drugs, now seems more open to the concept that a given compound need not be entirely good or evil. Psychiatrist Michael Mithoefer of the Medical University of South Carolina received FDA permission for a small (twenty patient) study on the use of Ecstasy in sufferers of PTSD. The initial goal of Mithoefer's study, which began April 16, 2004, is to see if the drug is safe for people who have never previously used it. He said he does not expect definitive answers from this small sample. Mithoefer commented, "This is a pilot study to see if there's any suggestion that MDMA can be useful." Doblin concurs, "We are at the forefront of studying risk and benefit. We hope that there's enough respect for science that people will judge us on the basis of our data." According to FDA pharmacologist Katherine Bonson, that is exactly what her agency wants. She said at an Ecstasy conference organized by the Lindesmith Center in February 2004, "We really need to see something. So if you give us data that makes it look like a good drug, we'll approve the drug." If Ecstasy wins FDA approval, advocates insist that the DEA will have no choice but to reschedule the drug so it can be used by medical professionals.

The legalization of drugs such as Ecstasy for medical purposes is often in direct opposition to the war on drugs' concept of a drug-free society. Central to the issue of drug legalization is the effect such legislation would have on drug use. As the case of Ecstasy shows, prohibition—the opposite strategy—can have the unintended effect of increasing drug use. Such surprises make legislators understandably reluctant to change the legal status of certain drugs. The uncertainty about what can happen when drugs are legalized or prohibited creates an environment that doubtless encourages the status quo.

Chapter 1

Is Prohibition an Effective Strategy in the War on Drugs?

Chapter Preface

Conducting the war on drugs is extremely expensive. One of the ways that the government generates revenue for this war is through civil asset forfeiture laws. The Fifth Amendment to the Constitution guarantees that no one will "be deprived of . . . property, without due process of law." However, the U.S. Supreme Court has ruled that under certain circumstances, property can be confiscated and sold by the federal government without any arrest, conviction, or due process for the owner. This is known as civil asset forfeiture, and it has become one of the principal weapons in the war on drugs.

Originally designed to punish major drug traffickers and members of organized crime who were making millions of dollars from the sale of illegal drugs, civil asset forfeiture also affects low-level drug dealers and innocent citizens alike. Individuals accused—but not arrested or convicted—of drug-related crimes can lose cash, cars, and other property through this aggressive pursuit of drug prohibition. Critics of civil asset forfeiture, including such disparate organizations as the American Civil Liberties Union (ACLU) and the National Rifle Association (NRA), claim that it deprives defendants and property owners of the protections that are critical to the U.S. criminal justice system and thus abridges their civil liberties. Alan Schlosser, managing attorney for the Northern California ACLU argues, "The irresistible attraction of forfeiture as a law enforcement weapon is that it provides an end run around the procedural safeguards of the criminal justice system."

In an effort to narrow the scope of federal forfeiture laws and offer property owners greater procedural protection, a bipartisan Congressional coalition crafted the Civil Asset Forfeiture Reform Act of 2000. Conservative congressman Henry Hyde, author of the act, explains why the bill was necessary:

> Enlisted twenty-five years ago as a legitimate auxiliary tool in the so-called war on drugs, the legal doctrines of civil asset forfeiture have since been perverted to serve an entirely improper function in our democratic system of government—official confiscation from innocent citizens of their money and property with little or no due process of law or judicial protection.

State and federal governments profit from civil asset forfeiture laws. Most states have laws directing that asset forfeiture profits go to education rather than back into law enforcement. However, many law enforcement agencies have found a way to circumvent their own state's laws using the federal government. When police seize cash or assets, instead of going to state court, they call a federal agency—such as the Drug Enforcement Administration (DEA). The DEA accepts the seizure, keeps a portion of the money, and gives the rest back to the police. Because the DEA is called in, the seizure is considered a federal case and bypasses state courts—and state laws—completely. This is not illegal, and most states insist that their police forces need the money to fight the war on drugs.

Controversial because they threaten civil liberties and create a conflict of interest for police departments, civil asset forfeiture laws are just one of the weapons in the government's war on drugs. Authors in the following chapter debate the effectiveness of prohibition as a strategy to fight drug abuse.

Drug Prohibition Is Effective

by John P. Walters

About the author: *John P. Walters is director of the Office of National Drug Control Policy, a position often referred to as "drug czar."*

The charge that "nothing works" in the fight against illegal drugs has led some people to grasp at an apparent solution: legalize drugs. They will have taken false heart from news from Britain [in July 2002], where the government acted to downgrade the possession of cannabis to the status of a non-arrestable offense.

According to the logic of the legalizers, it's laws against drug use, not the drugs themselves, that do the greatest harm. The real problem, according to them, is not that the young use drugs, but that drug laws distort supply and demand. Violent cartels arise, consumers overpay for a product of unknown quality, and society suffers when the law restrains those who "harm no one but themselves."

Better, the argument goes, for the government to control the trade in narcotics. That should drive down the prices (heroin would be "no more expensive than lettuce," argues one proponent), eliminate violence, provide tax revenue, reduce prison crowding, and foster supervised injection facilities.

Sounds good. But is it realistic? The softest spot in this line of reasoning is the analogy with alcohol abuse. The argument goes roughly like this: "Alcohol is legal. Alcohol can be abused. Therefore, cocaine should be legal." Their strongest argument, by contrast, is that prohibition produces more costs than benefits, while legalized drugs provide more benefits than costs.

Many Criminals Use Drugs

But legalizers overstate the social costs of prohibition, just as they understate the social costs of legalization. Take the statistic that more than 1.5 million Americans are arrested every year for drug crimes. Legalizers would have us believe that otherwise innocent people are being sent to prison (displacing "true" criminals) for merely toking up. But only a fraction of these arrestees are ever sentenced to prison. And there should be little question that most of those sentenced have earned their place behind bars.

Some 24% of state prison drug offenders are violent recidivists, while 83% have prior criminal histories. Only 17% are in prison for "first time offenses," while nominal "low-level" offenders are often criminals who plea-bargain to escape more serious charges. The reality is that a high percentage of all criminals, regardless of the offense, use drugs. In New York, 79% of those arrested for any crime tested positive for drugs.

"Legalizers overstate the social costs of prohibition, just as they understate the social costs of legalization."

Drug abuse alone cost an estimated $55 billion in 1998 (excluding criminal justice costs), and deaths directly related to drug use have more than doubled since 1980. Would increasing this toll make for a healthier America? Legalization, by removing penalties and reducing price, would increase drug demand. Make something easier and cheaper to obtain, and you increase the number of people who will try it. Legalizers love to point out that the Dutch decriminalized marijuana in 1976, with little initial impact. But as drugs gained social acceptance, use increased consistently and sharply, with a 300% rise in use by 1996 among 18–20 year-olds.

Britain, too, provides an instructive example. When British physicians were allowed to prescribe heroin to certain addicts, the number skyrocketed. From 68 British addicts in the program in 1960, the problem exploded to an estimated 20,000 heroin users in London alone by 1982.

The idea that we can "solve" our complex drug problem by simply legalizing drugs raises more questions than it answers. For instance, what happens to the citizenship of those legally addicted? Will they have their full civil rights, such as voting? Can they be employed as school bus drivers? Nurses? What of a woman, legally addicted to cocaine, who becomes pregnant? Should she be constrained by the very government that provides for her habit?

Won't some addicts seek larger doses than those medically prescribed? Or seek to profit by selling their allotment to others, including minors? And what about those promised tax revenues—how do they materialize? As it is, European drug clinics aren't filled with productive citizens, but rather with demoralized zombies seeking a daily fix. Won't drugs become a disability entitlement?

Drug Laws Are Not the Problem

Will legalization eliminate violence? The *New England Journal of Medicine* reported in 1999 on the risks for women injured in domestic violence. The most striking factor was a partner who used cocaine, which increased risk more than four times. That violence is associated not with drug laws, but with the drug. A 1999 report from the Department of Health and Human Services showed that two million children live with a parent who has a drug problem. Studies indicate that up to 80% of our child welfare caseload involves caregivers who abuse substances. Drug users do not harm only themselves.

Legalizers like to argue that government-supervised production and distribution of addictive drugs will eliminate the dangers attributed to drug prohibition. But when analyzing this "harm reduction" argument, consider the abuse of the opiate OxyContin, which has resulted in numerous deaths, physicians facing criminal charges, and addicts attacking pharmacies. OxyContin is a legally prescribed substance, with appropriate medical uses—that is, it satisfies those conditions legalizers envision for cocaine and heroin. The point is clear: The laws are not the problem.

Former Sen. Daniel Patrick Moynihan observed that drugs place us in a dilemma: "We are required to choose between a crime problem and a public health problem." Legalization is a dangerous mirage. To address a crime problem, we are asked to accept a public health crisis. Yet if we were to surrender, we would surely face both problems—intensified.

The War on Drugs Should Focus on Reducing the Drug Supply

by Rogelio E. Guevara

About the author: *Rogelio E. Guevara is chief of operations for the Drug Enforcement Administration (DEA).*

The Drug Enforcement Administration (DEA) employs a universal approach in enforcing the provisions of the controlled substances and chemical diversion trafficking laws and regulations of the United States. As a single mission agency, DEA is strictly focused on reducing drug trafficking and abuse in America, which continues to bring misery to America's cities and children. DEA's strong presence, both domestically and internationally, enables the agency to focus its resources on the most substantial drug trafficking organizations impacting the United States.

DEA's primary duty is to provide the best drug law enforcement agency to the American people, thereby reducing America's abuse of illicit drugs. America's efforts to reduce drug abuse have resulted in various successes. However, there is still much work to be done. Worldwide drug trafficking generates billions of dollars in illicit proceeds, sometimes used by criminal and terrorist organizations to carry out horrific acts against law-abiding citizens and established governments, including the United States.

To combat America's drug threat, DEA has instituted a number of strategic enforcement and intelligence programs and initiatives including:

• DEA's Priority Drug Trafficking Organization (PDTO) initiative will focus substantial resources in its 21 nationwide field divisions on local, regional, national and international drug organizations significantly impacting the drug supply;

• DEA's Intelligence Division vigorously focuses on intelligence driven targeting, in support of DEA's strategic goal to identify, target, investigate, disrupt

Rogelio E. Guevara, testimony before the U.S. House Subcommittee on Crime, Terrorism, and Homeland Security, House Judiciary Committee, Washington, DC, May 6, 2003.

and dismantle the most substantial drug trafficking groups;

• DEA's Operational Support Division has implemented significant changes regarding their management, technology, facilities and oversight, which has resulted in cost effective operations [and] more efficient, expeditious and systematically run programs;

• DEA's Demand Reduction Program, an element of our enforcement strategy, complements DEA's investigative operations by educating the media, law enforcement, the public at large and anti-drug groups, through initiatives such as Operation X-Out and Meth in America: Not in Our Town. . . .

The mission of DEA is to enforce the Controlled Substances laws and regulations of the United States and to bring to the criminal and civil justice system of the U.S., or any other competent jurisdiction, those organizations involved in the growing, manufacturing or distribution of controlled substances appearing in or destined for illicit traffic in the United States.

The Department of Justice Strategy

On March 19, 2002, the Attorney General announced a six-part drug strategy for the Department of Justice, which was squarely focused on reducing the availability of illegal drugs to Americans. Given the inherent relationship between drug supply and drug demand, the Department's strategy plays a pivotal role in achieving the President's overall goal of reducing drug use. Specifically, the Attorney General's strategy mounts a comprehensive multi-level attack on drug trafficking and money laundering organizations, as the central means of accomplishing Priority III of the President's National Drug Control Strategy—Disrupting the Drug Market. That strategy consists of six key elements:

> *"[The] DEA is strictly focused on reducing drug trafficking and abuse in America."*

Reduce the supply of drugs available in the United States by 10 percent.

Through the Organized Crime Drug Enforcement Task Force (OCDETF), engage the talent and resources of all of the federal law enforcement agencies to identify and target the major trafficking organizations responsible for the U.S. drug supply across the nine OCDETF regions.

Create, for the first time, a unified national list of drug organization targets—the Consolidated Priority Organization Target (CPOT) list—developed collaboratively by federal enforcement agencies.

Emphasize financial investigations to eliminate the infrastructure of drug organizations and remove the profits from these organizations through asset forfeiture.

Undertake a substantial redirection of resources to the drug importation and bulk distribution "hot spots" so that federal resources are realigned, commensurate with the current drug threat.

Conduct expanded investigations that move simultaneously in many districts against the different parts of the targeted organizations in order to eliminate their ability to supply illegal drugs to Americans.

DEA's Strategy

To accomplish this mission, DEA has specific long-range goals and objectives to target and immobilize major drug trafficking organizations operating at all levels of the drug trade. DEA directs investigative resources toward every angle of drug trafficking groups, using both traditional and innovative drug control approaches. This overall strategic approach is based on the recognition that the major drug traffickers, operating both internationally and domestically, have insulated themselves from the drug distribution networks but remain closely linked to the proceeds of their trade. Consequently, the identification and forfeiture of illicitly derived assets is a powerful means to successfully destroy the economic base of the drug trafficking organization, as well as a means of proving a connection between violators and a criminal drug conspiracy at the time of prosecution.

DEA's investigative efforts continue to be directed against major international drug trafficking organizations and their facilitators at every juncture in their operations—from the cultivation and production of drugs in foreign countries, to their passage through the transit zone, and eventual distribution on the streets of America's communities. DEA's Strategic Plan takes into account its management infrastructure and the current drug trafficking situation affecting the United States and works to identify the characteristics and exploit the vulnerabilities of all three levels of the drug trade. By focusing directly on the agency's investigative priority targeting system, DEA responds to each of the following levels, simultaneously:

International Targets: DEA will eliminate the power and control of the major drug trafficking organizations and dismantle their infrastructure by disrupting and dismantling the operations of their supporting organizations that provide raw materials and chemicals, produce and transship illicit drugs, launder money worldwide and halt the operations of their surrogates in the United States.

National/Regional Targets: DEA will continue an aggressive and balanced enforcement program with a multijurisdictional approach designed to help focus Federal and interagency resources on illegal drug traffickers, their organizations and key members who have control of an area within a region of the United States, and the drugs and assets involved in their activities.

Local Initiatives: DEA will continue to assist States and localities in attacking the violence that plagues our cities, rural areas and small towns to protect our citizens from the impact of drugs and help restore a positive quality of life. (DEA considers this an important part of its overall strategy to complement the state and local efforts with specialized programs that bring DEA's intelligence, expertise and leadership into specific trouble spots throughout the nation.)

Management and Infrastructure: DEA will develop a secure and effective infrastructure and ensure that management oversight provides DEA personnel with the tools necessary to get the job done. DEA must also have the systems and structures to monitor its programs carefully, comply with reporting and information sharing requirements and manage its finite resources efficiently.

Domestic Drug Trends and Trafficking Patterns

The drug market in the United States is one of the most diverse and profitable illegal enterprises in the world. Drug trafficking organizations exploit legal and geographic vulnerabilities and demonstrate a high degree of flexibility in their operations to evade law enforcement. Consequently, the deployment of DEA's counter-drug resources remains flexible in order to respond to the dynamics of the illicit drug trade.

Marijuana is the most widely abused and most readily available illicit drug in the United States and is available in varying degrees in every state in the union. Although precise estimates for the source of marijuana consumed in the United States cannot be made, marijuana smuggled into the United States, whether grown in Mexico, Colombia, or Jamaica, accounts for a large share of the marijuana available in the United States. High potency marijuana also enters the country from Canada. However, based on eradication statistics, domestic production is increasing. In the United States, cannabis is mainly cultivated in remote locations and frequently on public lands.

Mexican-based traffickers, with extensive networks in the United States, control poly-drug smuggling and wholesale distribution from hub cities to retail markets throughout the country. Mexican marijuana primarily enters the United States through entry points along the Southwest Border. Multi-ton amounts are often smuggled in tractor-trailers.

Colombian organizations control the worldwide supply of cocaine and move cocaine by land, sea and air. These groups have ceded an increasing role in cocaine trafficking to Mexican-based trafficking organizations that smuggle cocaine from Mexico into the United States. Colombian traffickers control wholesale-level cocaine distribution in the Northeast, while Mexican traffickers control distribution throughout the West and Midwest.

Southeastern ports, most notably Miami, Houston and New Orleans, are the primary maritime arrival zones, while cities along the Southwest Border are arrival and distribution points for overland cocaine movement. Chicago is a critical distribution hub for Mexican-based cocaine trafficking organizations, while New York City remains under the control of Colombian-based organizations.

Four Sources of Heroin

Heroin is readily available in many U.S. cities, as evidenced by its high purity at the street-level. Heroin from the four source areas—South America, Southeast Asia, Mexico and Southwest Asia—reaches the United States. Virtually all heroin produced in Mexico and South America is destined for the U.S. market.

Since the mid-1990s, when Colombian traffickers penetrated the market with high-purity, low-priced heroin, South American heroin has dominated the market in the eastern half of the country. Couriers traveling on commercial airlines are the primary smugglers of Colombian heroin to the United States, and their primary entry points are Miami and New York. Mexican heroin continues to dominate the market west of the Mississippi and is generally smuggled overland through Southwest Border states. Southwest and Southeast Asian heroin are available in the Northeast and North Central sections of the country.

Domestic methamphetamine production, trafficking and abuse are concentrated in the western, southwestern and mid-western sections of the United States. Although outlaw motorcycle gangs traditionally controlled methamphetamine production and trafficking, criminal groups composed of Mexicans and Mexican-Americans now produce most of the domestic methamphetamine. Methamphetamine produced in large-capacity laboratories, primarily located in the western and southwestern United States or Mexico, is transported via passenger vehicle across the country. Many of the largest methamphetamine laboratories can be found in California. Thousands of small independent laboratories, especially in the Midwest, produce gram or ounce quantities of methamphetamine, primarily for personal use or small-scale distribution.

> *"[The DEA's goal is to] reduce the supply of drugs available in the United States by 10 percent."*

MDMA (Ecstasy, XTC, Hug Drug), a hallucinogen with stimulant properties that is primarily produced in the Netherlands, remains the most prevalent of all the so-called club drugs in the United States. Often distributed at nightclubs and "raves," all-night dance parties, it is widely abused by middle-class teenagers and young professionals. In Fiscal Year [FY] 2001, the U.S. Customs Service seized approximately 7.2 million MDMA tablets. MDMA tablets smuggled into the United States from Europe are destined for distribution primarily in New York City, Miami and Los Angeles.

Other Dangerous Drugs

Often referred to as designer or club drugs, these illicit drugs, primarily synthetic, vary widely in their psychoactive effects and are most commonly encountered at nightclubs and "raves." In addition to MDMA, the most widely available club drugs include the depressant/predatory drug GHB and the hallucinogens PCP and LSD. These drugs have gained popularity principally due to the false perception that they are not as harmful, nor as addictive, as mainstream drugs such as cocaine and methamphetamine. The United Nations recently stated that, if current trends continue, "synthetic drugs" like MDMA and predatory drugs will be the number one drug problem in the world.

The synthetic substances, 5-MeO-DIPT, known by the street name "Foxy" or "Foxy Methox," and alpha-methyltryptamine (AMT), are being reported as new drugs of abuse in limited areas of the United States.

These substances, which produce hallucinogenic effects, are indicative of a trend in which many non-controlled synthetic substances are sold to capitalize on the current popularity of club drugs, especially MDMA. Recognizing this problem, DEA temporarily placed these two drugs in Schedule I, in April 2003.

Domestic DEA Operations

In 1973, DEA was comprised of 2,868 Special Agents and support personnel. Today, DEA has 8,475 authorized positions worldwide, including Special Agents, Intelligence Analysts, Diversion Investigators and Chemists. DEA's first budget was $74 million. In 2003, our enacted appropriation was $1.6 billion. Domestically, DEA maintains 21 Field Divisions, with offices in every State and the Special Operations Division at DEA Headquarters. At the core of DEA's operational successes lie specific programs and initiatives to combat America's greatest drug trafficking threats.

In April 2001, DEA initiated the Priority Drug Trafficking Organization (PDTO) initiative. The PDTO system was developed as a clear and specific enforcement objective targeting drug trafficking organizations by disrupting the networks that link them. PDTOs are regionally identified by field divisions as investigations of drug trafficking organizations that control the highest known level of the drug trafficking hierarchy.

PDTO investigations must reveal that the organization is stable and deals violently with members of its organization, competitors, clients, law enforcement officers, or citizens. Large-scale drug trafficking organizations use sophisticated techniques such as business fronts and the use of the Internet to facilitate their criminal activity. Their methodology consists of money laundering schemes, established lines of command and control, establishment of drug manufacturing, importation, transportation and distribution cells and diversion of controlled substances or precursor chemicals.

Since April 2001, DEA has initiated 1,276 PDTO cases. Of those cases, 158 organizations have been disrupted and 187 have been dismantled. Currently, there are 911 open, active PDTO investigations within DEA.

Concentration of Federal Resources

The greatest impact in combating drug trafficking organizations has been made when the full concentration of federal resources are brought to bear on these individuals and organizations through the efforts of the Department of Justice's OCDETF program. Just as when the program was originally initiated, DEA remains the leading initiator of OCDETF cases within the federal law enforcement community. The OCDETF program functions through the investigative, intelligence and support staffs of DEA; the Federal Bureau of Investigation; the Bureau of Alcohol, Tobacco, Firearms and Explosives and components of the Department of Homeland Security, as well as the efforts of the U.S. Attorneys, the Internal Revenue Service, the U.S. Coast Guard and state and local law enforcement agencies.

The primary goal of each OCDETF investigation is to reduce the availability of drugs in America by strategically targeting and eliminating those trafficking organizations responsible for supplying the largest amounts of drugs. The OCDETF member agencies determine connections to related investigations, nationwide, in order to identify and dismantle the entire structure of the drug trafficking organization (DTO). OCDETF investigations emphasize disrupting the financial dealings and dismantling the financial infrastructure that supports the DTO. DEA's State and Local Task Forces and High Intensity Drug Trafficking Area (HIDTA)-funded groups are engaged as partners with the OCDETF program and enhance the effectiveness and success of the OCDETF program.

> *"The primary goal of each ... investigation is to reduce the availability of drugs in America."*

Complementing DEA's PDTO and OCDETF initiatives, the DEA State and Local Task Force (SLTF) Program continues to foster productive relationships and enhance cooperation and coordination with our state and local counterparts in the enforcement of federal drug laws. These SLTFs address drug problems of concern in the geographic regions where they operate. State and local agencies that participate in this program are actually force multipliers, which add additional resources to DEA. Statistically, DEA SLTFs account for approximately 40 percent of all DEA case initiations and seizures.

Sharing of Resources and Expertise

It is important to emphasize that there are no real operational differences between the types of cases conducted by DEA Task Forces and DEA's regular enforcement groups. This program provides numerous advantages to both the DEA and participating agencies. DEA is able to share resources and expertise with state and local law enforcement, thereby increasing investigative results. The SLTF Program also allows state and local officers to be federally deputized, thus extending their jurisdiction. The SLTF Program is a significant asset to DEA and America's efforts to curb drug trafficking and abuse.

And finally, the HIDTA program is a national strategy providing Federal assistance in coordinating law enforcement efforts of local, state and Federal entities in areas where major drug production, manufacturing importation or distribution flourish to such a degree that they have harmful effects on other parts of the country. DEA maintains a strong ongoing commitment to the HIDTA program, addressing regional drug problems of concern. The DEA continues to achieve success in HIDTA-funded initiatives through cooperation and coordination with our state and local counterparts in the enforcement of federal drug laws.

DEA currently oversees and directly supervises 48 HIDTA-funded task forces located in DEA offices, consisting of 527 Task Force Officers. Over 300 DEA Special Agents work within HIDTA initiatives to share and develop narcotics intelligence and pursue joint investigations. DEA's commitment to the HIDTA program has resulted in significant HIDTA program successes, in furtherance of the Department of Justice's Domestic Drug Enforcement Strategy.

Notable Investigations

In furtherance of our mission, DEA has conducted numerous significant investigations. I would like to share a few of DEA's notable investigations with the Subcommittee.

• In July 2001, the DEA Miami HIDTA Task Force initiated an international investigation that identified a worldwide MDMA distribution network operating in Colombia, Israel, the Netherlands and the United States. Title III intercepts, undercover operations and search warrants resulted in the seizure of approximately 2 million MDMA pills and more than $2 million. Nine of the organizational leaders were arrested in Spain, Colombia and the United States. The investigation also determined that Israeli organized crime elements were financing the smuggling operation and obtaining the MDMA from the sources of supply in Holland. In January 2003, as a result of the international scope of this investigation, the authorities in Switzerland froze additional accounts of the organization totaling $1.5 million. The investigation is active and continuing.

• In September 2001, the FBI initiated the undercover investigation in Houston, Texas. The target was attempting to obtain $25 million worth of East-bloc military weapons for the AUC, a Colombian terrorist organization, in exchange for cocaine and U.S. currency. In April 2002, DEA Houston HIDTA Major Drug Squad (MDS) 6 became involved in the investigation. To date, the investigation has revealed that the original PDTO target has been a long-time member of an international drug trafficking organization responsible for the importation of more than 50 tons of cocaine into the United States. The undercover operation resulted in the arrest of four defendants in connection with the weapons deal, three of which occurred in Costa Rica.

> *"The Government of Mexico ... and the DEA have achieved great successes in drug interdiction and eradication."*

• In October 2002, an international MDMA investigation conducted in Belgium, Israel and the United States culminated with three arrests in New York City. The case began with the seizure of 1.4 million tablets of MDMA in Antwerp, Belgium, by the Belgian Federal Police—the largest MDMA seizure in Europe to date and the third largest MDMA seizure in the United States. The shipment had a retail value of approximately $42 million. During the course of the investigation, the Israeli National Police identified the shipment as part of an ongoing investigation targeting a group of Israeli nationals. These individuals were affiliated with violent, organized crime elements in Israel.

• Oliver Beasley, identified as a major cocaine and heroin distributor in the Pittsburgh, Pennsylvania area, was the leader of an organization responsible for the distribution of 50–100 kilograms of cocaine and at least 12 kilograms of heroin, per month. Direct evidence has corroborated that at least 11 heroin overdose deaths, from January 2002 to March 2002 in the Pittsburgh area, were attributed to the heroin bearing the stamps of this organization. To date, 45 individuals have been indicted and arrested. The seizure of the organization's assets total in excess of $8.6 million dollars, including U.S. currency, real estate, jewelry, vehicles and businesses, 12 weapons, three and a half kilograms of heroin, a half-kilogram of crack cocaine and three-quarters kilogram of cocaine.

International Operations

DEA's Office of International Operations maintains 79 offices in 58 countries. These offices support DEA domestic investigations through foreign liaison, training for host country officials, bilateral investigations and intelligence gathering. The DEA's international presence is an invaluable asset in the pursuit of drug traffickers in all areas of the world. Foreign operations enables DEA to share intelligence and coordinate and develop a worldwide drug strategy, in co-operation with our host countries. The DEA's foreign operations are managed in five sections: Southeast Asia, Central America/Mexico, South America, Europe/Middle East and the Caribbean.

Southeast Asia covers fifteen country offices. Intelligence indicates that, although there has been a marked decrease in the amount of Southeast Asian heroin seized in the U.S., Southeast Asian heroin continues to pose a threat to the United States. A shift in U.S. heroin trafficking trends could easily result in the resurgence of Southeast Asian heroin. Southeast Asian heroin has the broadest U.S. geographical distribution. The most visible trafficking organizations operating in Bangkok are the West African groups. In addition, DEA offices in Southeast Asia have reported an increase in methamphetamine production/abuse. The methamphetamine epidemic has negatively affected many U.S. strategic partners in this area, including the Philippines, Japan and Thailand.

DEA has supported significant investigations in Southeast Asia. In April 2002, an investigation with host country counter-parts culminated in the seizure of approximately 317 kilograms of heroin and the arrest of 13 subjects. This investigation is significant, as it was the first time that the exchange of "real-time intelligence" had led to a major seizure in China.

Central America/Mexico covers fifteen country offices. Current reporting indicates that the Southwest Border remains the point of entry for the majority of all illicit drugs smuggled into the United States. The Mexico-Central America corridor is currently the predominant route for cocaine movement to the United

States, with an estimated 72 percent of the cocaine transiting this corridor. Mexico also supplies heroin, methamphetamine and a significant amount of the marijuana consumed in the United States.

The U.S. diplomatic and DEA presence in Mexico is one of the largest outside the United States. The Government of Mexico (GOM) and DEA have achieved great successes in drug interdiction and eradication. Bilateral cooperation and the exchange of information have been unprecedented under President Vincente Fox-Quesada's administration. Under his Administration, the GOM has pursued every major drug trafficking organization (DTO). However, despite recent successes, Mexico still faces daunting and significant challenges in the areas of counter-narcotics, its legal system and anti-corruption effort.

Significant arrests of prominent Mexican DTOs have been made by the GOM. . . . In March 2002, Special Forces of the Mexican Army, in conjunction with the Mexican Organized Crime Unit, arrested Benjamin Arellano-Felix, leader and patriarch of the Arellano-Felix drug trafficking organization. Mexican authorities charged Arellano-Felix with money laundering, organized delinquency and trafficking in marijuana, cocaine and heroin. He is also indicted in the Southern District of California with operating a Continuing Criminal Enterprise, money laundering and drug conspiracy charges. Arellano-Felix led one of the most powerful and violent drug cartels in Mexico since the 1980s, transporting ton quantities of marijuana, cocaine, methamphetamine and heroin into the United States, through the Tijuana and Mexicali corridors.

Largest Exporter of Cocaine

The South America section covers fifteen country offices. The DEA in South America and, in particular, the Bogota, Colombia Country Office (BCO), is aggressively targeting international drug trafficking organizations, in addition to facilitating the objectives of the Andean Regional Initiative.[1] The BCO continues to focus on the dismantling of trafficking organizations with international implications—specifically, those with a connection to the United States. Colombia has long been the largest exporter of cocaine to the U.S. and has become a major supplier of heroin, as well. In addition, the BCO is focusing its efforts on the importation and diversion of precursor chemicals. The BCO's Special Investigative Units (SIU) and the Andean Programs have been very successful in mounting cases against major traffickers and having these traffickers extradited to the U.S. for prosecution.

Enforcement actions in the BCO demonstrate DEA's commitment in the war against drug trafficking and abuse and terrorism. In 2002, several high ranking members of the Revolutionary Armed Forces of Colombia (FARC) and the United Self-Defense Forces of Colombia (AUC) were indicted in the United

---

1. The Andean Regional Initiative is a foreign aid program for Bolivia, Brazil, Colombia, Ecuador, Panama, Peru, and Venezuela that provides money for counternarcotics, economic, and social programs.

States for drug trafficking. This investigation highlighted the link between groups and individuals under investigation for drug trafficking, as well as terrorist activity. This case represented the first time that drug trafficking charges were brought in the United States against members of foreign terrorist organizations.

In November 2002, the BCO successfully concluded a two-year investigation with the arrests of 16 defendants. The arrests included the principal targets in Colombia and Ecuador responsible for the 13-ton shipment of cocaine seized from the vessel M/V Svesda Maru. In June 2002, the BCO concluded the yearlong investigation, Operation Julieta, by arresting 21 individuals in Colombia responsible for shipping multi-kilograms of heroin and cocaine to the United States.

> *"Among current important ... initiatives ... [is] a program to target use of the Internet to illegally obtain controlled drugs."*

The Caribbean section covers seven foreign country offices and four domestic offices. The Caribbean has long been an important transit zone for drugs entering the United States and Europe from South America. The drugs are transported through the region, to both the United States and Europe, through a wide variety of routes and methods, primarily marine vessels. The Caribbean remains a major transit route for South American cocaine destined for the United States and other world markets. The Caribbean is also an important transit point for marijuana and heroin destined for the United States, as well as a major money-laundering center for illicit drug proceeds.

The Caribbean Offices strive to strengthen the region's collective ability to track, interdict, arrest and prosecute successfully money laundering and drug smuggling organizations that operate in the Caribbean.

Operation Containment

Europe/Middle East covers 156 countries, with 24 DEA country offices. With various drug trafficking organizations' methods of operation and tentacles stretching around the globe, DEA offices in these regions are combating the aggressive activities of numerous DTOs. These include the new methods of operation of the Albanian DTOs, the influx of MDMA and multi-ton shipments of cocaine from South America in containerized shipments.

The DEA initiated Operation Containment, an enforcement program involving the Central Asian States, India, Pakistan, Turkey, the Balkan countries, Russia, Germany and the United Kingdom. The goal of Operation Containment is to reduce the amount of Afghan heroin flowing to Western Europe through enhanced interdiction efforts, intelligence sharing and database connectivity. During Operation Containment's "Interdiction Blitz," from June 10, 2002 through July 10, 2002, the following drug seizures were made: 1705 kilograms of heroin, 125 kilograms of hashish, 1.5 kilograms of liquid cocaine, 1.6 kilograms of powder cocaine, 250,000 tablets of amphetamines, 690 tablets of MDMA, 5329 kilograms of cannabis, 352 kilograms of opium, 1574 metric tons of toluol, (precursor), 1008 kilograms of poppy straw and 2013 opium plants.

Special Operations Division

DEA's Special Operations Division (SOD), created in 1995, is a DEA led Division with participation from the Department of Homeland Security, the Federal Bureau of Investigation (FBI), the Internal Revenue Service (IRS) and Department of Justice's (DOJ) Criminal Division. SOD's mission is to establish seamless law enforcement strategies and operations aimed at dismantling national and international trafficking organizations by attacking their command and control communications. Special emphasis is placed on those major drug trafficking organizations that operate across jurisdictional boundaries on a regional, national and international level. The unique investigative support provided by SOD allows the program to act as a "force multiplier" for drug law enforcement because it provides an effective and efficient medium for communication, intelligence sharing and coordination among America's major drug law enforcement agencies.

Significant operations supported by SOD include Operation Webslinger, the first national operation that targeted organizations utilizing the Internet to traffic the predatory drugs GHB, GBL and 1,4 BD (BD). Operation Webslinger culminated in September 2002 and resulted in the arrest of 170 individuals and the seizure of 3,600 gallons of GHB, GBL and BD; 2 clandestine laboratories; 4.75 pounds of methamphetamine; 1.3 kilograms of MDMA; 2,500 vials of steroids; 17 properties; 10 vehicles; 44 weapons; and $2.4 million in U.S. currency. SOD also supported Operation Double Trouble, a money laundering operation that targeted international money brokers responsible for laundering drug proceeds. To date, this operation has resulted in the arrest of 62 individuals and the seizure of 170 kilograms of cocaine, 7 kilograms of heroin, 10 weapons, 4 vehicles and $12.4 million in U.S. currency.

Operation Mountain Express III, a nationwide investigation targeting pseudoephedrine suppliers for Mexican methamphetamine "super labs," revealed that proceeds from sales of Canadian pseudoephedrine were being funneled through traditional "hawalah" networks to individuals in the Middle East. This operation resulted in the arrest of 136 individuals, the seizure of 35.8 tons of Canadian origin pseudoephedrine, 179 lbs. of methamphetamine, six methamphetamine labs and $4.5 million.

Operation Northern Star employed a comprehensive strategy targeting the entire methamphetamine trafficking process, including the suppliers of precursor chemicals, chemical brokers, transporters, manufacturers, distributors and the money launderers who helped conceal their criminal proceeds. DEA and the Royal Canadian Mounted Police announced the arrests of over 65 individuals in ten cities, throughout the United States and Canada. The arrests resulted from an 18-month international investigation targeting the illegal importation of pseu-doephedrine, an essential chemical used in methamphetamine production. As part of this investigation, agents targeted six executives from three Canadian chemical companies. All sold bulk quantities of pseudoephedrine to metham-phetamine manufacturers in the United States, with the full knowledge that their sales were intended for the illegal production of the highly addictive and dangerous drug methamphetamine.

Intelligence Division

The Intelligence Division provides dedicated analytical support to DEA in-vestigations, programs and operations worldwide. The headquarters component advises on all matters pertaining to the formulation, direction, coordination and management of DEA's global drug intelligence and information exchange pro-gram. Intelligence functions include policy development and management, guidance on sensitive activities and maintenance and development of methods and techniques, domestic intelligence, international intelligence and the El Paso Intelligence Center (EPIC). The Intelligence Division also is active in counter-ing terrorism. DEA has over 700 Intelligence Analysts assigned to field divi-sions; foreign offices; and headquarters functions, including EPIC and the Avia-tion Intelligence Group.

EPIC concentrates primarily on drug movement, illegal aliens and weapons violations in the United States and the Western Hemisphere. A number of EPIC programs are dedicated to port-seizure analysis and the establishment of links between recent enforcement actions and ongoing investigations. EPIC coordi-nates training for state and local officers concerning interdiction and conceal-ment methods used for drugs and drug currency. EPIC also provides tactical in-telligence information to the officers within the first critical week after a seizure or a stop.

In FY 2002, 32 percent of EPIC's inquiries were related to counterterrorism. EPIC has supported the FBI, the Department of Defense, the United States Coast Guard, other federal and state and local agencies by processing almost a million database accesses, providing over 33,000 investigative leads and for-warding over 6,000 communiqués to investigators. The Office of Special Intel-ligence (NS) also is involved, routinely researching its databases for leads. NS has been critical in the identification of impending terrorism activities.

DEA's Intelligence Division is committed to interagency cooperation. Each designated HIDTA has at least one intelligence element, usually called an In-vestigative Support Center (ISC). HIDTA intelligence elements serve as hubs for the sharing of drug intelligence among federal, state and local law enforce-ment HIDTA-funded participating agencies. DEA's commitment to HIDTA shows in the assignment of nearly 10 percent of our analytical resources to HIDTAs. EPIC also plays a critical role in support of the HIDTA funded task forces by dedicating specific intelligence resources to facilitate HIDTA requests. Additionally, DEA provides leadership to the Counterdrug Intelligence Coordination Group and the Counterdrug Executive Secretariat and provides, on a reimbursable basis, at least three employees to the Central Intelligence Agency to support that agency's counterdrug programs.

DEA's Intelligence Division has been active in international cooperation, strengthening the Bilateral Drug Intelligence Working Groups. Mutually beneficial meetings have been held with the partners: Germany, Canada and Australia. To expand this initiative, meetings also were conducted with China.

Office of Diversion Control

The mission of DEA's Office of Diversion Control (OD) is to prevent the diversion of legitimately produced controlled substances and listed chemicals while ensuring adequate supplies for legitimate needs. In fulfilling its mandate under the Controlled Substances Act, among many functions, OD maintains a national registration program for all controlled substances handlers (those who manufacture, distribute, dispense, import or export such substances); conducts major diversion investigations, unilaterally or together with state/local authorities; serves as the U.S. Competent Authority in fulfilling national obligations under United Nations drug and chemical control treaties; establishes national drug production quotas; controls the import/export of controlled drugs and listed chemicals; and maintains liaison with the drug and chemical industry, associations and related professions.

> *"The DEA remains committed to our primary goal of targeting and arresting the most significant traffickers in the world today."*

Among current important OD initiatives are a national program to prevent and detect diversion of the powerful narcotic OxyContin®; international partnership initiatives to prevent and detect global diversion of key chemicals used in illicit cocaine, heroin and amphetamine-type stimulant (e.g., MDMA) production; and a program to target use of the Internet to illegally obtain controlled drugs. In a continual effort to streamline/improve efficiency of service to DEA registrants, OD is in the process of "re-engineering" the registration program to allow interactive Internet provision of registration services and is embarked on a major E-commerce initiative. This initiative will provide for the secure use of the Internet to conduct controlled substance prescription and ordering functions.

One notable Diversion case concerned the owner and six physicians of the Carolina Neurology and Pain Management Center in Myrtle Beach, South Carolina, who were named in a 59-count federal indictment. Each defendant was charged with conspiracy to unlawfully distribute and dispense Oxycodone, as well as a variety of other controlled substances. Due to the large amounts of controlled substances distributed for non-legitimate medical reasons at the clinic, several patients died. The defendants also were charged with money laundering in excess of $5,000,000 during the period between June 1997 and July 2001.

DEA employs over 500 Diversion Investigators, who are assigned to domestic field divisions, foreign offices and Headquarters elements. The Diversion Control Program is a fee-funded activity with respect to its controlled pharmaceutical functions.

Office of Training

The Drug Enforcement Administration's Office of Training is the nation's preeminent law enforcement training organization for national and international drug law enforcement training. The Office of Training provides technical and non-technical training to DEA personnel and appropriate domestic and foreign law enforcement officers, to improve individual and organizational performance and assist in achieving mission and performance goals.

The primary purpose of the DEA Training Academy is to train the agency's four core constituencies: Basic Agents, Basic Diversion Investigators, Basic Intelligence Research Specialists and Basic Forensic Scientists. In addition, the Academy provides for professional and executive development training, certification training and specialized training. The Academy also is used to conduct drug law enforcement seminars for state and local law enforcement personnel, and through the use of specially equipped classrooms, international drug training seminars for foreign law enforcement officials. DEA training includes Executive and Professional Development training, state and local training, clandestine laboratory training and various international training programs. During FY 2002, DEA's Office of Training provided instruction to over 7,800 DEA and other federal, state, local and international students. DEA anticipates training approximately the same number of personnel in FY 2003.

Operational Support Division

The Operational Support Division is responsible for the management and operation of DEA's Offices of Administration, Investigative Technology, Information Systems and Forensic Sciences. Numerous improvements have been realized in the areas of investigative technology, information technology, laboratory services, clandestine laboratory cleanups, audit requirements and domestic and laboratory replacements and renovations.

For example, the Office of Investigative Technology implemented a Centralized Call Data Delivery system for intercepted cellular pen register data for the field. This system enables each division to obtain cellular call data without the need to establish a dedicated connection to individual cellular companies, thus generating substantial cost savings to DEA. The Office of Information Systems was the first component in the Department of Justice to electronically transmit information through the Department's Joint Automated Booking System (JABS) to the FBI's Integrated Automated Fingerprint Identification System, through the Firebird Booking Station. This system provides rapid identification of individuals under arrest or detention, minimizes duplication of data entry during booking and it promotes data sharing among Department law enforcement agencies and other authorized parties, through an interface with the Nationwide JABS.

The Operational Support Division has improved hazardous waste disposal by implementing significant cost savings and efficiencies with a new five year hazardous waste cleanup contract and developing an alternative clean up program. In addition, significant improvements have been made in DEA's audit requirements, as apparent in the recently completed KPMG 2002 Financial Audit, in which DEA went from three IT material weaknesses in 2001 to none in 2002.

Supply Reduction Is Linked to Demand Reduction

While DEA is principally a law enforcement agency, demand reduction is an important element of DEA's overall enforcement strategy. Through investigations such as Operation Webslinger and Operation Pipe Dreams, an investigation that targeted national distributors of drug paraphernalia, DEA carries out its enforcement mission while achieving the complementary goal of raising public awareness regarding the dangers of drug abuse and drug trafficking.

DEA also provides training in support of national conferences held by a variety of federal, state and local agencies. These conferences bring together law enforcement, health, prevention and education groups to craft a specific strategy to deal with methamphetamine abuse unique to their states. . . . For example, DEA hosted Methamphetamine Conferences in Arkansas, Oklahoma, Kentucky, Hawaii and at the Midwest Governors' Summit in Iowa. DEA's Demand Reduction Program also spearheaded the following campaigns:

Methamphetamine has become the number one drug problem of rural and small-town America. As a law enforcement agency, DEA felt this message was an important one to put out to the American people. This public awareness campaign has led to numerous congressional offices requesting DEA participation in "Meth Town Hall Meetings," allowing Members to bring awareness about the problem to their constituents.

Operation X-Out shows how deeply integrated supply reduction and demand reduction are. X-Out combines enforcement operations against MDMA and predatory drug traffickers with public news conferences and town hall discussions in communities about the devastating effects of club drugs. Local citizens, drug prevention experts and victims of drug-inspired crimes participate and articulate how the community can actively engage and stop the spread of club drugs in their community. . . .

Demand Reduction Is the Primary Goal

The DEA remains committed to our primary goal of targeting and arresting the most significant traffickers in the world today. In particular, we will continue to work in close partnership with our local, state, federal and international counterparts to target drug trafficking groups, who spread misery and false hope to America's citizens. . . .

Drugs know no boundaries and do not make distinctions between big city and small town America, between color and ethnicity, whether rich or poor. It is the responsibility of every American to contribute in the fight against illegal drugs.

An International Drug Prohibition Effort Is Necessary

by Benjamin Gilman

About the author: *Benjamin Gilman is chairman emeritus of the House International Relations Committee. He retired in 2002, after serving thirty years in the U.S. Congress.*

Editor's Note: This viewpoint was originally given as a statement at the Inter-Parliamentary Drug Conference in Bolivia on February 21, 2001.

In our common fight against the scourge of illicit drugs, whose purveyors know no borders, nor respect any boundaries, no nation can go it alone. We all need each other's help, and this conference proves that fact.

These inter-parliamentary sessions have served to create greater global understanding on the dimensions of the drug problem, and how various portions of the fight are the responsibilities of the international community together in the battle against this scourge. When we all collectively take action on this challenge, we can and will win. Producer nations, transit nations, user nations, and those which produce precursor chemicals, all must do their part. Bolivia's success here in virtually eliminating its coca production, along with amazing progress as well in Peru, shows the skeptics and naysayers that with strong political will, and international community support, the battle against illicit drugs can, in fact, be won. Success comes when governments like Bolivia exercise the political will, show courage, and in turn gain the support of their people and the international community in our common fight.

Here in the Andean nations, we have long witnessed the destruction and havoc both to governments and to the environment from the illicit drug trade and the drug manufacturing process. The destruction of the rain forests by the slash-and-

Benjamin Gilman, statement at the Fourth Annual Inter-Parliamentary Drug Conference, Santa Cruz, Bolivia, February 21, 2001.

burn drug crop planting, and the poisoning of the rivers with run-off precursor chemicals, are byproducts of illegal drug production in the Andean ridge.

A recent Colombian Army report indicated that drug production contaminated the soil of that beleaguered nation with 200,000 tons of chemicals a year causing deforestation at a pace that was rapidly destroying the country's rain forests.

> *"In our common fight against the scourge of illicit drugs . . . no nation can go it alone."*

We in the major user-nations, whether in the Americas, Europe, Asia or Africa, have also seen the havoc these illicit drugs create in our communities and among our young people. There are few nations who can afford to sit on the sidelines and watch this destruction of the land and our people.

Precursor Chemicals Come from Europe

Europe, in particular, has a major new role to play here in the Andean ridge, where all of the world's cocaine originates. Europe—especially nations like Germany, Holland and others—are providing a great deal of the precursor chemicals which are often times "diverted" in transit to illicit drug production here in the Americas. In all of the world's illicit drug production—whether natural or synthetic drugs—European precursors, illegally diverted, play a key role in this drug production.

Meanwhile, recent trends show as much as 30 percent of the cocaine oftentimes produced by some of these European precursor chemicals here in the Andes now goes to Europe. Once the United States was the sole destination of this region's deadly cocaine, no more.

In Europe last year [2000] alone, 43 tons of deadly cocaine were seized coming from Colombia and Peru combined, transiting Venezuela, Bolivia or Brazil. I repeat, 43 tons of cocaine seized in Europe came from this region. Just a few short years ago, those of us who followed the drug trade talked merely in terms of kilos being seized; now it's multi-tons. I was recently in Ireland, where there was a major seizure of cocaine located under the seats of a Continental Airline flight from Newark to Shannon, Ireland. We are all clearly linked together in this common fight.

When we work together to prevent production at the source and interdiction of these drugs before they reach our shores, we can reduce demand by raising price and lowering purity.

I am hopeful that our European friends will recognize the environmental destruction this illicit drug production causes in this part of the world, and will also come to realize that places like Colombia produce none of the precursor chemicals used to create these illicit drugs. Many of these chemicals come from Europe. We in the USA, as well as they, can do a better job in controlling these key chemical ingredients.

More than $1 Billion in Aid to Colombia

In addition, with just a little more adequate advance shipping notice from Europe on huge shipments of precursor chemicals to producer nations like Colombia to allow the anti-drug police to check out the bona fides of the purported end users, we all might be able to make better progress on this front.

We could also use more European help for the UNDCP [United Nations International Drug Control Programme] and alternative development for this region, as the poor coca farmers face loss of their lucrative and once in-demand, illicit crops. The UNDCP's entire budget is less than $100 million to fight a worldwide plague conducting business exceeding $400 billion. We need more help from our European friends with our good UNDCP.

We in the United States are willing to do our share in this region. The U.S. has contributed more than $100 million here in Bolivia alone to help fight drug production and to support alternative development, which go hand in hand. In Colombia, we have provided more than a billion dollars in both police and military aid, as well as social and judicial aid. We support Peru as well in this common fight.

The drugs from these nations now transit to the whole world, and around the globe. We must all do our share together. I welcome this conference to help advance these goals. The days of finger pointing are over, and together we must join in this common struggle and not give in to the naysayers.

The Cost of Drug Prohibition Is Justified

by Lou Dobbs

About the author: *Lou Dobbs is the anchor and managing editor of the CNN news program* Lou Dobbs Tonight.

We've spent hundreds of billions of dollars on law enforcement, prevention and treatment since President Richard Nixon declared the war on drugs in 1971. Yet the use of illicit drugs continues to plague our country. The federal government spends nearly $1 billion a month to fight the war on drugs, but users spend more than five times that much a month to buy drugs.

Beyond the horrific human toll of 20,000 drug-induced deaths each year, illegal drugs cost our economy more than $280 billion annually, according to the Substance Abuse and Mental Health Services Administration.

Incredibly, there are those who choose to ignore the human devastation and the economic cost of the drug plague. Many of them are pseudo-sophisticated baby boomers who consider themselves superior and hip in their wry, reckless disregard of the facts. They may also smoke marijuana, advocate its legalization, and rationalize cocaine by calling it a recreational drug.

And there is a surprising list of libertarians and conservatives, including [conservative writer] William F. Buckley and Nobel laureate economist Milton Friedman who advocate the legalization or decriminalization of drugs.

Another Nobel laureate, Gary S. Becker, professor of economics at the University of Chicago, told me: "It (legalization) would certainly save a lot of resources for society. We could tax drug use so it could even lead to government revenue. We would be able to greatly cut the number of people in prison, which would save resources for state and local government."

Drugs Are Illegal Because They Are Bad

But the cost of drug abuse goes well beyond the expense to control supply and demand. Drug users cost the country $160 billion each year in lost productivity. Parental substance abuse is responsible for $10 billion of the $14 billion spent nationally each year on child welfare costs. And drugs are involved in seven out of every 10 cases of child abuse and neglect.

Pete Wilson, the former governor of California, is a strong opponent of drug legalization. Wilson says the problem that advocates of legalization fail to acknowledge is that drugs are addictive in nature, and are therefore not just another commodity.

"Drugs did not become viewed as bad because they are illegal," Wilson says. "Rather, they became illegal because they are clearly bad."

Although the war on drugs certainly has not captured the American public's attention to the extent that it should, there has been success in efforts to curb drug use and supply. According to the University of Michigan's "Monitoring the Future" study, the percentage of high school seniors who reported using any drug within the past month decreased from 39 percent in 1978 to 26 percent in 2001. There are a total of 9 million fewer drug users in America now than there were in 1979. And coca cultivation was 15 percent lower in Colombia in 2002, due to the combined efforts of the United States and Colombian governments.

> *"There has been success in efforts to curb drug use and supply."*

Drug czar John Walters, director of the Office of National Drug Control Policy, is optimistic about the war on drugs.

"We have to remember that, since we got serious in the '80s, overall drug use is half of what it was—and that's progress," Walters told me. . . .

I would say that is quite a lot of progress. But the job is only half done.

Drug Prohibition Is Counterproductive

by Timothy Lynch

About the author: Timothy Lynch is the director of the Cato Institute's Project on Criminal Justice. The Cato Institute is a nonprofit public policy research institute.

America's drug policies are never seriously debated in Washington. Year after year, our elected representatives focus on two questions: How much more money should we spend on the drug war? and, How should it be spent? In the months preceding elections, politicians typically try to pin blame for the drug problem on one another. After the election, the cycle begins anew.

Outside the capital, however, there is growing unease about the war on drugs. More and more Americans are concluding that the drug war has been given a chance to work—and has failed. Voters in California, Arizona, Oregon, Washington, Nevada, Alaska, and Maine have rejected the lobbying efforts of federal officials and approved initiatives calling for the legalization of marijuana for medicinal purposes. Two sitting governors, Jesse Ventura of Minnesota and Gary Johnson of New Mexico, have declared the drug war a failure. As public opinion continues to turn against the war, we can expect more elected officials to speak out.

Federal officials do not yet appreciate the extent of public dissatisfaction with the war on drugs. Congress continues to propose and enact laws with such platitudinous titles as "The Drug-Free Century Act." Not many people outside the capital are even paying attention to those laws, and even fewer take the rhetoric seriously.

Drug War Support Continues

To be sure, some people of good will continue to support the drug war. Their rationale is that we may not be close to achieving a "drug-free" society, but our present situation would only deteriorate if the government were to stop prose-cuting the drug war. The burden of persuasion on that proposition has always rested with drug reformers. But nowadays it is a burden reformers happily ac-cept, buoyed as they are by the realization that momentum in the debate is shift-ing in their direction.

Reformers are as eager as ever to debate the efficacy of the drug laws—while supporters of the drug war discuss the issue only grudgingly. Reformers ask: Why should an adult man or woman be arrested, prosecuted, and imprisoned for using heroin, opium, cocaine, or marijuana? The answer, according to the most prominent supporters of the drug war, is simple: Drug use is wrong. It is wrong because it is immoral, and it is immoral because it degrades human be-ings. The prominent social scientist James Q. Wilson has articulated that view as follows: "Even now, when the dangers of drug use are well understood, many educated people still discuss the drug problem in almost every way ex-cept the right way. They talk about the 'costs' of drug use and the 'socioeco-nomic factors' that shape that use. They rarely speak plainly—drug use is wrong because it is immoral and it is immoral because it enslaves the mind and destroys the soul."

William J. Bennett, America's first drug czar, has expressed a similar view: "A citizen in a drug-induced haze whether on his backyard deck or on a mat-tress in a ghetto crack house, is not what the Founding Fathers meant by the 'pursuit of happiness.' . . . Helpless wrecks in treatment centers, men chained by their noses to cocaine—these people are slaves."

Wilson, Bennett, and their supporters believe that to eradicate this form of slavery, the government should vigorously investigate, prosecute, and jail any-one who sells, uses, or possesses mind-altering drugs. The criminal sanction should be used—in Bennett's words—"to take drug users off the streets and de-ter new users from becoming more deeply involved in so hazardous an activity."

For more than 25 years, the political establishment has offered unflagging support for the ban on drugs. In 1973, President [Richard] Nixon created the Drug Enforcement Administration, a police agency that focuses exclusively on federal drug-law violations. President [Ronald] Reagan designated nar-cotics an official threat to America's national security; he also signed leg-islation authorizing the military to as-sist federal and state police agencies in the drug war. In 1988, Congress

> *"More and more Americans are concluding that the drug war has been given a chance to work—and has failed."*

created the Office of National Drug Control Policy; President [George] Bush appointed Bennett national drug czar to centralize control and coordinate activi-ties of federal agencies in the drug war. President [Bill] Clinton appointed a for-mer military commander, Gen. Barry McCaffrey, as drug czar.

Drug War Efforts Escalate

Since the early 1970s, Congress has been escalating the federal government's drug-war efforts. In 1979, the federal government spent $900 million on various antidrug programs; in 1989, it spent $5 billion; by 1999, it was spending nearly $18 billion.

According to the Office of National Drug Control Policy, vigorous law-enforcement tactics help reduce drug abuse chiefly by reducing demand and disrupting supply. Enforcement of the drug laws reduces demand by increasing social disapproval of substance abuse; arrest and threatened imprisonment also offer a powerful incentive for addicts to take treatment seriously. Drug enforcement disrupts supply by detecting and dismantling drug rings, which facilitate the movement of drugs from suppliers to the streets.

Congress has devoted billions of dollars to these tasks, and there have been palpable results. To begin with, the criminal-justice system has grown much larger: There are more police officers, prosecutors, judges, and prison guards than ever before. The number of arrests, convictions, and prisoners has increased exponentially; so has the amount of seized contraband. In February 1999, the *New York Times* reported that "every 20 seconds, someone in America is arrested for a drug violation. Every week, on average, a new jail or prison is built to lock up more people in the world's largest penal system."

> *"The supply of drugs has not been hampered in any serious way by the war on drugs."*

There is certainly a lot of government activity; but is the Office of National Drug Control Policy really achieving its twin objectives of reducing demand and disrupting supply? The demand for illegal drugs remains strong. According to the National Household Survey on Drug Abuse, 11 million Americans can be classified as "current users" (past month) of marijuana and 1.75 million Americans as current users of cocaine. As startling as those numbers are, they represent only the tip of the proverbial iceberg. Millions of other individuals can be classified as "occasional users," and tens of thousands of people use less popular illicit drugs, such as heroin and methamphetamine. In short: The government's own statistics admit that millions and millions of Americans break the law every single month.

The supply of drugs has not been hampered in any serious way by the war on drugs. A commission on federal law-enforcement practices chaired by former FBI director William Webster recently offered this blunt assessment of the interdiction efforts: "Despite a record number of seizures and a flood of legislation, the Commission is not aware of any evidence that the flow of narcotics into the United States has been reduced." Perhaps the most dramatic evidence of the failure of the drug war is the flourishing of open-air drug markets in Washington, D.C.—the very city in which the drug czar and the Drug Enforcement Administration have their headquarters.

Even though law enforcement has been unable to seriously disrupt either the supply of or the demand for illegal drugs, many hesitate to draw the conclusion that the drug war has failed. They choose to focus on the evils of drug use, and the need to keep up the fight against it, on the grounds that even an incomplete success is better than a surrender. But a fair appraisal of the drug war must look beyond drug use itself, and take into account all of the negative repercussions of the drug

> *"It is undeniable that the criminalization of drug use has created an immense and sophisticated black market."*

war. It is undeniable that the criminalization of drug use has created an immense and sophisticated black market that generates billions of dollars for gangster organizations. The criminal proceeds are often used to finance other criminal activity. Furthermore, rival gangs use violence to usurp and defend territory for drug sales. Innocent people die in the crossfire.

The Drug War Squanders Taxes

Then there is the cost. Billions of taxpayer dollars are squandered every year to keep drugs from entering the country. The government cannot even keep narcotics out of its own prisons—and yet it spends millions every month trying to keep contraband from arriving by air, land, and sea.

Prosecuting the war also involves a disturbingly large number of undesirable police practices: Paramilitary raids, roadblocks, wiretaps, informants, and property seizures have all become routine because of the difficulty of detecting drug offenses. Countless innocent people have had their phones tapped and their homes and cars searched. A criminal-justice system that devotes its limited resources to drug offenders is necessarily distracted from investigating other criminal activity—such as murder, rape, and theft.

Unfortunately, the most prominent supporters of the drug war have refused to grapple with these grim consequences of their policy. Drug legalization, they retort, would undermine the moral sanction against drug use. William Bennett has actually indulged in a comparison that would equate alternative drug policies—such as decriminalization—with surrender to the Nazis: "Imagine if, in the darkest days of 1940, [former British prime minister] Winston Churchill had rallied the West by saying, 'This war looks hopeless, and besides, it will cost too much. Hitler can't be that bad. Let's surrender and see what happens.' That is essentially what we hear from the legalizers."

After decades of ceaseless police work, it is safe to say that Bennett is confusing perseverance with bullheadedness. One thoughtful analyst, Father John Clifton Marquis, recognized—as long ago as 1990—that "when law does not promote the common good, but in fact causes it to deteriorate, the law itself becomes bad and must be changed. . . . Authentic moral leaders cannot afford the arrogant luxury of machismo, with its refusal to consider not 'winning.'"

Marquis is correct; and this is precisely why Bennett's World War II imagery is misplaced. The notion that the drug czar is somehow leading an army against an evil foe is an example of what Marquis calls "arrogant machismo." A more apt analogy would be America's 15-year experience with alcohol prohibition: Americans rejected Prohibition because experience showed the federal liquor laws to be unenforceable and because alcohol prohibition led to gang wars and widespread corruption. The war on drugs has created a similar set of problems.

Lessons of Prohibition

The most valuable lesson that can be drawn from the Prohibition experience is that government cannot effectively engineer social arrangements. Policymakers simply cannot repeal the economic laws of supply and demand. Nor can they foresee the unintended consequences that follow government intervention. Students of American history will someday wonder how today's lawmakers could readily admit that alcohol prohibition was a disastrous mistake, but simultaneously engage in a reckless policy of drug prohibition.

Drug policy in America needs to be reinvented, starting with a tabula rasa. Policymakers ought to address the issue in an open, honest, and mature manner. A growing number of Americans are coming to the conclusion that the law should treat substances such as marijuana and cocaine the same way it treats tobacco, beer, and whiskey: restricting sales to minors and jailing any user who endangers the safety of others (by, for example, operating an automobile while under the influence). Education, moral suasion, and noncoercive social pressure are the only appropriate ways to discourage adult drug use in a free and civil society.

The War on Drugs Should Focus on Reducing Demand

by Joseph G. Lehman

About the author: *Joseph G. Lehman is executive vice president of the Mackinac Center for Public Policy, a research and educational institute based in Midland, Michigan.*

The economics of the drug war dictate its futility. When public policy is pitted against economic reality, reality wins. A new approach to the drug problem is needed because the war on drugs, as it is currently prosecuted, has no more chance of success than a war on geometry.

Drug policy in the United States is largely "supply-side"—it aims primarily to restrict availability of certain substances. Our supply-side policies include training anti-narcotics battalions to support aerial herbicide spraying of Colombian drug crops, authorizing deadly force for border patrols, detaining travelers suspected of drug activity, inspecting commercial shipments, seizing property of suspected drug dealers, mandating lengthy incarceration for convicted dealers and regulating financial dealings to impede or expose drug transactions.

Drug War Spending Increases

The cost of these policies is climbing. Drug war spending in the mid-1980s was about $10 billion annually. Today it's more than $40 billion—$19 billion in state and local spending, and the rest for federal anti-drug efforts in nearly every cabinet-rank department.

These costly policies are supposed to make drugs harder to get, but by that criterion the drug war fails. Peter Reuter, senior fellow at the RAND Corp., writes in a recent *Milken Institute Review* that cocaine and heroin street prices have declined when adjusted for inflation during the last two decades.

Reuter also found that availability of drugs has not decreased significantly. While the risk of being imprisoned for drug dealing quintupled as the drug war expanded, the percentage of high school seniors reporting that cocaine and marijuana are available to them has remained steady for 10 years and 25 years, respectively.

We spend $40 billion annually to extinguish our $50 billion illegal drug market, so why do we fail? Basic economics suggest many reasons, but here are three:

> *"Private demand-reduction programs are probably more effective."*

• The potential to supply drugs is huge. Eradication of U.S.-bound drug crops in Bolivia and Peru in the 1990s merely shifted drug production to other countries, including Colombia, where we are today spending $1.3 billion in similar elimination efforts. And if we somehow manage to wipe out the drug crops there, farmers elsewhere will supply our willing buyers.

• There is immense profit in illegal drugs. Drugs are extremely cheap to make compared with their street prices. The massive price markups compensate dealers and producers for risking harsh legal penalties.

• There is persistent strong demand for drugs. The robust demand . . . is fairly unresponsive to massive spending on drug interdiction, three-fourths of which is for capturing and penalizing dealers and users.

The Success of Demand Reduction

Is success more likely with a "demand-side" approach?

Demand for drugs decreases if potential users deem drugs unfashionable or otherwise undesirable. Specific drugs go in and out of fashion for reasons that are difficult to shape government policy around, but government policy is not the only choice. Two proven ways to influence drug attitudes and desires—education and rehabilitation treatment—can be done by government or private groups.

Private demand-reduction programs are probably more effective. The first line of defense against drugs, parental teaching and discussion, is believed to be the most effective education "program." But the popular government drug program for schools, Drug Abuse Resistance Education (DARE), is consistently rated negatively by independent studies.

Worse, DARE may lull parents into believing their children learn enough about drugs at school. The National Parents' Resource Institute for Drug Education found that conversations about drugs between parents and children dropped 27 percent from 1991–96—strong growth years for the billion-dollar DARE program.

Rehabilitation treatment can stem drug demand, particularly when administered privately. Government drug treatment programs often report a success rate of less than 20 percent. Phoenix House, the nation's largest private, nonprofit drug treatment organization, claims 60 percent success for 70,000 addicts and dependent people over three decades. The Christian program Teen Challenge achieves an 86-percent "cure" rate. Offsetting the cost of treatment, RAND estimates that costs due to crime and lost productivity drop $7.46 for every dollar spent on treatment.

To the tragedy of drug abuse the drug war adds all the tragedies of war—violent deaths, innocent casualties, lost freedoms, squandered resources and corrupted institutions. Effective drug abatement efforts, especially those intended to reduce demand, must rely on family, religious and other private institutions. Force-oriented government policies aimed at restricting drug supplies will fail as long as there is strong demand for illicit substances. That is economic reality.

The United States Should Not Pressure Other Countries to Comply with Its Prohibition Efforts

by Dan Gardner

About the author: *Dan Gardner is a journalist for the* Ottawa Citizen, *a newspaper published in Ottawa, Canada.*

On June 6, 1998, a surprising letter was delivered to Kofi Annan, secretary-general of the United Nations. "We believe," the letter declared, "that the global war on drugs is now causing more harm than drug abuse itself."

The letter was signed by statesmen, politicians, academics and other public figures. Former UN Secretary-General Javier Perez de Cuellar signed. So did George Shultz, the former U.S. secretary of state, and Joycelyn Elders, the former U.S. surgeon general. Nobel laureates such as Milton Friedman and Argentina's Adolfo Perez Esquivel added their names. Four former presidents and seven former Cabinet ministers from Latin American countries signed.

The drug policies the world has been following for decades are a destructive failure, they said. Trying to stamp out drug abuse by banning drugs has only created an illegal industry worth $400 billion, "or roughly 8 percent of international trade."

The letter continued: "This industry has empowered organized criminals, corrupted governments at all levels, eroded internal security, stimulated violence and distorted both economic markets and moral values." It concluded that these were the consequences "not of drug use per se, but of decades of failed and futile drug war policies."

This powerful statement landed on Annan's desk just as the UN was holding a special assembly on global drug problems. Going into that meeting, the governments of the world appeared all but unanimous in the belief that the best way to combat drug abuse was to ban the production, sale or possession of certain drugs.

Drug prohibition, most governments believe, makes harmful substances less available to people and far more expensive than they otherwise would be. Combined with the threat of punishment for using or selling drugs, prohibition significantly cuts the number of people using these substances, thus saving them from the torment of addiction and reducing the personal and social harms drugs can inflict. For these governments—and probably for most people in most countries—drug prohibition is just common sense.

Still, the letter to Annan showed that this view is far from unanimous. In fact, a large and growing number of world leaders and experts think the war on drugs is nothing less than a humanitarian disaster.

But governments are all but unanimous in supporting drug prohibition. It's not easy to imagine alternatives to a policy that has been in place for decades, especially when few people remember how the policy came into being in the first place, or why.

"War on drugs" is a compelling sound bite, whereas the damage drug prohibition may do is complex and impossible to summarize on a bumper sticker.

But the core reason the war on drugs so completely dominates the official policies of so many nations is simple: The United States insists on it.

"Turning the Whole World Dry"

The "international" war on drugs is a policy conceived, created and enforced by the U.S. government. Originally, nations were cajoled, prodded or bullied into joining it. Then it became international orthodoxy, and today most national governments are enthusiastic supporters of prohibition. To the extent that they debate drug policy at all, it is only to question how strictly or harshly prohibition should be enforced, not whether the basic idea is sound.

The few officials and governments that do stray, even slightly, outside the prohibition orthodoxy are cajoled, manipulated or bullied to get back in. The U.S. government does everything it can to prevent the views of conscientious objectors from being heard.

Drugs such as marijuana, cocaine and opium are linked in modern minds to organized crime, street violence and junkies wasting away in crack dens. But they weren't always thought of this way.

"A . . . growing number of world leaders and experts think the war on drugs is nothing less than a humanitarian disaster."

These drugs were used for centuries before they were criminalized in the 20th century. Like alcohol today, they were produced, sold and purchased legally. And like alcohol, the producers and sellers of these drugs usually were ordinary merchants and companies that conducted their business according to the laws of the day. They fought for market share with advertisements and settled disputes with lawsuits, like any other business.

These legal markets for drugs clearly had their harms. As in every age and every society, a small minority of the people who used what are now illegal drugs became addicted and suffered. But the legal availability of what are now illegal drugs did not create burgeoning plagues of drug addiction any more than the legal availability of alcohol today has spawned an epidemic of alcoholism.

For many well-intentioned activists of the late 19th and early 20th centuries, that wasn't good enough. In the United States, where the puritan dream of building a morally righteous "City on the Hill" always has been a potent social force, anti-drug activism took its strongest hold.

The first goal was banning alcohol, but many in the American temperance movement had even grander designs. William Jennings Bryan, a former secretary of state and a pioneer in the push to ban alcohol and other drugs, insisted in 1919, when alcohol was about to be made illegal, that the United States must "export the gift of Prohibition to other countries, turning the whole world dry." In 1900, the Rev. W.S. Crafts, an official in the Theodore Roosevelt administration, had called for an even broader "international civilizing crusade against alcohol and drugs."

Most of the early crusaders genuinely believed a ban would end drug problems: Simply make drugs illegal, and no one would sell, buy or use them. As the American preacher

> *"The core reason the war on drugs so completely dominates the official policies of so many nations is simple: The United States insists on it."*

Billy Sunday joyously proclaimed when the United States banned alcohol in 1920, "The reign of tears is over. The slums will soon be a memory. We will turn our prisons into factories and our jails into storehouses and corncribs. Men will walk upright now, women will smile, and children will laugh."

In 1920, when alcohol was banned in the United States, a rich and powerful criminal class emerged. And with it came a stupendous rise in violence and corruption. Gangsters protected themselves from the law by buying off officials. They fought for market share not with ads but guns.

And since they couldn't be sued or supervised by government regulators, gangsters and smugglers often provided alcohol that was adulterated or even poisonous, killing tens of thousands and leaving more blind or paralyzed.

These developments shocked Americans. Just 13 years after the Constitution had been amended to create Prohibition, it was changed again to legalize alcohol.

More than Alcohol

But other drugs, which had been banned only gradually with few apparent repercussions because of the vastly lower demand for them, were not legalized.

Instead, the energy of the American anti-alcohol campaign turned on them. Under the leadership of Harry Anslinger, Prohibition agent turned anti-narcotics chief, the American government expanded its bans on drugs at home and took up the "international civilizing crusade" with zeal.

The precedent for international drug prohibition had been set in conferences in 1909 and 1911. At the time, a few nations, notably Canada and Britain, were interested in international regulation of opium, but it was the United States that instigated these conferences and prodded the talks toward total criminal prohibition. Though

> *"The 'international' war on drugs is a policy conceived, created and enforced by the U.S. government."*

delayed by the two world wars, such negotiations eventually led to a full ban.

"It was only in 1945 that the United States within the international community had the political clout to internationalize these ideas of prohibition," said David Bewley-Taylor, a professor at the University of Wales and author of *The United States and International Drug Control, 1909–1997.*

Several international protocols were signed in the 1940s and 1950s. The United States also worked behind the scenes to internationalize its prohibition efforts—sometimes using questionable pressure tactics.

Charles Siragusa, a U.S. narcotics agent during the early years of international drug prohibition, noted in his 1966 memoirs that foreign police "almost always worked willingly with us. It was their superiors in government who were sometimes unhappy that we had entered their countries. Most of the time, though, I found that a casual mention of the possibility of shutting off our foreign aid programs, dropped in the proper quarters, brought grudging permission for our operations almost immediately."

The use of foreign aid as leverage in expanding U.S. drug policies was occasionally made explicit. The 1984 National Drug Strategy for Prevention of Drug Abuse and Drug Trafficking said that "U.S. decisions on foreign aid and other matters" should be "tied to the willingness of the recipient country to execute vigorous enforcement programs against narcotic traffickers."

It was not an idle threat. In 1980, the United States suspended most foreign aid to Bolivia when it deemed the Bolivian government unresponsive to American concerns about cocaine.

Major UN conventions on drugs passed in 1961, 1971 and 1988. These conventions, now the basic international laws of drug prohibition, all were initiated by the U.S. government. Today, almost every nation has signed the UN conventions.

Yet it's important to remember that international drug prohibition came together only gradually, in steps, over decades. Whether prohibition should be the basic method of dealing with drug problems never has been debated seriously at the international level.

American Arm Twisting

The object of American policy today is not only to have nations committed to its general approach of drug prohibition. As Charles Siragusa's memoirs show, the United States long has attempted to carry out its anti-drug activities in other countries and to have its favored policies and programs implemented abroad. It also has worked doggedly to block other countries from trying any drug policy not in line with its own strict-prohibition approach.

Formally, at least, the key instrument of American influence is the "certification" process. Acting under a 1986 directive from Congress, the president, through the State Department, each year reports on the level of cooperation and effort other nations are putting into anti-drug measures. Decertification can result in economic sanctions, international isolation, even an end to U.S. foreign aid.

For third-world countries, that would be a disaster. Not surprisingly, the U.S. report, which is released in March, is always preceded by a flurry of drug crackdowns and anti-drug initiatives in targeted nations. Mexicans call it the "February surprise."

These efforts to curry American favor are meant to avoid the fate of Colombia. Decertified in the mid-1990s, Colombia under President Ernesto Samper spun into political crisis even though the full force of U.S. economic sanctions wasn't used.

> *"The use of foreign aid as leverage in expanding U.S. drug policies was occasionally made explicit."*

Colombia was forced to abandon other priorities and launch a furious attack on drug trafficking. Many experts feel it was that switch of priorities that weakened the central government, damaged the economy and, ultimately, allowed Colombia's rebels to seize 40 percent of the nation's territory. These developments in turn led to spectacular increases in drug production and even greater instability. . . .

U.S. Policies Were Not Criticized

There is considerable opposition to drug prohibition in Latin America, as evidenced by the signatures of many Latin American presidents, ministers and other officials on the 1988 protest letter sent to Annan. Many Latin Americans feel the U.S.-led war on drugs has hurt their countries deeply, by creating powerful drug cartels that corrupt their governments, destabilize their economies and spread bloody mayhem in their streets.

Still, there is virtually no serious official opposition to U.S. policies. Senior Latin American officials often publicly criticize what they see as an exaggerated American emphasis on drug supply rather than on domestic drug demand. But they virtually never criticize the core policy of prohibition.

In part, this false unanimity stems from the old fears of losing American foreign aid and trade access. But another reason is hinted at in the 1998 protest letter itself: All of the senior government officials who signed were "the former president of Colombia," "the former president of Costa Rica," and so on. Only those whose careers are all but over seem willing to criticize the core idea behind American drug policy.

The Latin American elites who dominate their governments have close business, educational and social ties with the United States. For Colombia's elite, Miami is practically a second capital. To be refused a visa to the United States is to have careers, even social lives, crippled.

> *"Whether prohibition should be the basic method of dealing with drug problems never has been debated seriously at the international level."*

Monica de Greiff, a former Colombian justice minister, says it's even a blemish on one's name at home. "If you don't have a visa, [people] will say, 'Um, why don't you have a visa? You must be doing something wrong if you don't have a visa,'" she said.

One of those who says he has felt the effects of this weapon is her father, Gustavo de Greiff. As Colombia's prosecutor general in the early 1990s, de Greiff was renowned in his own country and the United States for his success in hunting and prosecuting drug traffickers.

But at the height of this fame, he publicly declared the drug war to be futile and destructive. His formerly close relations with the United States immediately soured, he says. Not long after, the United States accused de Greiff of corruption. Ultimately, he lost his American visa.

The State Department denies that the United States retaliates against dissenting Latin American officials. In a written response to the *Citizen*, an official stated: "Our law provides that if we have persuasive evidence that somebody is complicit in the commission of a number of types of crimes, one of which is drug trafficking, he doesn't get a visa to enter the United States. This is never done because somebody is critical."

Monica de Greiff doesn't accept this. She says the fear of losing an American visa stunts democratic dialogue in South America. "The idea of legalization is bigger, it's spreading [in Colombia]," she says.

But "people, because of what happened for example to my father, they will never, never take a strong position on that, even if they talk privately about it."

Lies About Holland

Despite the American goal of universal support for drug prohibition, a few countries have taken slightly different directions. The Netherlands is the most famous of these.

Holland is a signatory to international prohibition agreements and continues aggressively to fight most forms of drug trafficking. But since the mid-1970s, the Dutch have made it possible to possess marijuana and sell it in tightly regulated shops. Possession of small amounts of other drugs also is not normally punished. "Harm-reduction" programs, such as providing clean needles to heroin addicts, are central to Dutch policy.

For taking this route, Holland has been fiercely attacked. In a series of statements in 1998, Barry McCaffrey, the outgoing head of the White House's office of National Drug Control Policy, savaged Dutch policy. Dutch teenagers used marijuana at three times the rate of American teens, McCaffrey claimed. "The murder rate in Holland is double that in the United States. The per capita crime rates are much higher than [in] the United States—that's drugs." The Dutch approach, he said, was "an unmitigated disaster."

None of what he said was true.

While figures vary from study to study, most research shows that far fewer Dutch teenagers use marijuana than do American teens. The American murder rate is actually 4½ times higher than the Dutch rate. And while the "unmitigated disaster" claim is vague, it seems unsupportable given that the rate of heroin abuse—considered a key drug indicator—is nearly three times higher in the United States than in Holland.

UN Succumbs to U.S. Pressure

Subtler forms of pressure and influence are used by the United States in a forum that is central to international drug policy: the UN.

The UN has two main bodies that control international drug policies and programs: the International Narcotics Control Board (INCB) and the UN International Drug Control Program (UNDCP). The INCB, made up of 13 people, monitors compliance with international agreements on drugs. The UNDCP handles the UN's drug programs.

"[The United States] also has worked doggedly to block other countries from trying any drug policy not in line with its own strict-prohibition approach."

Many public health officials identify the INCB as being most active in enforcing strict prohibition.

More recent events in Australia strengthen the idea of the INCB as enforcer. Australia also has been working toward the creation of "safe injection rooms"—clean, medically supervised sites where heroin addicts can inject heroin without fear of arrest. The United States strongly opposes such projects. In November 1999, the INCB warned the Australians that if they went ahead, the INCB might embargo Tasmania's opium poppy industry—exactly the same "hint" made by the U.S. State Department in 1996.

"The American influence on the narcotics board is overwhelming and unfortunate," the health minister for the Australian Capital Territory, Michael Moore, told the *Canberra Times*. Pennington agrees. "INCB has throughout been led by the policies of the U.S. State Department." The State Department said it was unable to comment on these views.

U.S. influence can be felt at other levels in the UN, too. For example, the UN's World Health Organization (WHO) was subjected to intense U.S. pressure when it commissioned a report on cocaine use in the early 1990s. Two years of research involving dozens of experts in 22 cities and 19 countries led to a finished report in 1995. On March 15 of that year, the WHO issued a press release announcing the publication of the results. The project, the WHO proudly noted in the press release, was "the largest global study on cocaine use ever undertaken."

But the WHO never issued the report.

WHO spokesman Gregory Hartl says that after the press release was issued, the organization asked several experts to peer-review the report. After "two to three years," some of the experts reported, and the WHO decided the report was "technically unsound"—despite the fact that in 1995, responding to complaints from the United States, the WHO had defended the report as "important and objective."

The WHO has no plans to do further research on cocaine.

The Secret Report

The unreleased document is critical of existing drug policies and many of the beliefs about cocaine that support those policies. . . .

According to a former senior UN International Drug Control Program official, this landmark report was withheld because the United States pressed the WHO to bury it. If it was released, American officials warned, the United States would pull its funding from the section of WHO responsible for the report. The U.S. State Department says it is unable to comment on this allegation.

However, Hartl confirms that this threat was made. In a May 1995 meeting, according to the WHO's records, Neil Boyer, the American representative to the organization, "took the view that [the WHO's] program on substance abuse was headed in the wrong direction."

As proof, Boyer cited the cocaine study, along with "evidence of the WHO's support for harm-reduction programs and previous WHO association with organizations that supported the legalization of drugs." Boyer concluded that "if WHO activities relating to drugs failed to reinforce proven drug-control approaches, funds for the relevant programs should be curtailed."

Despite such pressure, Australia's Pennington says public health officials around the world are increasingly dissenting from a status quo that sees criminal prohibition as central to drug policy. Friction is growing, he says, between officials who want to try novel approaches, such as harm-reduction methods, and the American government, with its insistence on sticking strictly to the war on drugs.

That conflict has yet to seriously break into the international political arena. But if the growing opposition to the war on drugs starts to find a voice among senior world leaders—as the 1998 protest letter to Annan showed it might—it will be increasingly difficult for the American government to cajole, manipulate or bully other countries. Someday, the nations of the world may finally hold an open debate on the wisdom of international drug prohibition.

The Cost of Drug Prohibition Is Not Justified

by David Boaz

About the author: *David Boaz is the executive vice president of the Cato Institute, a libertarian think tank in Washington, D.C.*

Ours is a federal republic. The federal government has only the powers granted to it in the Constitution. And the United States has a tradition of individual liberty, vigorous civil society, and limited government: just because a problem is identified does not mean that the government ought to undertake to solve it, and just because a problem occurs in more than one state does not mean that it is a proper subject for federal policy.

Perhaps no area more clearly demonstrates the bad consequences of not following such rules than drug prohibition. The long federal experiment in prohibition of marijuana, cocaine, heroin, and other drugs has given us unprecedented crime and corruption combined with a manifest failure to stop the use of drugs or reduce their availability to children.

Prohibition: A Guaranteed Failure

In the 1920s Congress experimented with the prohibition of alcohol. On February 20, 1933, a new Congress acknowledged the failure of alcohol Prohibition and sent the Twenty-First Amendment to the states. Congress recognized that Prohibition had failed to stop drinking and had increased prison populations and violent crime. By the end of 1933, national Prohibition was history, though in accordance with our federal system many states continued to outlaw or severely restrict the sale of liquor.

Today Congress confronts a similarly failed prohibition policy. Futile efforts to enforce prohibition have been pursued even more vigorously in the 1980s and 1990s than they were in the 1920s. Total federal expenditures for the first 10 years of Prohibition amounted to $88 million—about $733 million in 1993 dol-

David Boaz, testimony before the U.S. House Subcommittee on Criminal Justice, Drug Policy, and Human Resources, Government Reform and Oversight Committee, Washington, DC, June 16, 1999.

lars. Drug enforcement cost about $22 billion in the Reagan years and another $45 billion in the four years of the [H.W.] Bush administration. The federal government spent $16 billion on drug control programs in FY [fiscal year] 1998 and has approved a budget of $17.9 billion for FY 1999. The Office of National Drug Control Policy reported in April 1999 that state and local governments spent an additional $15.9 billion in FY 1991, an increase of 13 percent over 1990, and there is every reason to believe that state and local expenditures have risen throughout the 1990s.

Those mind-boggling amounts have had some effect. Total drug arrests are now more than 1.5 million a year. There are about 400,000 drug offenders in jails and prison now, and over 80 percent of the increase in the federal prison population from 1985 to 1995 was due to drug convictions. Drug offenders constituted 59.6 percent of all federal prisoners in 1996, up from 52.6 percent in 1990. (Those in federal prison for violent offenses fell from 18 percent to 12.4 percent of the total, while property offenders fell from 14 percent to 8.4 percent.)

The Federal Effort Has Been a Dud

Yet as was the case during Prohibition, all the arrests and incarcerations haven't stopped the use and abuse of drugs, or the drug trade, or the crime associated with black-market transactions. Cocaine and heroin supplies are up; the more our Customs agents interdict, the more smugglers import. In a letter to the *Wall Street Journal* published on November 12, 1996, Janet Crist of the White House Office of National Drug Policy claimed some success:

> Other important results [of the Pentagon's anti-drug efforts] include the arrest of virtually the entire Cali drug cartel leadership, the disruption of the Andean air bridge, and the hemispheric drug interdiction effort that has captured about a third of the cocaine produced in South America each year.

"However," she continued, "there has been no direct effect on either the price or the availability of cocaine on our streets."

That is hardly a sign of a successful policy. And of course, while crime rates have fallen in the past few years, today's crime rates look good only by the standards of the recent past; they remain much higher than the levels of the 1950s.

As for discouraging young people from using drugs, the massive federal effort has largely been a dud. Despite the soaring expenditures on antidrug efforts, about half the students in the United States in 1995 tried an illegal drug before they graduated from high school. According to the 1997 National Household Survey on Drug Abuse, 54.1 percent of high school seniors reported some use of an illegal drug at least once during their lifetime, although it should be noted that only 6.4 percent reported use in the month before the survey was conducted. Every year from 1975 to 1995, at least 82 percent of high school seniors have said they find marijuana "fairly easy" or "very easy" to obtain. During that same period, according to federal statistics of dubious reliability, teenage marijuana use fell dramatically and then rose significantly, suggesting that cultural factors have more effect than "the war on drugs."

The manifest failure of drug prohibition explains why more and more people—from Baltimore mayor Kurt Schmoke to Nobel laureate Milton Friedman, conservative columnist William F. Buckley Jr., and former secretary of state George Shultz—have argued that drug prohibition actually causes more crime and other harms than it prevents.

Drug Prohibition Leads to Increased Crime Rates

Congress should recognize the failure of prohibition and end the federal government's war on drugs. First and foremost, the federal drug laws are constitutionally dubious. As previously noted, the federal government can only exercise the powers that have been delegated to it. The Tenth Amendment reserves all other powers to the states or to the people. However misguided the alcohol prohibitionists turned out to be, they deserve credit for honoring our constitutional system by seeking a constitutional amendment that would explicitly authorize a national policy on the sale of alcohol. Congress never asked the American people for additional constitutional powers to declare a war on drug consumers.

Second, drug prohibition creates high levels of crime. Addicts are forced to commit crimes to pay for a habit that would be easily affordable if it were legal. Police sources have estimated that as much as half the property crime in some major cities is committed by drug users. More dramatically, because drugs are illegal, participants in the drug trade cannot go to court to settle disputes, whether between buyer and seller or between rival sellers. When black-market contracts are breached, the result is often some form of violent sanction, which usually leads to retaliation and then open warfare in the streets.

Our capital city, Washington, D.C., has become known as the "murder capital" even though it is the most heavily policed city in the United States. Make no mistake about it, the annual carnage that stands behind America's still outrageously high murder rates has nothing to do with the mind-altering effects of a marijuana cigarette or a crack pipe. It is instead one of the grim and bitter consequences of an ideological crusade whose proponents will not yet admit defeat.

"As was the case during Prohibition, all the arrests and incarcerations haven't stopped the use and abuse of drugs."

Third, drug prohibition channels over $40 billion a year into the criminal underworld. Alcohol prohibition drove reputable companies into other industries or out of business altogether, which paved the way for mobsters to make millions through the black market. If drugs were legal, organized crime would stand to lose billions of dollars, and drugs would be sold by legitimate businesses in an open marketplace.

Fourth, drug prohibition is a classic example of throwing money at a problem. The federal government spends some $16 billion to enforce the drug laws every year—all to no avail. For years drug war bureaucrats have been tailoring their budget requests to the latest news reports. When drug use goes up, taxpayers are told the government needs more money so that it can redouble its efforts against a rising drug scourge. When drug use goes down, taxpayers are told that it would be a big mistake to curtail spending just when progress is being made. Good news or bad, spending levels must be maintained or increased.

Fifth, the drug laws are responsible for widespread social upheaval. "Law and order" advocates too often fail to

> *"Drug prohibition creates high levels of crime."*

recognize that some laws can actually cause societal disorder. A simple example will illustrate that phenomenon. Right now our college campuses are relatively calm and peaceful, but imagine what would happen if Congress were to institute military conscription in order to wage a war in Kosovo, Korea, or the Middle East. Campuses across the country would likely erupt in protest—even though Congress obviously did not desire that result. The drug laws happen to have different "disordering" effects. Perhaps the most obvious has been turning our cities into battlefields and upending the normal social order.

Drug prohibition has created a criminal subculture in our inner cities. The immense profits involved in a black-market business make drug dealing the most lucrative endeavor for many people, especially those who care least about getting on the wrong side of the law.

Drug dealers become the most visibly successful people in inner-city communities, the ones with money, and clothes, and cars. Social order is turned upside down when the most successful people in a community are criminals. The drug war makes peace and prosperity virtually impossible in inner cities.

Breaking Up Families

Sixth, the drug laws break up families. Too many parents have been separated from their children because they were convicted of marijuana possession, small-scale sale of drugs, or some other non-violent offense. Will Foster used marijuana to control the pain and swelling associated with his crippling rheumatoid arthritis. He was arrested, convicted of marijuana cultivation, and sentenced to 93 years in prison, later reduced to 20 years. Are his three children better off with a father who uses marijuana medicinally, or a father in jail for 20 years?

And going to jail for drug offenses isn't just for men any more. In 1996, 188,880 women were arrested for violating drug laws. Most of them did not go to jail, of course, but more than two-thirds of the 146,000 women behind bars have children. One of them is Brenda Pearson, a heroin addict who managed to maintain a job at a securities firm in New York. She supplied heroin to an addict friend, and a Michigan prosecutor had her extradited, prosecuted, and sentenced to 50 to 200 years. We can only hope that her two children will remember her when she gets out.

Seventh, drug prohibition leads to civil liberties abuses. The demand to win this unwinnable war has led to wiretapping, entrapment, property seizures, and other abuses of Americans' traditional liberties. The saddest cases result in the deaths of innocent people: people like Donald Scott, whose home was raided at dawn on the pretext of cultivating marijuana, and who was shot and killed when he rushed into the living room carrying a gun; or people like the Rev. Accelyne Williams, a 75-year-old minister who died of a heart attack when police burst into his Boston apartment looking for drugs—the wrong apartment, as it turned out; or people like Esequiel Hernandez, who was out tending his family's goats near the Rio Grande just six days after his 18th birthday when he was shot by a Marine patrol looking for drug smugglers. As we deliberate the costs and benefits of drug policy, we should keep those people in mind.

Students of American history will someday ponder the question of how today's elected officials could readily admit to the mistaken policy of alcohol prohibition in the 1920s but continue the policy of drug prohibition. Indeed, the only historical lesson that recent presidents and Congresses seem to have drawn from the period of alcohol prohibition is that government should not try to outlaw the sale of alcohol. One of the broader lessons that they should have learned is this: prohibition laws should be judged according to their real-world effects, not their promised benefits.

"Drug laws break up families."

Intellectual history teaches us that people have a strong incentive to maintain their faith in old paradigms even as the facts become increasingly difficult to explain within that paradigm. But when a paradigm has manifestly failed, we need to think creatively and develop a new paradigm. The paradigm of prohibition has failed. I urge members of Congress and all Americans to have the courage to let go of the old paradigm, to think outside the box, and to develop a new model for dealing with the very real risks of drug and alcohol abuse. If the Congress will subject the federal drug laws to that kind of new thinking, it will recognize that the drug war is not the answer to problems associated with drug use.

Medical Marijuana

In addition to the general critique above, I would like to touch on a few more specific issues. A particularly tragic consequence of the stepped-up war on drugs is the refusal to allow sick people to use marijuana as medicine. Prohibitionists insist that marijuana is not good medicine, or at least that there are legal alternatives to marijuana that are equally good. Those who believe that individuals should make their own decisions, not have their decisions made for them by Washington bureaucracies, would simply say that that's a decision for patients and their doctors to make. But in fact there is good medical evidence about the therapeutic value of marijuana—despite the difficulty of doing adequate research on an illegal drug. A recent National Institutes of Health panel concluded that smoking marijuana may help treat a number of conditions, including nausea and pain. It can be particularly effective in improving the appetite of AIDS and cancer patients. The drug could also assist people who fail to respond to traditional remedies.

More than 70 percent of U.S. cancer specialists in one survey said they would prescribe marijuana if it was legal; nearly half said they had urged their patients to break the law to acquire the drug. The British Medical Association reports that nearly 70 percent of its members believe marijuana should be available for therapeutic use. Even President George Bush's Office of Drug Control Policy criticized the Department of Health and Human Services for closing its special medical marijuana program.

> *"A particularly tragic consequence of the stepped-up war on drugs is the refusal to allow sick people to use marijuana as medicine."*

Whatever the actual value of medical marijuana, the relevant fact for federal policymakers is that in 1996 the voters of California and Arizona authorized physicians licensed in the state to recommend the use of medical marijuana to seriously ill and terminally ill patients residing in the state without being subject to civil and criminal penalties.

In response to those referenda, however, the Clinton administration announced, without any intervening authorization from Congress, that any physician recommending or prescribing medicinal marijuana under state law would be prosecuted. In the February 11, 1997, Federal Register the Office of National Drug Control Policy announced that federal policy would be as follows: (1) physicians who recommend and prescribe medicinal marijuana to patients in conformity with state law and patients who use such marijuana will be prosecuted; (2) physicians who recommend and prescribe medicinal marijuana to patients in conformity with state law will be excluded from Medicare and Medicaid; and (3) physicians who recommend and prescribe medicinal marijuana to patients in conformity with state law will have their scheduled-drug DEA registrations revoked.

The announced federal policy also encourages state and local enforcement officials to arrest and prosecute physicians suspected of prescribing or recommending medicinal marijuana and to arrest and prosecute patients who use such marijuana. And adding insult to injury, the policy also encourages the IRS to issue a revenue ruling disallowing any medical deduction for medical marijuana lawfully obtained under state law.

Clearly, this is a blatant effort by the federal government to impose a national policy on the people in the states in question, people who have already elected a contrary policy. Federal officials do not agree with the policy the people have elected; they mean to override it, local rule notwithstanding—just as the Clinton administration has tried to do in other cases, such as the California initiatives dealing with racial preferences and state benefits for immigrants.

Congress and the administration should respect the decisions of the voters in Arizona and California; and in Alaska, Nevada, Oregon, and Washington, where voters passed medical marijuana initiatives in 1998; and in other states where such initiatives may be proposed, debated, and passed. One of the benefits of a federal republic is that different policies may be tried in different states. One of the benefits of our Constitution is that it limits the power of the federal government to impose one policy on the several states.

Mandatory Minimums

The common law in England and America has always relied on judges and juries to decide cases and set punishments. Under our modern system, of course, many crimes are defined by the legislature, and appropriate penalties are defined by statute. However, mandatory minimum sentences and rigid sentencing guidelines shift too much power to legislators and regulators who are not involved in particular cases. They turn judges into clerks and prevent judges from weighing all the facts and circumstances in setting appropriate sentences. In addition, mandatory minimums for nonviolent first-time drug offenders result in sentences grotesquely disproportionate to the gravity of the offense. Absurdly, Congress has mandated minimums for drug offenses but not for murder and other violent crimes, so that a judge has more discretion in sentencing a murder than a first-time drug offender.

"More than 70 percent of U.S. cancer specialists in one survey said they would prescribe marijuana if it was legal."

Rather than extend mandatory minimum sentences to further crimes, Congress should repeal mandatory minimums and let judges perform their traditional function of weighing the facts and setting appropriate sentences.

Not a Criminal Problem

Drug abuse is a problem, for those involved in it and for their family and friends. But it is better dealt with as a moral and medical than as a criminal problem—"a problem for the surgeon general, not the attorney general," as Mayor Schmoke puts it.

The United States is a federal republic, and Congress should deal with drug prohibition the way it dealt with alcohol Prohibition. The Twenty-First Amendment did not actually legalize the sale of alcohol; it simply repealed the federal prohibition and returned to the several states the authority to set alcohol policy. States took the opportunity to design diverse liquor policies that were in tune with the preferences of their citizens. After 1933, three states and hundreds of counties continued to practice prohibition. Other states chose various forms of alcohol legalization.

Congress should withdraw from the war on drugs and let the states set their own policies with regard to currently illegal drugs. The states would be well advised to treat marijuana, cocaine, and heroin the way most states now treat alcohol: It should be legal for licensed stores to sell such drugs to adults. Drug sales to children, like alcohol sales to children, should remain illegal. Driving under the influence of drugs should be illegal.

With such a policy, Congress would acknowledge that our current drug policies have failed. It would restore authority to the states, as the Founders envisioned. It would save taxpayers' money. And it would give the states the power to experiment with drug policies and perhaps devise more successful rules.

Repeal of prohibition would take the astronomical profits out of the drug business and destroy the drug kingpins that terrorize parts of our cities. It would reduce crime even more dramatically than did the repeal of alcohol prohibition. Not only would there be less crime; reform would also free police to concentrate on robbery, burglary, and violent crime.

The War on Drugs has lasted longer than Prohibition, longer than the War in Vietnam. But there is no light at the end of this tunnel. Prohibition has failed, again, and should be repealed, again.

Drug Prohibition Violates Civil Liberties

by Lance Lamberton

About the author: *Lance Lamberton was the deputy director of the White House Office of Policy Information for the Reagan administration.*

In determining the proper boundaries of government action consistent with a free society, it is instructive to explore whether drug prohibition is an appropriate response to actions that are clearly self-destructive to some. Following from concern over the harmful effects of drugs, the prevailing view is that government has a responsibility to protect its citizens from that harm through prohibition. Yet that position runs directly counter to the foundation and maintenance of a free society. Indeed, in today's context, drug prohibition represents one of the single greatest threats to our liberties.

Foremost to understanding the threat prohibition poses to liberty is a proper understanding of rights. According to the Declaration of Independence, we are endowed "with certain inalienable Rights, that among these are Life, Liberty, and the Pursuit of Happiness." The underlying assumption is that one's life is one's own. Thus the choices a person makes with his own life properly belong to him.

This principle is not hard to embrace. The idea that the individual owns his own life is accepted almost implicitly, especially in countries with a tradition of free thought and institutions, such as the United States. Yet it is a principle readily abandoned when it comes to drugs. Underlying the idea that government, and not the individual, has the right to determine what one may or may not ingest is the assumption that government, and not the individual, has ultimate authority over, and ownership of, life itself. Taken to its logical conclusion, this principle leads to slavery.

This does not mean government has no right to restrict and prohibit harmful behavior. But it must do so only to enhance and protect freedom of action. The old axiom that "my freedom to swing my arms ends where your nose begins"

Lance Lamberton, "The Drug War's Assault on Liberty," *The Freeman: Ideas on Liberty*, vol. 50, August 2000.

applies here. The essential point is that the individual has the right to do whatever he wants with his own life, since he has a property in that life, provided that he does not interfere with the same freedom of another.

With drug prohibition, the government attempts to coerce citizens into abstaining from something it deems harmful. This, in essence, is criminal behavior elevated to the status of law because it involves the initiation of force, or threat of force, against a class of citizens (illicit drug users) who are engaged in voluntary, non-coercive behavior. Moreover, the policy is doomed to failure as witnessed by the daily news reports on the government's drug war, which clearly show that the government will *never* be able to stop individuals from taking drugs short of imposing an Orwellian *1984* level of surveillance on its citizens. And judging from the ready availability of drugs in prison, even that is unlikely to work.

Taking Drugs Is Not a Crime

The bottom line is that "criminal" action implies a victim, where force, or the threat of it, is imposed *on another.* However, what the individual freely does to himself—such as taking drugs—does not constitute the imposition of force, and is therefore not a crime. On the contrary, it is the prosecution of the drug war that is the crime.

The devastating impact of the drug war on society, along with its inevitable failure, is a consequence of its protagonists' failure to recognize a salient fact of human nature—namely, there will always be some individuals strongly driven to take drugs because they provide pleasure or block pain, and no legal sanctions, no matter how severe, will prevent that. Furthermore, the more draconian the drug enforcement the more draconian the consequences by every measure imaginable, from diminished civil liberty to increased violent crime.

Criminal activity normally involves no more than a small fraction of any given population. Yet when laws are dramatically at variances with the legitimate exercise of freedom, wide-scale disobedience is often the result. Such was the case with alcohol prohibition, conscription during the War Between the States and the Vietnam War, civil disobedience during America's civil rights movement, and general disregard for the national 55-mph speed limit.

> *"Drug prohibition represents one of the single greatest threats to our liberties."*

Prohibition also fails to acknowledge the power of markets. By making a desired substance illegal, prohibition increases profitability by making the substance scarcer and more risky to handle. In the pursuit of self-interest, and in light of the enormous profits earned from the illicit drug trade, there will always be a plentiful supply of risk-takers willing to run the gamut of government interdiction efforts to meet the demand for drugs. Ironically, the scarcer drugs become because of prohibition, the more profitable they become for dealers and the greater the incentive to sell them.

Thus it is profit, and the pleasure derived from taking drugs, that thwarts the increasingly militant calls for an "all out" drug war. Not surprisingly, when government attempts to deny basic individual sovereignty, it must intrude with reckless abandon on other rights to enforce its objectives. Protection from unreasonable search and seizure, as guaranteed by the Fourth Amendment to the Constitution, is a prime target for the drug warriors. Calls for universal drug testing are beginning to surface, regardless of any concern for probable cause. Former New York Mayor Ed Koch and others have even

> *"When laws are dramatically at variance with the legitimate exercise of freedom, wide-scale disobedience is often the result."*

called for shooting down planes merely suspected of carrying drugs.

Tragically, the war on drugs, allegedly being prosecuted to protect human life, has instead claimed many innocent lives. Take, for example, those caught in the crossfire between warring gangs of drug dealers fighting over turf, or trigger-happy drug-enforcement agents who raid the wrong homes and accidentally kill residents defending their families against violent assault. Additional fatalities in the drug war include deaths attributed to drug overdoses or poisoned drugs owing to the adulteration and unknown potency of drugs traded on the illicit market. The war on drugs has also become a significant factor in the spread of AIDS; almost 7,000 intravenous drug users a year have died of AIDS from sharing needles.

Legalization Would Not Increase Drug Use

Despite this tragic loss of life, prohibitionists claim that legalization will result in a dramatic increase in use, thereby dwarfing the number of fatalities directly attributable to prohibition. However, considering that 80 percent of deaths from ingestion of heroin and cocaine is caused by their adulteration on the black market, leaving 20 percent who die as a result of factors that would exist after legalization, it would require a 400 percent increase in use to equal the current death toll. This is unlikely; at the end of alcohol prohibition, estimates of increased consumption have ranged from zero to 250 percent.

On the contrary, it could be argued that consumption of hard drugs such as heroin and cocaine would actually decline with legalization, especially among vulnerable youth in the inner cities. This is because tens of thousands of hardcore users would no longer be pushing drugs to non-users in order to make money to support their own habits, a common and well-known practice throughout the drug culture. When we look at how alcohol is marketed and distributed, we can see how legalization will put the neighborhood "pusher" out of business.

In addition to the death toll coming from prohibition, the costs related to drug enforcement are staggering. Since President [Ronald] Reagan launched his much-heralded "war" in the early 1980s, the United States has spent nearly $300 billion to stem the flow, with indirect costs put at $67 billion annually as government continues to beef up the budgets of law enforcement agencies and the military to prosecute the drug war.

The courts are so overwhelmed with drug cases that the administration of justice is being hampered to an intolerable degree. For example, in 1998 more than 400,000 Americans serving prison terms (one in four imprisoned) were doing so for drug offenses, up from 50,000, or one in ten, in 1980.

Prohibition also has the unfortunate consequence of corrupting law enforcement agents lured by the easy availability of huge sums of tax-free income in return for their cooperation in the drug trade. According to reporters Jack Nelson and Ronald J. Ostrow, "Law enforcement corruption, sparked mostly by illegal drugs, has become so rampant that the number of federal, state and local officials in federal prisons has multiplied five times in four years, from 107 in 1994 to 548 in 1998."

On the civil liberties front, the drug war has led to the property of non-drug users being confiscated without due process. In operations labeled "zero-tolerance," leased boats are searched (sometimes without satisfying the legal standard of probable cause) and then seized from their owners when even minute quantities of drugs are found onboard. Indeed, fully 80 percent of total asset seizures related to the drug war occur without a criminal charge being filed.

Another casualty in the war on drugs is legitimate scientific research with drugs such as LSD and MDMA. In addition, marijuana has been almost universally prohibited for use as a treatment for glaucoma, which leads to blindness, and for ameliorating the severe side effects of chemotherapy.

Individual Responsibility Is the Key to Liberty

Inherent in the prohibitionist position is the failure to recognize individual responsibility and autonomy as operating principles for an efficacious life. While taking drugs involves the freedom to engage in what may be self-destructive behavior, it also, and more importantly, involves the principle of allowing for life-enhancing activity. The freedom to fail is also the freedom to succeed, and vice versa. Ultimately, only the individual can determine what is in his best interest. While that is not a fail-safe mechanism, the alternative

> *"Protection from unreasonable search and seizure, as guaranteed by the Fourth Amendment . . . is a prime target for the drug warriors."*

is tyranny. Drug prohibitionists embrace that alternative by presuming to know what is best for others, and in the pursuit of their vision of the good life they are willing to impose that vision on others by force.

To counter the argument for individual responsibility, prohibitionists claim that drugs necessarily hurt others and society at large. Discounting the preponderance of evidence that prohibition imposes a much greater cost on society than legalization ever could, the fact remains that even for those who use drugs in a life-threatening way, it is *their lives* that they threaten. Society, and even loved ones, do not have a property right in the life of the drug abuser. To assume otherwise is collectivism, pure and simple.

If prohibitionists were interested in consistency, their line of reasoning would take them down a path I doubt many of them would want to follow. Would they propose banning tobacco or alcohol consumption because of potentially harmful effects? How about high cholesterol foods? With heart disease being the single greatest killer of Americans today, are prohibitionists prepared to follow their own logic and ban bacon and eggs? And what about high-risk occupations and activities such as stunt-car driving, hang gliding, and motorcycling?

Assuming you could successfully ban such activities and substances, what would be the implications for the role that risk-taking plays in enhancing the enjoyment of life? While most people avoid risk in the realm of health or physical activity, others are drawn to it because it enriches their lives. The very essence of individuality implies that different people have different requirements in achieving happiness.

> *"On the civil liberties front, the drug war has led to the property of non-drug users being confiscated without due process."*

Drug prohibitionists, however, will claim that illicit drugs can never have any other effect than to debilitate and destroy. Yet even among the most dangerous drugs, "addiction" is far from guaranteed. Dosage has everything to do with a drug's potentially harmful affects, and if doses are low enough, and taken infrequently enough, no long-term or short-term ill effects will result.

Besides, the critical point, which cannot be emphasized enough, is that ownership of one's life entitles one to do with it what one chooses, even if that choice leads to self-destruction.

In light of the futility in waging the war on drugs, what leads the government to pursue it and most Americans to support it? Part of the answer lies in the coercive nature of government itself. If war, as Randolph Bourne stated, is "the health of the state," then the American government is on a very healthy diet.

The Government Must Protect Rights

Since government is predicated on the use of force, it oft-times sees its reason for being in exercising it. If this power is used to protect rights, it is a benevolent force. But the temptation to abuse that power is sometimes irresistible. While the line between using government force in retaliation against initiators and being the initiator itself is a clear one, it is line easily crossed.

There is also a need on the part of government to fight an enemy, take on a menace, and be the paternalistic guardian of the people. Indeed, if officeholders do not have the commodity of fear and the specter of menace to incite people to rally around them for support, they risk, in a democracy, repudiation at the polls from bored and fickle voters, and in a dictatorship, the violent overthrow of the government.

Hollywood and the media have certainly done their parts in feeding the current frenzy. Grisly news reports on the drug war and its victims boost ratings

> *"The real undoing of the drug war will be the eventual realization that government cannot alter human nature."*

and provide ample grist for sensationalized TV specials and movies. This in turn creates the popular illusion that it is the drugs themselves that cause the violence and crimes associated with them, rather than their prohibition. Yet we have only to look back to the era of alcohol prohibition to identify the real source of drug-related violence. In the ten years following the end of alcohol prohibition, the murder rate from assault by firearms went down from a prohibition high of 16 per 100,000 of population in 1933 to less than nine per 100,000 by 1943.

America's drug war is also a manifestation of the historical pendulum swinging toward social conservatism. Operating in cycles that run on the order of 20 years, America is reacting to the social excesses of the 1960s. Sexual mores have become more restrictive, drinking is less socially acceptable, and smokers' rights have become severely circumscribed.

Indeed, the current trend—popular among both conservatives and "liberals"—is to place under cultural and political assault activities that give pleasure and hold the potential for harm. The "safety at any cost" approach toward regulating consumer choices, championed by environmental and consumer activists such as Ralph Nader, is but one variant of the kind of government paternalism now in vogue.

America Has a Heritage of Political Liberty

America's puritanical heritage, while dramatically at variance with its heritage of political liberty, has endured as well as it has owing to the lure of messianic perfectionism. Few countries in the West are as "blessed" as the United States with the number and intensity of moral crusaders determined to use government to impose their moral values on others by force.

This puritanical impulse is enjoying a major resurgence in the United States. Historically, America has been a magnet for cultural extremes, ranging from the free love communes of the sixties to the abstinent Shaker communities of the early nineteenth century. In the history of the Western world, no other country embarked on the bizarre path of alcohol prohibition, despite alcohol's deep historical, cultural, and economic roots.

The U.S. Constitution and Bill of Rights have held America's crusading impulse in check. Nevertheless, it persists, ebbing and flowing as circumstance and public opinion dictate.

Another factor fueling the drug war is an undeniable increase in drug use, a trend that started in the sixties. Yet can the increase in any way correlate with the hysteria that has overtaken America in the decades that followed? Indeed, deaths attributed to drug use are but a small percentage of deaths related to alcohol and tobacco. And despite hyperbolic claims by politicians and the media over the threat that drugs pose to our society and culture, the economy continues to grow, life expectancies continue to increase, technological advances continue unabated, and Americans in all walks of life continue to build lives of meaning and value, both for themselves and their families.

The most tragic consequences related to drug use persist in America's inner cities. Yet here it is government paternalism that is the culprit, leading people without hope into lives of drug dependency. As the debilitating effects of welfare dependency strangle motivation and opportunity, the seductive lure of drug profits or the temporary relief that drugs bring provides a market for drugs that otherwise would not exist.

Government Intrusion Must Be Stopped

Predicting the future is always a risky business, but when it comes to determining what path Americans will choose concerning drug policy, both history and a proper understanding of human nature give us some guideposts.

People eventually tire of moral crusades. No matter how lofty or seemingly righteous, there comes a time when people's energy and direction must go elsewhere. For example, the wave of progressive reform that began at the end of the nineteenth century eventually burned itself out, to be replaced by the relative social liberalism of the roaring twenties. The strident anti-communism of the McCarthy era in the fifties gave way to the New Left that engulfed America's universities in the sixties.

But the real undoing of the drug war will be the eventual realization that government cannot alter human nature and that society is no longer willing to pay the price required; in money, social disruption, and reduced liberty, to prosecute this war. In the past decade especially, many prominent voices have been raised against prohibition, and no doubt many others will join them in the near future. Moreover, prohibitionists are finding themselves compelled to respond in public to the growing call for legalization to an extent that would have been unheard of ten years ago.

Yet until the current level of support for prohibition burns itself out, vigilance and the courage to speak out are required if we are to avoid the permanent establishment of new forms of government intrusion into our personal lives. That is the real threat facing us today.

Drug Prohibition Discriminates Against Minorities

by Human Rights Watch

About the author: *Human Rights Watch is an independent, nongovernmental organization that conducts fact-finding investigations into human rights abuses in all regions of the world and publishes those findings in books and reports.*

Since the mid 1980s, the United States has undertaken aggressive law enforcement strategies and criminal justice policies aimed at curtailing drug abuse. The costs and benefits of this national war on drugs are fiercely debated. What is not debatable, however, is its impact on black Americans. Ostensibly color blind, the war on drugs has been waged disproportionately against black Americans.

Our research shows that blacks comprise 62.7 percent and whites 36.7 percent of all drug offenders admitted to state prison, even though federal surveys and other data detailed in this report show clearly that this racial disparity bears scant relation to racial differences in drug offending. There are, for example, five times more white drug users than black. Relative to population, black men are admitted to state prison on drug charges at a rate that is 13.4 times greater than that of white men. In large part because of the extraordinary racial disparities in incarceration for drug offenses, blacks are incarcerated for all offenses at 8.2 times the rate of whites. One in every 20 black men over the age of 18 in the United States is in state or federal prison, compared to one in 180 white men.

Shocking as such national statistics are, they mask even worse racial disparities in individual states. In seven states, for example, blacks constitute between 80 and 90 percent of all drug offenders sent to prison. In at least fifteen states, black men are admitted to prison on drug charges at rates that are from 20 to 57 times greater than those of white men. These racial disparities in drug offenders admitted to prison skew the racial balance of state prison populations. In two states, one in every 13 black men is in prison. In seven states, blacks are incarcerated at more than 13 times the rate of whites.

The imprisonment of blacks for drug offenses is part of a larger crisis of over-incarceration in the United States. Although prison should be used as a last resort to protect society from violent or dangerous individuals, more people are sent to prison in the United States for nonviolent drug offenses than for crimes of violence. Throughout the 1990s, more than one hundred thousand drug offenders were sent to prison annually. More than 1.5 million prison admissions on drug charges have occurred since 1980. The rate at which drug offenders are incarcerated has increased ninefold. According to retired General Barry McCaffrey, director of the Office of National Drug Control Policy, the nation's war on drugs has propelled the creation of a vast "drug gulag." Drug control policies bear primary responsibility for the quadrupling of the national prison population since 1980 and a soaring incarceration rate, the highest among western democracies.

Black Americans Bear a Heavier Burden

Human Rights Watch presents in this report original as well as previously published statistics that document the extraordinary extent to which Americans, and especially black Americans, have been burdened with imprisonment because of nonviolent drug offenses. We have conducted the first state-by-state analysis of the impact of drug offenses on the admission to prison of blacks and whites. The statistics we have compiled present a unique—and devastating—picture of the price black Americans have paid in each state for the national effort to curtail the use and sale of illicit drugs.

We have focused on the imprisonment of drug offenders at the state level because aggregate national data masks the remarkable differences among the states regarding the degree to which they put drug offenders in prison and the extent to which the use of prison as a penal sanction for drug offenders is racially disproportionate. As discussed in this report, these substantial state differences are primarily the result of public penal policies and law enforcement priorities, not different rates of drug offending.

With this report Human Rights Watch seeks to bring renewed attention to extreme racial disparities in one area of the criminal justice system—the incarceration of drug law

"Ostensibly color blind, the war on drugs has been waged disproportionately against black Americans."

offenders, i.e., persons whose most serious conviction offense is a nonviolent drug law violation. The high rates of incarceration for all drug offenders are cause for concern. But the grossly disparate rates at which blacks and whites are sent to prison for drug offenses raise a clear warning flag concerning the fairness and equity of drug law enforcement across the country, and underscore the need for reforms that would minimize these disparities without sacrificing legitimate drug control objectives.

Drug offenders in the United States face penal sanctions that are uniquely severe among western democracies. Drug sentences, even for those guilty of retailing or possessing small drug quantities, can compare to or exceed sentences for serious violent crimes such as armed robbery, rape, and even murder. Supporters of imprisonment for drug offenders insist it removes major traffickers and dangerous criminals from society, deters prospective offenders, and enhances community safety and well-being. Critics point to compelling data showing that few of the

> *"Black men are admitted to state prison on drug charges at a rate . . . 13.4 times greater than that of white men."*

drug offenders who end up in prison are higher level dealers or traffickers and, indeed, that the prior criminal records of many incarcerated drug offenders are limited to drug offenses or consist of other nonviolent crimes. The massive use of imprisonment has failed to decrease the availability of drugs or raise their price, and adult drug use has not changed appreciably since the end of the 1980s. Most observers believe imprisonment has had little impact on the number of drug dealers on the streets. Even many police officials acknowledge that for every low level dealer incarcerated, another emerges to take his place. Moreover, according to an authoritative independent study of mandatory minimum prison sentences for drug offenders, such sentences are "not justifiable on the basis of cost-effectiveness at reducing cocaine consumption, cocaine expenditures or drug-related crime."

Racial Bias Versus Sheer Indifference

Prison is a legitimate criminal sanction—but it should be used sensibly, justly, parsimoniously, and with due consideration for the principles of proportionality and respect for human dignity required by international human rights law. The incarceration of hundreds of thousands of low-level nonviolent drug offenders betrays indifference to such considerations. Moreover, many drug offenders receive egregiously long prison sentences, particularly because of the prevalence of mandatory sentencing laws for drug offenses that do not permit judges to calibrate sentences to the conduct and level of culpability of each defendant. Many factors—the transformation of crime and punishment into key issues in electoral debates, the persistence of drug abuse, the desire to "send a message" and communicate social opprobrium, ignorance about drug pharmacology, and concern about crime, among others—have encouraged politicians and public officials to champion harsh prison sentences for drug offenders and to turn a blind eye to the extraordinary human, social, and economic costs of such policies. They have also turned a blind eye to the war on drugs' staggering racial impact.

It is difficult to assess the extent to which racial bias or sheer indifference to the fate of black communities has contributed to the development and persistence of the nation's punitive anti-drug strategies. Certainly the emphasis on penal sanctions in the fight against drugs cannot be divorced from longstanding public association of racial minorities with crime and drugs. Cocaine use by white Americans in all social classes increased in the late 1970s and early 1980s, but it did not engender the "orgy of media and political attention" that catalyzed the war on drugs in the mid-1980s when smokable cocaine in the form of crack spread throughout low income minority neighborhoods that were already seen as dangerous and threatening. Even though far more whites used both powder cocaine and crack cocaine than blacks, the image of the drug offender that has dominated media stories is a black man slouching in an alleyway, not a white man in his home. When asked to close their eyes and envision a drug user, Americans overwhelmingly picture a black person.

Poor minority urban neighborhoods have been the principal "fronts" of the war on drugs. Massive street sweeps, "buy and bust" operations, and other police activities have heavily targeted participants in street level, retail drug transactions in these neighborhoods. Not surprisingly, comparably few of the people arrested there have been white. Racial profiling—or the police practice of stopping, questioning, and searching minorities in vehicles or on the street based solely on their appearance—has also contributed to racially disproportionate drug arrests, although there are no reliable estimates of the number. More blacks have also been prosecuted federally for crack offenses than white, and thus have disproportionately felt the effects of the higher sentences for crack versus powder cocaine mandated in federal law.

Many Americans would agree that punitive drug policies relying on harsh penal sanctions would have been changed long ago if whites were incarcerated on drug charges at the same rate as blacks. It is deeply troubling that in the United States the political majority has maintained criminal justice policies that so disproportionately burden a racial minority, particularly when those policies coupled with felony disenfranchisement laws further politically weaken that minority. Politicians have been able more easily to reap the electoral advantages of endorsing tough policies because the group that suffered most from those policies—black Americans—lacked the numbers to prevail in the political arena.

> *"The grossly disparate rates at which blacks and whites are sent to prison for drug offenses raise a clear warning flag."*

Human Rights Watch fully acknowledges the public's legitimate interest in curtailing the abuse of dangerous drugs. But the importance of drug control should not be permitted to override fundamental principles of equal protection of the laws and racial equality. In an equitable criminal justice system, sanctions should be imposed equally on offending populations.

Policies with Unjustified Discriminatory Impacts Must End

Under state and federal constitutional law, racial disparities in law enforcement are constitutional as long as they are not undertaken with discriminatory intent or purpose. International human rights law wisely does not impose the requirement of discriminatory intent. The International Convention on the Elimination of all Forms of Racial Discrimination (CERD), to which the U.S. is a state party, defines race discrimination as conduct that has the "purpose or effect" of restricting rights on the basis of race. It proscribes race-neutral practices curtailing fundamental rights that unnecessarily create statistically significant racial disparities even in the absence of racial animus. It requires remedial action whenever there is an unjustifiable disparate impact upon a group distinguished by race, color, descent, or national or ethnic origin, even where there may be no intent to discriminate against that group. Under CERD, governments may not engage in "malign neglect," that is, they may not ignore the need to secure equal treatment of all racial and ethnic groups, but rather must act affirmatively to prevent or end policies with unjustified discriminatory impacts.

> *"More blacks have . . . disproportionately felt the effects of . . . higher sentences for crack versus powder cocaine."*

Assessing whether the severe impact of drug law enforcement on blacks is justifiable requires scrutiny of the drug war's goals and methods, and consideration of available alternatives. Human Rights Watch believes there are numerous policy alternatives to current patterns of criminal law enforcement that would reduce adverse racial disparities while continuing to respond to social concerns about public drug dealing and drug abuse. In the context of nationwide debates over the use of the criminal law to address drug abuse, doubts about the fairness and justice of enforcing those laws disproportionately against minorities take on even greater significance. It is hard to justify policies that result in the grossly disproportionate incarceration of a racial minority when there are feasible and cost-effective alternative approaches to address drug abuse and drug dealing that would not have such an effect.

Even if blacks and whites were sent to prison on drug charges at comparable rates, Human Rights Watch would still urge reconsideration of the heavy U.S. reliance on incarceration in its drug policies. In choosing strategies to address drug abuse and drug dealing, the country must consider the negative consequences of high incarceration rates, particularly in minority communities. No functioning democracy has ever governed itself with as large a percentage of its adults incarcerated as the United States. The direct and collateral consequences of imprisonment may be acceptable when violent offenders are put behind bars, but they are much harder to justify for nonviolent drug offenders.

In the poor urban minority communities from which most black drug offenders are taken, the high percentage of men and, increasingly, women sent to prison may also undermine their communities' moral and social cohesion. By damaging the human and social capital of already disadvantaged neighborhoods, the "war on drugs" may well be counterproductive, diminishing opportunities for social and economic mobility and even contributing to an increase in crime rates.

The racially disproportionate nature of the war on drugs is not just devastating to black Americans. It contradicts faith in the principles of justice and equal protection of the laws that should be the bedrock of any constitutional democracy; it exposes and deepens the racial fault lines that continue to weaken the country and belies its promise as a land of equal opportunity; and it undermines faith among all races in the fairness and efficacy of the criminal justice system. Urgent action is needed, at both the state and federal level, to address this crisis for the American nation.

America Must Reassess Drug Fighting Policies

U.S. political leaders must acknowledge the excessive and racially disproportionate incarceration of nonviolent drug offenders and grapple forthrightly with ways to eliminate it. The first step is to reevaluate the current strategies for fighting drugs. Policy makers in each state, as well as in the federal government, should reassess existing public policy approaches to drug use and sales to identify more equitable but still effective options. In particular, they should examine the costs and benefits of relying heavily on penal sanctions to address drug use and drug trafficking and should look closely at law enforcement strategies to identify ways to make them more racially equitable.

We believe each state as well as the federal government should subject current and proposed drug policies to strict scrutiny and modify those that cause significant, unwarranted racial disparities. In addition, we believe the state and federal governments should:

• Eliminate mandatory minimum sentencing laws that require prison sentences based on the quantity of the drug sold and the existence of a prior record. Offenders who differ in terms of conduct, danger to the community, culpability, and other ways relevant to the purposes of sentencing should not be treated identically. Judges should be able to exercise their informed judgment in crafting effective and proportionate sentences in each case.

• Increase the availability and use of alternative sanctions for nonviolent drug offenders. Drug defendants convicted of nonviolent offenses should ordinarily not be given prison sentences, even if they are repeat offenders, unless they have caused or threatened specific, serious harm—for example, when drug sales are made to children—or if they have upper level roles in drug distribution organizations.

• Increase the use of special drug courts in which addicted offenders are given the opportunity to complete court supervised substance abuse treatment instead of being sentenced to prison.

• Increase the availability of substance abuse treatment and prevention outreach in the community as well as in jails and prisons.

• Redirect law enforcement and prosecution resources to emphasize the arrest, prosecution, and incarceration of importers, manufacturers, and major distributors, e.g., drug king pins, rather than low level offenders and street level retail dealers.

Eliminate Racial Profiling

• Eliminate different sentencing structures for powder cocaine and crack cocaine, drugs that are pharmacologically identical but marketed in a different form. Since more blacks are prosecuted for crack cocaine offenses and thus subjected to the higher penalties for crack offenses that exist in federal and some state laws, the crack-powder sentencing differential aggravates without adequate justification the racial disparities in imprisonment for drug offenses.

• Eliminate racial profiling and require police to keep and make public statistics on the reason for all stops and searches and the race of the persons targeted.

• Require police to keep and make public statistics on the race of arrested drug offenders and the location of the arrests.

To facilitate more inter-state criminal justice analyses, the Bureau of Justice Statistics of the U.S. Department of Justice should annually compile and publish state-by-state statistics on the racial impact of the criminal justice system as it applies to drug offenders, including statistics on arrests, convictions, sentences, admissions to prison, and prison populations.

Incarceration Rates Are Rapidly Increasing

In the year 2001, the total number of people in U.S. prisons and jails will surpass two million. The state and federal prison population has quadrupled since 1980 and the rate of incarceration relative to the nation's population has risen from 139 per 100,000 residents to 468. If these incarceration rates persist, an estimated one in twenty of America's children today will serve time in a state or federal prison during his or her lifetime.

There is a considerable range in prison incarceration rates among U.S. states. Minnesota has the lowest rate, 121 prisoners per 100,000 residents, and Louisiana the highest, with a rate of 763. Seven of the ten states with the highest incarceration rates are in the South. Almost every state has a prison incarceration rate that greatly exceeds those of other western democracies, in which between 35 and 145 residents per 100,000 are behind bars on an average day. The District of Columbia, an entirely urban jurisdiction, has a rate of 1,600. Thirty-two states have mandatory minimum sentencing laws for drug offenses. Mandatory sentences are not responsible for all excessive drug sentences. In Oklahoma, for example, a jury in 1997 gave a sentence of 93 years to Will Forster, an employed father of three with no prior criminal record who grew marijuana plants in his basement.

Chapter 2

Should U.S. Drug Policies Be Liberalized?

The Drug Policy Debate: An Overview

by Mary H. Cooper

About the author: *Mary H. Cooper is a staff writer for* CQ Researcher.

Ronald G. is every parent's nightmare. Shortly after he began snorting heroin nine years ago, the 51-year-old Maryland man started selling the drug to feed his own gnawing habit. He pushed heroin for three and a half years in the nearby drug markets of Washington, D.C., contributing to the surging heroin use among the capital's teenagers and young adults.

After undercover police infiltrated Ronald's narcotics ring, he was convicted of conspiracy to distribute heroin and sentenced to 84 months in prison.

Yet to some observers, Ronald is as much a victim of failed social policies as a villain who peddles drugs to kids. When Ronald was 12, his alcoholic father took a fatal spill down a flight of stairs. Ronald started drinking in his late teens but remained steadily employed for three decades, got married and had three children.

After losing his job as a Red Cross bloodmobile driver, Ronald, then 42, became depressed over his inability to find another job and succumbed to a friend's invitation to snort his first line of heroin. It was the beginning of a journey through hell that he is still trying to end.

"When I lost the job, heroin became my buddy," Ronald recalls. "It told me not to worry, that it was just a job. It starts out that way, but after a while it becomes your personality. Soon my job became selling drugs, and heroin was the boss."

The drug's hold over Ronald continued in prison, where narcotics were readily available. Finally, lured by the promise of early release, he successfully completed a drug-treatment program and was released after serving 42 months of his sentence. As a condition of parole, he enrolled in an outpatient drug-treatment program.

But he returned to heroin, entered another outpatient program and then relapsed again. This time, he enrolled in a six-month residential program run by

Second Genesis, a drug and alcohol rehabilitation program in the Washington, D.C., area, where he is today.

"Here, I've gotten the information about myself that I needed to put my life back on track and realize how I've made a mess of my life, as well as my family's and a few friends', too," he says. "At my age, I should be thinking about retirement, but by doing drugs I've delayed my future."

Despite Efforts, Drug Use Is Widespread

The "war on drugs," the federal government's 30-year-old effort to curb the use of marijuana, heroin, cocaine and other banned substances, was launched to go after men like Ronald. The campaign has consumed billions of dollars in an array of efforts to eradicate drugs at their source at home and abroad; stop their importation at the border; disrupt street markets; discourage their use through prevention and education programs; and help drug abusers overcome their addictions. Virtually every major federal agency is involved.

Despite these efforts, drug use remains widespread. Ronald is one of more than 13 million Americans who regularly used illicit drugs in 1998, the latest year for which data are available. He's also one of more than 975,000 Americans who used heroin at least once in 1998—double the number of users in 1993. Similarly, marijuana and cocaine use by teenagers roughly doubled during the 1990s. Although there was a slight decline in teenage drug use from 1997 to 1998, almost 10 percent of youths ages 12 to 17 reported using illicit drugs in 1998.

Such statistics lead critics of U.S. drug policy to conclude that the Clinton administration's anti-crime efforts, including stiffer sentences for drug offenders, have been a dismal failure. Indeed, while the nation's jails and prisons are overflowing with drug offenders, the street prices of some of the most harmful illegal substances have fallen, even as drug purity levels have increased.

"Prohibition didn't work for alcohol in the 1920s, and it's never going to work for drugs," says Kevin B. Zeese, president of Common Sense for Drug Policy, based in Washington, D.C. "When something doesn't work, you have two choices: Face up to the fact and change course, or refuse to admit you're failing and escalate. And that's what's been happening over the past 20 years."

To the retired Army general leading the war on drugs, however, naysayers like Zeese fail to recognize important gains of current drug policies. "Drug

"Prohibition didn't work for alcohol in the 1920s, and it's never going to work for drugs."

use in America is down dramatically," says Barry R. McCaffrey, director of the Office of National Drug Control Policy—the nation's so-called drug czar. "In [1999] the percentage of young people ages 12 to 17 using drugs declined by 13 percent, the average age of first-time use went up and the overall use of pot and other drugs leveled off."

Drug Use Is Down over the Long Term

The real measure of the drug policy's effectiveness, McCaffrey says, is clear when viewed over the long term. "The highest rate of drug use in modern history was in 1979, when 14.1 percent of Americans used illegal substances," he says. "Today it's down to 6 percent."

McCaffrey is the first military professional to oversee federal drug policy and its $17.8 billion budget. Despite his background, he describes himself as a reluctant drug czar and even rejects the military terms used to describe his mandate. "The metaphor of a 'war on drugs' is inappropriate," he says. "Drug abuse is more like a cancer affecting American communities."

Indeed, McCaffrey says his experience in the military taught him that treatment is more effective than law enforcement in combating drug abuse. "As many as a third of the people in uniform were using drugs in the 1970s, and it absolutely wrecked our professional competence," he says. "We worked our way out of it, and we did so not by arresting people, but by running one of the largest drug-treatment programs the world had ever seen. It took us a decade. This is the mindset I brought into this issue."

McCaffrey argues that many critics, in their zeal to denounce the drug policy's failures, overlook the Clinton administration's support of drug prevention and treatment. "We can argue about courses of action, but not about facts, and the facts are that the treatment budget is now over $3.5 billion a year," he says. "The federal drug-prevention budget [from] 1996 to 2000 is up 52 percent, the treatment budget is up 34 percent and the research budget is up 35 percent."

> *"Critics insist that treatment and prevention [of drug abuse] continue to take a back seat to eradication, interdiction and domestic law-enforcement efforts."*

But critics insist that treatment and prevention continue to take a back seat to eradication, interdiction and domestic law-enforcement efforts to reduce the supplies reaching American streets. For evidence, they point to [the 2000] congressional approval of a $1.3 billion aid package to help Colombia eradicate its illegal coca and opium crops, the source of most of the cocaine and heroin in the United States. [President Bill] Clinton signed the measure into law on July 14, after a lengthy debate in Congress in which critics warned that U.S. forces would be sucked into Colombia's civil war without seriously curtailing the country's drug industry.

Innovative Approaches Come from the States

Some critics of current drug policy say the place to look for innovative approaches to the drug problem is not in Washington, D.C., but in the states. In recent years, voters in seven states and the District of Columbia have legalized the use of marijuana as a pain reliever for patients with cancer and other diseases. Many advocates of drug-policy reform point to California, where voters this fall [2000] will decide on a ballot initiative requiring non-violent drug offenders to get treatment rather than prison the first two times they are arrested.[1]

These and other initiatives fall within a category of policy alternatives that many advocates call "harm reduction."

"This is an approach that acknowledges that both drug use and drug prohibition are going to persist for the foreseeable future and that we

> *"A better way to reduce the harm caused by drug use and drug policies . . . would be to focus on '. . . violence . . . and the use of kids as dealers.'"*

need to focus on reducing the harms associated with both of them," says Ethan A. Nadelmann, director of the Lindesmith Center, a drug policy institute in New York City, and a leading advocate of drug-policy reform.

Not all critics of current policy agree with Nadelmann's assessment. "I deeply regret what's going on, because the alternatives that are being proposed, including the California initiative, are all hot air," says Mark Kleiman, a professor of policy studies at the University of California, Los Angeles, who was a Justice Department drug official during the Reagan administration. "The California initiative would require offenders to go to treatment, which most of them don't need and which for many of them won't work. But it never allows you to find out whether or not they're complying with a perfectly simple instruction, which is, 'Don't use.'"

A better way to reduce the harm caused by drug use and drug policies, Kleiman says, would be to focus on "the side effects of drug trafficking—violence, corruption, neighborhood disorder and the use of kids as dealers."

Coerced Abstinence

With this approach, often referred to as "coerced abstinence," all drug offenders on parole and probation would be subjected to periodic urine testing. Those who test positive for drug use would be punished with mild sanctions, such as a few days' incarceration. "Instead of sending people to prison, we'd put them on the street in a condition of restricted liberty," he says.

Although several congressional hearings have focused on the war on drugs in recent months, there are few indications of change in federal policy during [2000]. Voters in a number of states, however, will be able to choose drug-policy alternatives this fall.

As voters consider current efforts to curb drug abuse, these are some of the issues they will consider:

Should drug prohibition be relaxed?

For years, some critics of drug policy have advocated overturning the entire

---

1. The bill passed.

system of drug prohibition. Just as Prohibition in the 1920s led to a vast black market in alcohol and widespread violence as gangsters fought to control the lucrative trade in bootleg liquor, advocates of drug legalization say current drug laws have only increased crime and suffering.

"Legalization means we educate, regulate, tax and control the estimated $400-billion-a-year drug industry," wrote Gov. Gary E. Johnson, R-N.M., a leading supporter of legalization. "We need to make drugs a controlled substance just like alcohol."

Legalization Would Increase Drug Use

But while legalization would certainly result in reduced drug-related criminal activity, most experts say it would almost certainly lead to increased drug use. "Under a legal regime, the consumption of low-priced, low-risk drugs would increase dramatically," writes drug reform advocate James Q. Wilson, a professor of public policy at Pepperdine University in Malibu, Calif. "We do not know by how much, but the little evidence we have suggests a sharp rise."

Concern about rising drug use prompts many critics of current policies to take a more measured view of drug-law reform; or what Wilson calls a "third way" between the war on drugs and outright legalization. Some, notably billionaire financier George Soros, call for decriminalization of less-dangerous substances, such as marijuana, while retaining bars on access to heroin, cocaine and other addictive drugs.

"We should be aiming for some measure of legally regulating marijuana and then aiming for harm-reduction approaches with respect to the other drugs," says Nadelmann of the Soros-backed Lindesmith Center. "Let's stop pretending that we can be a drug-free society and acknowledge that drugs are here to stay. The challenge is not to get rid of drugs, but to have them cause the least possible harm."

An immediate goal of the harm reductionists, as Nadelmann and like-minded reformers are often called, is to decriminalize the use of marijuana by people suffering from certain diseases, such as glaucoma and cancer. Medical-marijuana initiatives have been approved in seven states—California, Alaska, Washington, Oregon, Maine, Nevada and Colorado—and the District of Columbia. In June [2000], Hawaii became the first state to legalize medical marijuana through the legislative process.

Medical Marijuana

Skeptics say the ballot initiatives defy federal law and undercut the authority of the medical establishment. "The medicinal use of marijuana is a medical issue that needs to be answered first and foremost by the medical community," says Steve Dnistrian, executive vice president of the Partnership for a Drug-Free America, a coalition of communications-industry representatives which works to reduce demand for illicit drugs. "We've got to work on a new way to get THC, marijuana's active ingredient, into the bloodstream because smoking it is not the best way."

At least one drug company is working on a form of medicinal marijuana that is not smoked. But like many critics of harm-reduction initiatives, Dnistrian suspects that medical-marijuana initiatives are just a cover for broader legalization efforts.

"This is a well-choreographed and well-financed plan by the same people who have been leading the charge for drug legalization and decriminalization for the past 25 to 30 years," he says, "so naturally we are a little bit suspicious of their true motives."

> *"The challenge is not to get rid of drugs, but to have them cause the least possible harm."*

Needle-exchange programs are another key priority for harm-reduction advocates. Needle sharing by injection drug users is a leading cause of the spread of HIV/AIDS, accounting for some 200,000 current cases. In April 1998, Health and Human Services Secretary Donna Shalala announced, "a meticulous, scientific review has now proven that needle-exchange programs can reduce the transmission of HIV and save lives without losing ground in the battle against illegal drugs."

Needle Exchange Was Not Approved

To the dismay of reformers, however, President Clinton decided not to approve federal AIDS funding for needle exchanges under pressure from critics who said such programs would send the wrong signal on drug use. "The federal government has been totally irresponsible in the way [it] handles AIDS prevention and drugs," says Zeese of Common Sense for Drug Policy. "Half the new AIDS cases come from intravenous drug use, and we could cut that rate in half and even reduce drug abuse if we had needle exchange funded fully as part of an AIDS-prevention program."

Supporters of current drug policy say some of the harm-reduction proposals already have been incorporated into the federal drug strategy. "If you're chronically addicted, our strategy says we're trying to organize effective drug treatment to help you break the cycle," McCaffrey says. "The term 'harm reduction' has to some extent been hijacked by some in America who are actually calling for the normalization of drug abuse. So I rarely use the term, but there's no question that much of what we're doing is precisely that."

To some critics, the most damaging effect of the harm-reduction argument is that it distracts attention from drug abuse itself. "This campaign is being fueled by the millions and millions of dollars that George Soros and others have committed to this effort," says Mitchell S. Rosenthal, president and founder of Phoenix House, a nonprofit organization in New York City that runs a nationwide network of drug-treatment programs. "I think it's unfortunate in two ways. First, it takes the focus away from what public policy ought to be about—the drugs—and makes the issue one of legalization, or veiled attempts at legalization, which to some extent is what the whole harm-reduction movement is about. Secondly, it is not helping more people access the treatment they need."

Nadelmann rejects the criticism. "Most people in the drug-policy reform movement do not support over-the-counter sales of heroin and cocaine and treating these drugs the way we do alcohol and cigarettes," he says. "The drug czar, the Partnership [for a Drug-Free America] and much of Congress tend to conflate all of our efforts as being all about legalization in sheep's clothing. Neither George Soros nor I are out-and-out legalizers. The general public has a hard time understanding the gray areas in all this. As a rhetorical matter, if someone says 'legalize,' it's instantly a headline, but the term 'harm reduction' just isn't going to make the cover of *Time* magazine."

Should mandatory-minimum sentences for drug offenses be abolished?

In the late 1960s and early '70s, as heroin use rose, Congress and a number of states passed mandatory-minimum sentencing laws, which forced judges to hand out fixed sentences, without parole, as a way to discourage drug use. The most stringent mandatory-sentencing laws were signed in 1973 by Gov. Nelson Rockefeller, R-N.Y., in response to the burgeoning heroin trade in Manhattan. Under the Rockefeller laws, as they are still known, selling small amounts of heroin or cocaine is a Class B felony, comparable in seriousness to armed robbery, first-degree rape and first-degree manslaughter, and brings 15 years to life with no possibility of parole.

Mandatory-Minimum Sentences Added

More stringent sentencing laws were introduced in the 1980s, including the federal Omnibus Anti-Drug Abuse Act of 1988, which added a mandatory-minimum sentence for possession of crack cocaine.

"When crack hit the newspapers in 1986 and began transforming the inner city and the drug trade, there was a sense of desperation, and a whole lot of new laws were written," says Peter Kerr, a spokesman for Phoenix House. "The drug laws of the 1970s and '80s are now reaping a toll. We've never had this many people in prison, and there are very few countries with as many as we have."

> *"An immediate goal of . . . harm reductionists . . . is to decriminalize the use of marijuana by people suffering from certain diseases."*

Today about 2 million men and women are being held in state and federal prisons. In fact, the United States has the largest prison population in the world, and is second only to Russia in the proportion of its population behind bars—almost seven inmates for every 1,000 people. Critics say the high incarceration rate has had no visible impact on drug use.

"The main effect of imprisoning drug sellers, we believe, is merely to open the market for another seller," write public-policy experts Anne Morrison Piehl, Bert Useem and John J. DiIulio Jr. For evidence that incarceration has failed to disrupt the market for illegal drugs, they note that the street price of cocaine and other drugs has actually fallen since 1980, at the same time that incarceration rates have increased.

"In sum, it seems to us that the imprisonment of large numbers of drug offenders is not a cost-effective use of public resources," they wrote.

Worse, Kerr says, mandatory-minimum laws deprive judges of their discretionary power to fit the sentence to the gravity of the crime. "The Rockefeller laws that don't allow discretion to judges don't make sense," he says. "A judge has to see whether this is a criminal who's made a fortune out of dealing drugs or a young person who's gotten snared into an addiction and could use treatment."

> *"Critics say the high incarceration rate has had no visible impact on drug use."*

The plight of non-violent, first-time drug offenders sentenced to years in prison for simple possession has prompted relatives and other critics to organize. In 1991, after her brother received a five-year sentence in federal prison for possession of 36 marijuana plants, Julie Stewart founded Families Against Mandatory Minimums (FAMM), which today has branches in 21 states.

FAMM says the case of 36-year-old Jan Warren illustrates the unfairness of drug-sentencing laws. Warren, who was pregnant and had a teenage daughter, was sentenced in 1987 to 15 years to life for selling 7.83 ounces of cocaine, though she had no prior convictions. At the time of her arrest, an accomplice plea-bargained and received a lighter sentence.

The judge, who said at Warren's sentencing that he "didn't want to do this," later called her sentence a "travesty."

Supporters of current policy tend to dismiss such claims of innocence. "There's a myth about mandatory minimums that a first-time offender who's busted with a dime bag of marijuana goes to jail for 10 years," Dnistrian says. "By and large, that never happens. You have to have a criminal record from here to Chicago."

McCaffrey agrees. "People are not arrested and prosecuted and jailed for first-time possession of a controlled drug for personal addiction," he says. "That almost doesn't happen. People end up behind bars because they break into your house or your car, they steal money from your business or they're addicted themselves and they're selling drugs to other people to pay for their drug habit. That's why they get arrested and prosecuted."

Law Enforcement Is Critical

But some of the strongest criticism of mandatory minimums comes from the law-enforcement community itself. "I believe that mandatory-sentencing laws for drug offenses are in some cases ridiculous," says Dennis Ray Martin, president of the American Police Hall of Fame and a spokesman for the National Association of Chiefs of Police in Saginaw, Mich. "We are filling our jails up, and it's come to the point where one of the top industries in the nation today is building prisons."

Martin, a former police chief of Maple Grove, Mich., says the most serious shortcomings of mandatory minimums are their ineffectiveness and unintended consequences. "Is the problem actually being addressed?" he asks. "We feel it is not. Personally, I would say the reality is that many of these people, once they are released, have not been positively affected by their incarceration. Many of them have families who have been left destitute, which has really created more problems for society than I think were anticipated."

Still other critics dismiss the controversy over mandatory minimums as a mere distraction from more serious flaws in drug-law enforcement. "Most of the people who go to prison on drug charges aren't the victims of mandatories," Kleiman says. "So if we abolished mandatories tomorrow, nothing important would improve. The question is not whether we have mandatories or not, but what the basis of drug sentencing should be. Right now, it's drugs and quantity, but we need fewer, shorter sentences and sentences more focused on conduct rather than on quantity."

Should parolees be required to abstain from drug use as a condition of their release?

Mandatory-minimum sentences for drug offenses have helped boost the prison population in the United States to about 2 million inmates. Of these, as many as three-quarters tested positive for drug use at the time of arrest. The main defect in current drug policies, law-enforcement officials say, is that drug addicts, once released, tend to return to their neighborhoods and the conditions that prompted them to take drugs in the first place and commit crimes.

"In order to purchase many of these illegal drugs, they have to do illegal acts," Martin says. "A lot of these people can't even hold a job, so they have to generate money in other ways, and that's usually by illegal breaking and entering. They'll steal a $300 television set, which may only bring $25 on the street. So they have to steal larger quantities of merchandise to generate the kind of money they need."

> *"The most serious shortcomings of mandatory minimums are their ineffectiveness and unintended consequences."*

Many experts agree that treatment is the key to stopping the revolving door of incarceration, release and rearrest. The Clinton administration's main effort to break that cycle is the drug court. Introduced in the late 1980s at the state and local level, drug courts require drug-involved offenders to undergo treatment as part of their sentences. Thanks in part to federal funding, there are more than 600 drug courts around the country.

"If you are arrested at 2 in the morning and you're dazed, drunk or drugged, you're a male street prostitute or you're breaking into a car when arrested, we would like to get you into the drug-court system at the front end," says McCaffrey, the administration's chief booster of drug courts. "If you go into treatment and get a job, we'll arrange the social services and medical care you need, we'll try and keep you out of prison and, indeed, try and not put a formal conviction on your record."

An essential element of the drug-court system, McCaffrey says, is its

> *"The longer drug addicts are in treatment, the more likely they are to overcome their addiction."*

coercive nature. "It doesn't work without the coercive threat of the drug court," he says. "Say you flunk your drug test because you have a chronically relapsing disorder. You're in misery, you're desperate and you've got this compulsion because you've neurologically modified your brain. When you flunk your drug test, we'll lock you up for a three-day weekend—no boyfriend, no TV—and then release you back into community life."

Treatment Works Better than Prison

Some drug-treatment professionals say this approach isn't enough to break the cycle of drug abuse. "We still have in New York and some other states mandatory minimums, where people who are convicted of possession or sale of certain amounts of drugs will have to do long, heavy sentences," says Rosenthal of Phoenix House. "That frequently puts people in jail for what are ludicrously long sentences, when in fact very often these addicted sellers would do much better sentenced in effect to two years of treatment or some lesser prison term with a treatment component in prison. That would be a very significant addition to public policy."

In Rosenthal's experience, the longer drug addicts are in treatment, the more likely they are to overcome their addiction. "We know from the research data that if you keep people in treatment for 12 to 18 months, both in and out of prison, and there's real continuity in treatment, you're going to see positive results over time," he says.

Other critics say the rationale behind both the drug-court system and long-term treatment—that drug abuse is largely a medical condition—is false.

"Most people who use illicit drugs aren't sick, so what are we treating them for?" Kleiman asks. "This policy assumes that if somebody does have a substance-abuse disorder, that somehow there's a treatment process they can go through and then they're cured. Come on. Some people get better, but some people don't. Drug abuse isn't like gonorrhea, where you can just give someone some penicillin to make them well."

A better alternative, in Kleiman's view, would require all people on parole or probation to undergo drug testing as a condition of release. Known as "coerced abstinence," this approach embraces drug testing and immediate, mild sanctions for drug use, generally only a few days in jail.

"The current system puts a lot of people in prison," he says. "If you're on parole and you test dirty, you're likely to spend 90 days in prison. I want to have a very predictable, mild sanction, which I think will involve less punishment and less drug use in the aggregate than the current system. If harm reduction had its ordinary language meaning, this would be a harm-reduction approach."

But advocates of harm reduction reject coerced abstinence on ideological grounds. "We believe that people should not be punished for what they put in their bodies," Nadelmann says. "People should be held responsible for their actions, whether they're under the influence or not. Therefore, anything that relies on urine testing in a punitive way by definition cannot be harm reduction."

Nadelmann also is skeptical of in-prison treatment programs, saying they fail to address the underlying problems that lead to drug abuse. "There are a lot of things wrong with coerced drug treatment," he says. "The best place to provide treatment, generally speaking, is outside the criminal-justice system, in the community, where people can get it before they get in trouble. We're hearing more and more stories of people getting arrested just so they can get access to treatment, which is almost ludicrous."

The obvious answer to that problem, Nadelmann says, "Everyone is talking about huge amounts of money flowing into things like coerced drug treatment and drug courts," he says. "At the same time, the money in the community for drug treatment—whether it's methadone maintenance [for heroin addicts] or programs for women who are pregnant and using drugs—all of that is drying up.

"I look at the whole push for more drug courts and coerced drug treatment as a mixed blessing. While I think it's doing some good in moving things somewhat in the right direction, I also think it's hugely corrupting of the long-term picture of what drug treatment should be about."

Drug Policies Should Be Liberalized

by the Unitarian Universalist Association

About the author: *The Unitarian Universalist Association (UUA) was formed in 1961 through the consolidation of two faith traditions, the Universalist Church of America and the American Unitarian Association. Today the UUA is a religious organization, of more than one thousand congregations that support each other with a theology of tolerance, interdependence, and compassion.*

For more than 30 years, American public policy has advanced an escalating "war on drugs" that seeks to eradicate illegal drugs from our society. It is increasingly clear that this effort has failed. Our current drug policy has consumed tens of billions of dollars and wrecked countless lives. The costs of this policy include the increasing breakdown of families and neighborhoods, endangerment of children, widespread violation of civil liberties, escalating rates of incarceration, political corruption, and the imposition of United States policy abroad. For United States taxpayers, the price tag on the drug offensive has soared from $66 million in 1968 to almost $20 billion in 2000, an increase of over 30,000 percent. In practice the drug war disproportionately targets people of color and people who are poverty-stricken. Coercive measures have not reduced drug use, but they have clogged our criminal justice system with non-violent offenders. It is time to explore alternative approaches and to end this costly war.

The war on drugs has blurred the distinction between drug use and drug abuse. Drug use is erroneously perceived as behavior that is out of control and harmful to others. Illegal drug use is thus portrayed as threatening to society. As a result, drug policy has been closed to study, discussion, and consideration of alternatives by legislative bodies. Yet many people who use both legal and illegal drugs live productive, functional lives and do no harm to society.

As Unitarian Universalists committed to a free and responsible search for truth, we must protest the misguided policies that shape current practice. We

Unitarian Universalist Association, "Alternatives to the War on Drugs," Unitarian Universalist Association Forty-First General Assembly Statement of Conscience, June 22, 2002. Reproduced by permission.

cannot in good conscience remain quiet when it is becoming clear that we have been misled for decades about illegal drugs. United States government drug policy-makers have misled the world about the purported success of the war on drugs. They tell the public that success is dependent upon even more laws restricting constitutional protections and the allocation of billions of dollars for drug law enforcement. They mislead the public about the extent of corruption and environmental degradation in other countries that the American war on drugs has left in its wake.

As Unitarian Universalists committed to the inherent worth and dignity of every person and to justice, equity, and compassion in human relations, we call for thoughtful consideration and implementation of alternatives that regard the reduction of harm as the appropriate standard by which to assess drug policies. We seek a compassionate reduction of harm associated with drugs, both legal and illegal, with special attention to the harm unleashed by policies established in the war on drugs.

As Unitarian Universalists committed to respecting the interdependent web of existence of which we are a part, we find irresponsible and morally wrong the practices of scorching the earth and poisoning the soil and ground water in other countries to stop the production of drugs that are illegal in the United States.

As a community of faith, Unitarian Universalists have both a moral imperative and a personal responsibility to ask the difficult questions that so many within our society are unable, unwilling, or too afraid to ask. In asking these questions and in weighing our findings, we are compelled to consider a different approach to national drug policy.

A Different Approach

To conceive and develop a more just and compassionate drug policy, it is necessary to transform how we view drugs and particularly drug addiction. Drug use, drug abuse, and drug addiction are distinct from one another. Using a drug does not necessarily mean abusing the drug, much less addiction to it. Drug abuse issues are essentially matters for medical attention. We do not believe that drug use should be considered criminal behavior. Advocates for harsh drug policies with severe penalties for drug use often cite violent crime as a direct result of drug use. Drugs alone do not cause crime. Legal prohibition of drugs leads to inflated street value, which in turn incites violent turf wars

"It is becoming clear that we have been misled for decades about illegal drugs."

among distributors. The whole pattern is reminiscent of the proliferation of organized crime at the time of alcohol prohibition in the early twentieth century. That policy also failed.

We believe that the vision of a drug-free America is unrealistic. Many programs for school children have misled participants and the public by teaching that all illicit drugs are equally harmful in spite of current scientific research to the contrary. "Just Say No" is not a viable policy. The consequences of the current drug war are cruel and counterproductive. At issue here are the health and well being of our families and our communities, our societal fabric and our global community. Alternatives exist.

Alternative Goals

Based on this perspective, we believe appropriate and achievable goals for reformed national drug policies include:

• To prevent consumption of drugs, including alcohol and nicotine, that are harmful to health among children and adolescents;

• To reduce the likelihood that drug users will become drug abusers;

• To minimize the harmful effects of drug use, such as disease contracted from the use of contaminated needles and overdosing as a result of unwittingly using impure drugs;

> *"To conceive and develop a more just and compassionate drug policy, it is necessary to transform how we view drugs and . . . addiction."*

• To increase the availability and affordability of quality drug treatment and eliminate the stigma associated with accessing it;

• To significantly reduce violent and predatory drug-related crime;

• To minimize the harmful consequences of current drug policy, such as racial profiling, property confiscation without conviction, and unnecessary incarceration; and

• To reduce the harm to our earth now caused by the practice of destroying crops intended for the production of drugs.

Alternative Policies

Instead of the current war on drugs, we offer the following policies for study, debate, and implementation:

• Shift budget priorities from spending for pursuing, prosecuting, and imprisoning drug-law offenders to spending for education, treatment, and research.

• Develop and implement age-appropriate drug education programs that are grounded in research and fact and that promote dialogue without fear of censure or reprisal.

• Undertake research to assess the effects of currently illegal drugs. Ensure that findings and conclusions are publicly accessible, serving as a basis for responsible decision-making by individuals and in arenas of public policy and practice.

• Research the sociological factors that contribute to the likelihood of drug use becoming habitual, addictive, and destructive, such as poverty, poor mental health, sexual or other physical abuse, and lack of education or medical treatment.

• Research and expand a range of management and on-demand treatment programs for drug abuse and addiction. Examples include nutritional counseling, job training, psychiatric evaluation and treatment, psychological counseling, parent training and assistance, support groups, clean needle distribution and exchange, substitution of safer drugs (e.g., methadone or marijuana), medically administered drug maintenance, disease screening, and acupuncture and other alternative and complementary treatments. Publish the results of studies of these programs.

• Require health insurance providers to cover in-patient and out-patient treatment for substance abuse on the same basis as other chronic health conditions.

• Make all drugs legally available with a prescription by a licensed physician, subject to professional oversight. End the practice of punishing an individual for obtaining, possessing, or using an otherwise illegal substance to treat a medical condition. End the threat to impose sanctions on physicians who treat patients with opiates for alleviation of pain.

• Prohibit civil liberties violations and other intrusive law enforcement practices. Violations of the right to privacy such as urine testing should be imposed only upon employees in safety-sensitive occupations.

• Establish a legal, regulated, and taxed market for marijuana. Treat marijuana as we treat alcohol.

• Modify civil forfeiture laws to require conviction before seizure of assets. Prohibit the eviction of family, friends, and co-habitants or the loss of government entitlements.

• Abolish mandatory minimum prison sentences for the use and distribution of currently illicit drugs. Legislation should specify only maximum prison sentences.

> *"We believe that the vision of a drug-free America is unrealistic."*

• Remove criminal penalties for possession and use of currently illegal drugs, with drug abusers subject to arrest and imprisonment only if they commit an actual crime (e.g., assault, burglary, impaired driving, vandalism). End sentencing inequities driven by racial profiling.

• Establish and make more accessible prison-based drug treatment, education, job training, and transition programs designed for inmates.

• End the financing of anti-drug campaigns in Central and South America, campaigns that include the widespread spraying of herbicides, contribute to the destruction of rainforests, and are responsible for uprooting peoples from their homelands.

Our Call to Act as a People of Faith

We must begin with ourselves. Our congregations can offer safe space for open and honest discussion among congregants about the complex issues of drug use, abuse, and addiction. Through acceptance of one another and encouragement of spiritual growth, we should be able to acknowledge and address our own drug use without fear of censure or reprisal.

We can recognize that drugs include not only currently illegal substances but also alcohol, nicotine, caffeine, over-the-counter pain relievers, and prescription drugs. We can learn to distinguish among use, abuse, and addiction. We can support one another in recognizing drug-related problems and seeking help. We can seek to understand those among us who use drugs for relief or escape. With compassion, we can cultivate reflection and analysis of drug policy. In the safe space of our own congregations, we can begin to prevent destructive relationships with drugs. We can lend necessary support to individuals and families when a loved one needs treatment for an addiction problem. We can encourage our congregations to partner with and follow the lead of groups representing individuals whose lives are most severely undermined by current drug policy—people of color and of low income. We can learn from health care professionals what unique patterns of substance abuse exist in our local areas. We can go beyond our walls and bring our perspective to the interfaith community, other nonprofit organizations, and elected officials.

Our Unitarian Universalist history calls us to pursue a more just world. Our faith compels us to hold our leaders accountable for their policies. In calling for alternatives to the war on drugs, we are mindful of its victims. Drug use should be addressed solely as a public health problem, not as a criminal justice issue. Dependence upon any illegal drugs or inappropriate use of legal drugs may point to deep, unmet human needs. We have a moral obligation to advocate compassionate, harm-reducing policy. We believe that our nations have the imagination and capability to address effectively the complex issues of the demand for drugs, both legal and illegal.

We reaffirm the spirit of our social witness positions taken on drugs in resolutions adopted from 1965 to 1991. Recognizing the right of conscience for all who differ, we denounce the war on drugs and recommend alternative goals and policies. Let not fear or any other barrier prevent us from advocating a more just, compassionate world.

Liberalizing Drug Policies Would Reduce Community Violence and Police Brutality

by Peter Moskos

About the author: *Peter Moskos is a member of the Department of Sociology at Harvard University. He worked as a Baltimore, Maryland, police officer for two years.*

In 1998 the Drug Enforcement Administration [DEA] sent its Mobile Enforcement Team into Benton Harbor, Mich., while state troopers patrolled the crime-ridden streets. With 42 arrests, the DEA struck a major blow at the drug ring responsible for some 90 percent of violent crime in the city.

In congressional testimony the following year, the DEA boasted: "After the intervention of law enforcement officers. . . . Benton Harbor was being brought back to life. . . . They brought a sense of stability to the area."

This was wishful thinking. Not only has there been no lasting effect on the drug trade, resentment of outside law enforcement in Benton Harbor recently has exploded into riots. Residents of the crime-ridden and depressed city see police as an occupying force.

Outsiders find it hard to believe that residents of dangerous communities—those most in need of police services—can be anti-police. Our drug laws create this paradox.

Police Are Subjected to Drug-Related Hostility

I policed ground zero in our "war" on drugs on the streets of Baltimore. Police in such circumstances, myself included, do the best they can. But faced with constant levels of drug-related violence and hostility, one should not expect the model for Officer Friendly.

Benton Harbor is not the first or last anti-police race riot. The pattern is always the same: a poor community ravaged by drugs, a history of real and perceived police misconduct, a racially charged spark, then riots.

Terrance Shurn was Benton Harbor's spark. He died after crashing his motorcycle June 16. He wouldn't stop for police. He might have been running to avoid a drug conviction. His license was suspended. Had I stopped him, I would have searched him, legally. I would have found the small bag of marijuana he was carrying. Suddenly, it's jail and a criminal drug conviction.

> *"Prohibition creates an illegal market based on cash, guns and violence."*

Most citizens in and out of our ghettoes, including drug users, despise drug dealers. But nobody supports heavy-handed drug enforcement.

Those at the receiving end of our drug policy know it simply doesn't work. People will riot as long as police keep locking them up without anything getting better.

Liberals are correct to note that rioting does not happen in the absence of poverty, poor education and poor policing. Conservatives are right to blame the individual rioters. But both sides miss the central point: The problems that lead to riots stem from the drug trade. Eighty years of failed drug prohibition have destroyed swaths of urban America.

While the damage from heroin and cocaine use is real and severe, prohibition creates an illegal market based on cash, guns and violence. While drug use can destroy an individual, the illegal and violent drug trade destroys whole neighborhoods.

The Drug War Is Unwinnable

If the war on drugs were winnable, we would already have won it. Drug prohibition criminalizes large segments of the population, even the majority in some areas. Police can't hire from some areas they police because not enough men reach hiring age without a drug conviction.

We need to accept the fact that drug addiction is a personal and medical problem. We need to push violent dealers off the street even if it means tolerating inconspicuous and peaceful indoor drug dealing.

Users don't belong in jail. Drug dealers see themselves as businessmen. Arrest one and another will quickly move to take the market. As long as addicts need to buy, somebody will sell.

How can tolerance lower drug use? We can learn from our already legal recreational drugs.

In 40 years cigarette smoking has decreased by half. This is a great victory

against drugs. Public education hammered home the harm and changed our culture's attitudes towards tobacco.

Alcohol prohibition was tried and failed. Few argue that alcohol is an absolute "good." But for the most part people are happy with their localities regulating sales, balancing the rights of individuals with the harm to society. For both tobacco and alcohol, high taxation discourages new users and raises money for education.

We should implement similar policies for drug use. Treat drug abuse as a medical problem. Separate the problems of drug use from the violence of the drug trade. Acknowledge that drugs are bad, but don't frame drug policy as a moral war against evil.

Until we do these things, people in communities such as Benton Harbor will be under siege and sparks will set off riots.

Drugs Should Be Legalized

by Meaghan Cussen and Walter Block

About the authors: *Meaghan Cussen coauthored this viewpoint in her junior year at the College of the Holy Cross in Worcester, Massachusetts, with Walter Block, a professor of economics at Loyala University in New Orleans, Louisiana.*

Drug dealers are a thing of the past. Violent crimes and theft are greatly reduced. Drug-related shoot-outs are unheard of. The streets of America begin to "clean up." Communities pull themselves together. Youths and adults once involved in crime rings are forced to seek legitimate work. Deaths due to infected intravenous needles and poisonous street drugs are eliminated. Taxpayers are no longer forced to pay $10,000,000,000 to fund drug-related law enforcement. The $80,000,000,000 claimed by organized crime and drug rings will now go to honest workers. What policy change will bring about such good news? The legalization of drugs! Both practically and philosophically speaking, addictive drugs should be legalized.

Drug Legalization Protects Civil Liberties

Many argue that drug prohibition protects addicts from themselves by exerting parental control over their behavior. This government-enforced control, the anti-drug laws, strictly monitors addicts' treatment of their own bodies. For example, the government decides that it wants to protect Fred Brown from destroying his body. The government, therefore, outlaws narcotics and, in effect, takes control of Fred's body. Under the United States Constitution and the anti-slavery laws, this hegemony should not happen. The guiding principles of the United States, iterated both in the Declaration of Independence and the Constitution, protect Fred's basic civil liberties to "pursue his own happiness" as long as he doesn't infringe on others' rights to life and property. With prohibition, Fred no longer has his constitutional right. He no longer controls his own body. Regulation has stripped him of his civil liberty. Fred's role of "owner of his own body" is taken away from him. This has in effect made him a slave.

Are we being hysterical in categorizing present drug law as a form of servitude? No, our drug laws amount to partial slavery. We must all question the practices of roadblocks, strip-searches, urine tests, locker searches, and money laundering laws. Philosophically speaking, drug prohibition severely threatens our civil liberties and is inconsistent with the anti-slavery philosophy and the founding documents of the United States. The legalization of drugs would give a basic civil liberty back to U.S. citizens, by granting them control over their own bodies.

Free Trade in Drugs

Free trade benefits all parties. It can be assumed that if drugs were legalized, and thus were a part of the market, both the buyer and the seller would gain. Each time a trade occurs, the welfare of both parties is improved. If Joe sold you his shirt for $10, he would benefit because he obviously values the $10 more than the shirt. If he didn't, he would not have traded it. You would also gain from the trade because you obviously value the shirt more than you do the $10. If you didn't, then you would not have agreed to the deal. Free trade in the drug market works the same way. If Joe sells you marijuana for $10, he gains because he values the money more, and you gain because you value the drugs more. Whether or not another person thinks you should value the drugs more is not the question. That third party is not involved in the trade. The amount of pleasure the drug brings you is your motivation for buying it. Trade is a positive-sum game. Both parties gain, at least in the *ex ante* [forward-looking] sense.

It cannot be denied that certain third parties will be offended by the drug transaction, on moral or ethical grounds. However, try to find any transaction that does not offend at least one person. Many people object to the sale of alcohol, cigarettes, birth control or animal products, but their feelings or beliefs do not stop these items from being sold. Marxists object to any market transactions because they see commercial activity as necessarily exploitative. There is obviously no pleasing everyone when it comes to market transactions. In our free enterprise economy, however, anyone who participates in the market will benefit from it [According to Walter Block,] ". . . For all third parties who say they will be aggrieved by a legalized drug trade, there will be many more benefiting from the reduction in crime. A third party can verbally oppose any given trade. But that opposition cannot be revealed through market choices in the same way that trade between the two parties indicates a positive evaluation of the transaction. Free trade of all goods contributes to the number of those who gain. In a free market economy, everybody has opportunity to participate in the market, and therefore, equal opportunity to gain in a positive sum transaction."

> *"Both practically and philosophically speaking, addictive drugs should be legalized."*

Not only would the legalization of drugs protect basic freedoms and lead to individual benefit through free trade, but it would also bring enormous benefits to society as a whole. The first and most important societal benefit is a reduction in crime.

Legalizing Drugs Would Reduce Crime

When addictive drugs are made legal, crime will decrease substantially, for four main reasons. First, the lowered price of narcotics will eliminate the theft and murder associated with their high prices. When drugs are legalized, law-abiding businesspeople will no longer be deterred by the illegality of drug commerce and will become willing to enter the market. With this increase of supply, assuming a less than proportional increase in demand, the price of narcotics will fall. Addicts who were formerly forced to steal, murder, and engage in illegal employment to earn enough money for their habits will be able to afford the lower prices. Therefore, these types of drug-related crimes will decrease.

Second, substance-related disputes such as gang wars and street violence will be reduced. Dealers will be able to use the courts to settle their disputes instead of taking the law into their own hands. Violations of rights within the drug business will be resolved through the judicial system, thereby decreasing gang violence, and saving the many innocent lives that often get caught in the crossfire.

> *"The legalization of drugs would give a basic civil liberty back to U.S. citizens, by granting them control over their own bodies."*

Third, the drug business creates great profits for cartels. Cartels are often international organizations, many of which support terrorism and add to violent crime in America. If the narcotics market were open, drug revenues would be equally distributed by free-market forces, and would have less of a chance of supporting terrorist organizations, crime rings, and cartel activity and profit.

Finally, and most obviously, with transport, sale, and possession legalized, formerly illegal activities will now become society-approved business transactions. Crime, an act that breaks the law, and in its very insurrectional essence leads to societal instability, will be greatly reduced through the legalization of the inevitable activity of drug transactions.

The prohibition of alcohol in the 1920s provides us with a perfect case in point. The high crime rates during this decade were due to the existence of the black market, spawned from the government-enforced illegalization of alcohol. The black market led to the formation of major crime rings. The underground market for alcohol grew and led many profit-hungry entrepreneurs into a risky lifestyle of crime. Many were jailed due to transport, sale, and possession.

When Prohibition ended, alcohol-related crime ceased. The profit balloon driven by the limited supply of the illegal substance was deflated. The black

market disappeared, along with all of the illegal activity associated with it. Crime rings were forced to disband and seek other means of income. How many crime rings exist today for the selling of alcohol? The answer is none. The reason is legalization.

Legalizing Drugs Will Reverse the Potency Effect

In contrast, drug-related crime is skyrocketing. As [James] Ostrowski notes, "The President's Commission on Organized Crime estimates a total of seventy drug market murders yearly in Miami alone. Based on that figure and FBI data, a reasonable nationwide estimate would be at least 750 murders a year. Recent estimates from New York and Washington are even higher." Anyone who questions whether prohibition is responsible for violence should note the relative peace that prevails in the alcohol and legal drug markets.

> *"The legalization of drugs ... would ... bring enormous benefits to society as a whole."*

The end of Prohibition also brought the end of the dangerous potency effect. During Prohibition, it was in the best interests of the sellers to carry more potent forms of alcohol. Hence, an alcohol dealer would be more likely to carry vodka and other hard liquor instead of beer and wine because of hard liquor's greater value (per unit of volume). Therefore, people began drinking vodka and other hard liquor, which because of their high potency are more dangerous than beer and wine. Alcohol-related deaths increased. This horrific result is known as the potency effect.

Fifty years after the repeal of Prohibition, the potency effect has been reversed. The average per capita consumption of alcohol has fallen to its lowest level ever. In fact, people have begun switching to weaker alcohol alternatives, such as wine coolers and nonalcoholic beer. The legalization of alcohol reversed the potency effect. The legalization of drugs will do the same.

For example, the risks involved in transporting marijuana, a low-potency drug, for the purpose of sale are extremely high. It is in the best interests of the dealer to carry more potent, thus more expensive, drugs, which is why he or she will be more likely to carry cocaine because of its greater value (per unit of volume). Because cocaine is more potent, it is also more dangerous. Addicts face increased health risks when using cocaine as opposed to using marijuana. These health risks grow as potency increases. Stronger and more dangerous drugs such as crack, "ice," and PCP are substituted for the weaker, relatively safer drugs. The results are often deadly.

Legalizing Drugs Offers Health Benefits

The legalization of drugs would eliminate serious health risks by assuring market-driven high quality substances and the availability of clean needles. Prohibition in the 1920s created a market for cheap versions of alcoholic products, such as bathtub gin. Alcohol was diluted or adulterated in often dangerous ways. Needless deaths occurred because of the poor quality of the product. So is drug prohibition worth the health risks? Fly-by-night goods cannot always be trusted. If narcotics were legalized, purity could be all but guaranteed. Drugstores, held accountable by customers, would deliver safe products. Brand names would bring competition into the market and assure safer, better products. Doctors would now be able to monitor the drug use of seriously addicted patients. Poor quality would be a thing of the past.

In addition, clean needles would be readily available. Drug vendors and health care organizations would be able to provide clean needles for their customers and patients respectively. Today, needles are shared because they are difficult to obtain. About twenty-five percent of AIDS cases are contracted through the sharing of intravenous needles. Legalizing drugs would eliminate this problem. [David Boaz notes,] "In Hong Kong, where needles are available in drugstores, as of 1987 there were no cases of AIDS among drug users."

When was the last time you heard of a diabetic contracting AIDS from contaminated needles? If insulin were prohibited, this situation would surely change for the worse.

Societal Benefits

Illegal drug sale creates a destructive atmosphere. When a criminal culture emerges, a community is torn apart. A booming black market fosters a large criminal presence. Casual recreational users are forced to come in contact with criminals to make their purchases, as prohibition makes it impossible to make a legal transaction. Additionally, basically good citizens often deal with and, unfortunately, become influenced by, the criminals of the area.

"When addictive drugs are made legal, crime will decrease substantially."

Inner-city youths, surrounded by the booming black market, are influenced by the sheer amount of money dealers make and often fall into a life of crime. These youths often see themselves as having the choice of remaining in poverty, earning "chump change," or pursuing a life of crime and making thousands of dollars a week. Which do you think all too many young people will choose?

The black market presence often leads to the corruption of police officers and public officials. Police, on average, make $35,000 a year. When they arrest the denizens of the drug world who make ten times that amount, it is often difficult not to be tempted into a life of crime.

Legalizing Drugs Reduces Police Corruption

Drug corruption charges have been leveled against FBI agents, police officers, prison guards, U.S. customs inspectors, even prosecutors. In 1986, in New

York City's 77th Precinct, twelve police officers were arrested for stealing and selling drugs. Miami's problem is worse. In June 1986, seven officers there were indicted for using their jobs to run a drug operation that used murders, threats, and bribery. Add to that two dozen other cases of corruption in the last three years in Miami alone.

We must question a policy that so frequently turns police officers into the very outlaws they are authorized to bring to justice. We must question a policy that leads to the enormous success of these willing to break the laws of our society. We must question a policy that leaves a criminal profession in a position of great influence over our youth and other honest citizens. Milton Friedman put it best when he wrote, "Drugs are a tragedy for addicts. But criminalizing their use converts the tragedy into a disaster for society, for users and non-users alike."

> *"Illegal drug sale creates a destructive atmosphere."*

The laws of the United States prohibit violent acts against other citizens. This is consistent with the founding principles of our nation, which allow each free individual to pursue life, liberty, and happiness. The laws of the United States should not prohibit the intake of narcotics that only have an immediate effect on the individual consumer. If I ingest a drug, I am doing possible harm only to myself, and no other. If I subsequently act violently on account of my altered state of mind, only then am I doing harm to others. It is the subsequent action that is harmful, not the drug taking itself. Since I am responsible for my actions, I should be arrested and punished only when I am violent. Alcohol is legal even though people commit rapes, murders, beatings, and other violent crimes when they are drunk. Yet if a person commits these crimes when intoxicated, he or she is held responsible for them. A mere substance should not and does not serve as an excuse for the violent acts. The ingestion of alcohol is not illegal per se. The same standard should be applied to the use of presently illegal drugs.

It should also be noted that every narcotic does not turn the user into a crazed, enraged lunatic capable of all sorts of violent crimes. In fact, it is just the opposite. Most drugs induce lethargy. Remember that opium, now illegal, was used quite often in England, China, and the United States, and tended to induce stupor. The use of traditional opiates did not render users violent. In fact, no drug is "as strongly associated with violent behavior as is alcohol. According to Justice Department statistics, 54 percent of all jail inmates convicted of violent crimes in 1983 reported having just used alcohol just prior to committing their offense," [says Ethan Nadelmann]. This statistic renders the prohibition of drugs rather than alcohol a legal inconsistency.

Legalizing Drugs Saves Taxpayers Money

According to the U.S. Department of Justice, federal, state, and local governments currently spend over $20 billion per year on drug enforcement. In 1992, there were more than one million arrests for drug law violations. In 1993, sixty percent of the seventy-seven thousand federal prisoners were incarcerated for drug-related crimes. Jails are crowded and large amounts of tax dollars are being spent on enforcement efforts that only aggravate the problem. We can add to this sum the amount of money spent on research and medical care for those infected with AIDS and other diseases caused by needle sharing.

With legalization, the tax dollars spent on enforcement would be saved. The availability of clean needles would reduce the rate of AIDS infections, and would consequently reduce the amount of money spent on medical care, to say nothing of the reduction in human misery.

If we continue with the same anti-drug policies, we are only helping drug lords get richer. Each time a bust occurs and a shipment is captured and destroyed, the criminals benefit. The seizure reduces supply and takes out one or more black market participants. According to the laws of supply and demand, with a decrease in drug supply, black market prices will rise, creating a larger profit for suppliers. So, every time we think we are winning a battle in the war, we are really strengthening the enemy rather than weakening it. The way to win is not by fighting the alligators, but by draining their swamp. It is better to ruin drug lords' businesses by deflating the profit balloon than by acting in a way (i.e., prohibition) that only benefits them. "By taking the profits out of [drugs], we could at one fell swoop do more to reduce their power than decades of fighting them directly," [says Jason Holloway].

Legalization Diminishes Illegal Profits

At present, governmental control of the drug lords, while minuscule, is as effective as it will ever be in any sector of society. Just think, even in jails, where the lives of residents are completely controlled by the government, drugs still have not been eliminated. If the government cannot even control the drug trade within its own house, how can it expect to control it within the entire nation? Are we to imprison the whole citizenry in an attempt? Legalization will take the profits out of the narcotics industry.

> *"Legalization will take the profits out of the narcotics industry."*

Many believe the elasticity of demand for narcotics is very high. If drugs are legalized and their prices fall, the amount purchased will increase by a large amount. This is not the case. In fact, the elasticity of demand for drugs in general is very low for three main reasons. First, narcotics are seen as necessities for drug users, not luxuries. "While one might severely reduce demand for [luxuries] in the face of an increased price, or even give it up entirely in the extreme, this does not apply to [necessities]," [according to Block]. This behavioral pattern indicates that drugs are indeed low elasticity goods. In fact, there is really no good reason to assume that many Americans would suddenly start to ingest or inject narcotics even if given the legal opportunity.

Second, most people recognize the danger of drugs and will avoid them no matter what the price. Third, if drugs are made legal, they will no longer have to be pushed. If they are sold over the counter to adults, criminals will no longer have to pawn these goods off on innocent youths. Competition will be high and dealers will have no reason to resort to this extreme measure. Certainly, market competition will

> *"We are not by any means winning the war on drugs."*

occur which may result in advertisements' targeting particular age groups. However, this would have a negligible effect compared to drug pushers' current youth-targeted tactics.

Finally, we should realize that legalization would cause potency to fall. With normalized supply, people will begin purchasing weaker, safer drugs. This normalized supply, along with the low elasticity of demand for narcotics, will lead to only a small increase in consumption.

Legalization Does Not Mean Approval

A main driver of anti-drug legislation is the concern that government would be sanctioning an immoral and destructive activity, viewed as sinful in many eyes of the population. However, the legalization of drugs does not mean that government and society would sanction their use. Alcohol and cigarettes are legal but we have pretty successful campaigns against these substances. Gossiping and burping are also legal, but you never see a government sponsored advertisement advocating catty behavior or belching in public. Are we as a society to prohibit automobile racing, extreme skiing, the ingestion of ice cream and fried foods because they may have a detrimental effect on human health? No. Dangers associated with these activities cannot be measured. ". . . Such inherently unquantifiable variables cannot be measured, much less weighed against each other. Interpersonal comparison of utility is incompatible with valid economic analysis," [Block notes]. We cannot allow such legal inconsistencies to take place.

Legalizing drugs would eliminate these inconsistencies, guarantee freedoms, and increase the efficiency and effectiveness of the government's anti-drug beliefs. If drugs were legalized, taxes could be cut, with the elimination of government expenditures on enforcement. All of the money saved could be used to promote anti-drug campaigns. Private organizations could take over the tasks of inspecting and regulating. A minimum age of twenty-one would be mandated for the consumption of drugs. Transactions would take place in a drugstore, with upstanding suppliers. Drugs could safely be administered, with clean needles, in hospitals where medical professionals could monitor and rehabilitate the addicted. MADD (Mothers Against Drunk Driving) is a good example of a successful anti-substance abuse campaign. Private, nonprofit groups like this one could help in the fight against drug abuse.

Currently, we are not by any means winning the war on drugs. Our futile attempts at enforcement only exacerbate the problem. We need to de-escalate the war rather than continue fighting the over twenty-three million adult Americans who are obviously determined to enjoy themselves as they see fit. We must also remember that those that need to be deterred the most, the hard-core drug users, are the least likely to be stopped. Our law enforcement is not working to contain and control the very people the anti-drug laws are designed to control. The war on drugs has done little to reduce narcotics use in the United States and has thus proved counterproductive. Philosophically and practically speaking, drugs should be legalized. This act would prevent our civil liberties from being threatened, reduce crime rates, reverse the potency effect, improve the quality of life in inner cities, prevent the spread of disease, save the taxpayer money, and generally benefit both individuals and society as a whole.

Mandatory Sentencing Is an Ineffective Policy in the War on Drugs

by the Center on Juvenile and Criminal Justice

About the author: *Originally established in 1985 as the Western Regional Office of the National Center on Institutions and Alternatives, the Center on Juvenile and Criminal Justice provides direct services, technical assistance, and policy research in the criminal justice field.*

It is clear that we cannot arrest our way out of the problem of chronic drug abuse and drug-driven crime. We cannot continue to apply policies and programs that do not deal with the root causes of substance abuse and attendant crime. Nor should we expect to continue to have the widespread societal support for our counter-drug programs if the American people begin to believe these programs are unfair.
—Barry R. McCaffrey, Director, Office of National Drug Control Policy

They [mandatory sentences] have not stemmed the drug trade. The only thing they've done is to fill the prisons.
—Retired Republican New York State Senator John Dunne.

As America entered the new millennium we culminated the most punishing decade in our nation's history. While the number of persons in jail and prison grew by 462,006 in the seven decades from 1910 to 1980, in the 1990s alone, the number of jail and prison inmates grew by an estimated 816,965. As the millennium turned, America's prison and jail populations approached the 2 million mark, with that dubious distinction likely to be achieved within a year of the release of this report [in 2000].

The cost of this massive growth in incarceration is staggering. Americans will spend nearly $40 billion on prisons and jails in the year 2000. Almost $24 billion of that will go to incarcerate 1.2 million nonviolent offenders. Meanwhile, in two of our nation's largest states, California and New York, the prison budgets outstripped the budgets for higher education during the mid-1990s.

The number of people behind bars not only dwarfs America's historical incarceration rates; it defies international comparisons as well. While America has about 5% of the world's population, almost one in four persons incarcerated worldwide are incarcerated in the US.

While substantial increases in all categories of inmates have contributed to America's mushrooming incarceration rates, the use of imprisonment for drug offenders has increased particularly sharply, drawing increased attention by researchers and policy makers alike.

In 1999, the Sentencing Project reported that between 1980 and 1997, drug arrests tripled in the United States. In 1997, four out of five drug arrests (79.5%) were for possession, with 44% of those arrests for marijuana offenses. Between 1980 and 1997, while the number of drug offenders entering prisons skyrocketed, the proportion of state prison space housing violent offenders declined from 55% to 47%.

An American Gulag

Fully 76% of the increase in admissions to America's prisons from 1978 to 1996 was attributable to non-violent offenders, much of that to persons incarcerated for drug offenses. Data like these prompted retired General Barry McCaffrey, Director of the Office of National Drug Control Policy, to refer to America's prison system as an "American gulag." And indeed, with an incarceration rate second to only Russia's, the drug czar's choice of language is fitting.

The hammer of incarceration for drug offenses has by no means fallen equally across race or age categories, with young, African American men suffering unprecedented rates of incarceration for drug offenses. According to the Sentencing Project, nearly one in three (32%) black men between the ages of 20 and 29 were under criminal justice control in 1995. A recent report by the Building Blocks for Youth Initiative found that black youth were admitted to state public facilities for drug offenses at 48 times the rate of white youth.

> "*Drug control policies bear primary responsibility for the quadrupling of the national prison population since 1980.*"

From 1986 to 1991, while the number of blacks imprisoned for violent offenses rose by about the same amount as whites (31,000 and 33,000, respectively), the number of blacks imprisoned for drug offenses increased four times as much as the increase for whites (66,000 vs. 15,000). This occurred at a time when survey data showed that five times as many whites were using drugs as blacks. The consequences of mass incarceration affect individuals and whole communities. The Sentencing Project and Human Rights Watch has reported that by 1998, 1.4 million African America men, or 13% of the black male adult population, had lost the right to vote due to their involvement in the criminal justice system.

More recently, Human Rights Watch released a report focusing on the extent to which African Americans "have been burdened with imprisonment because of nonviolent drug offenses." The findings of the report were sobering:

• While blacks make up about 13% of regular drug users in the US, they make up 62.7% of all drug offenders admitted to prison.

• While there are 5 times as many white drug users as black drug users, black men are admitted to state prison for drug offenses at a rate that is 13.4 times greater than that of white men. This drives an overall black incarceration rate that is 8.2 times higher than the white incarceration rate.

> *"Nearly one in four . . . prisoners in America is incarcerated for a non-violent drug offense."*

• In seven states, blacks constitute 80 to 90% of all drug offenders sent to prison. In 15 states, black men are admitted to state prison for drug charges at a rate that is 20 to 57 times the white male rate.

Human Rights Watch concluded, "Drug control policies bear primary responsibility for the quadrupling of the national prison population since 1980 and a soaring incarceration rate, the highest among western democracies. . . . No functioning democracy has ever governed itself with as large a percentage of its adults incarcerated as the United States."

Using the same data set examined by the Human Rights Watch researchers—the National Corrections Reporting Program—as well as data provided by the Justice Department's Bureau of Justice Statistics and the California Department of Corrections, the Justice Policy Institute sought to examine several questions:

• What proportion of the total current prison population is made up of persons incarcerated for drug offenses and what is America currently spending to incarcerate drug offenders?

• How has incarceration for drug offenders increased over time vs. incarceration for other categories of non-violent offenders and for violent offenders?

• How have drug commitments for whites and blacks changed over time?

• How have drug commitments for younger adults changed over time?

• Which states make the most prolific use of prison space for drug offenders?

• Do states that incarcerate a higher proportion of their citizens for drug offenses experience lower rates of drug use amongst their citizens than states that make more parsimonious use of prisons for drug offenders?

Huge Growth in Drug Incarcerations

Nationally, the overall increase in drug admissions to prison from 1986 to 1996 is astonishing. For the thirty-seven states examined, a total of 38,541 inmates were admitted to prison on drug charges in 1986. In 1996 that number had grown to 148,092—nearly four times as many admissions as only a decade earlier. As population figures change, it is more instructive to examine drug incarceration rates per 100,000. In 1986, for every 100,000 citizens there were 18 people admitted to prison for drug offenses. By 1996 the rate had more than tripled to 63 drug admissions per 100,000, a 247% increase.

By the year 2000, these increases resulted in 458,131 drug offenders incarcerated in America's prisons and jails—approximately the size of the entire US prison and jail population of 1980. This means that nearly one in four (23.7%) prisoners in America is incarcerated for a non-violent drug offense. Using federal, state and local average per prisoner annual costs, the price tag for incarcerating 458,131 nonviolent drug offenders comes to $9.4 billion annually.

This growth defies not only historical US prison populations, but international incarceration rates as well. America's imprisonment of drug offenders dwarfs the incarcerated drug populations of *all* of Europe. In fact, America has 100,000 more persons behind bars *just for drug offenses* (458,131), than the European Union has *for all offenses* (356,626), even though the EU has 100 million more citizens than the US.

Every state except West Virginia and Hawaii increased the number of admissions to prison for drug offenses in 1996 versus 1986. But, as we show, the ramifications of these two states' decreases need to be taken with a grain of salt. California incarcerated the most people for drug admissions in 1986 and again in 1996, 9,885 and 42,614 respectively—a quadrupling in drug incarcerations. No other state came close. New York incarcerated the second most with 14,658 in 1996, up from 4,464 in 1986; Texas was third, admitting 9,246 in 1996 compared to 5,805 in 1986.

Examining the rates of drug incarceration offers a more reasonable way to compare states to one another. California is the leader in this category as well with 134 Californians incarcerated for drug offenses for every 100,000 citizens of the state. California also led the nation in 1986 with 37 admissions to prison for drug offenses per 100,000. Texas, the third highest incarcerator in terms of raw numbers in 1996, had the second highest drug incarceration rate in 1986. However, Texas fell to 16th in 1996 with 49 drug incarcerations per 100,000.

> *"America has 100,000 more persons behind bars* **just for drug offenses . . .** *than the European Union has* **for all offenses."**

Texas' relative slide (during which time, it is important to remember, Texas still experienced a 39% increase in its drug commitment rate) is largely the result of having been surpassed by a number of states with very low rates in 1986 choosing to increase their reliance on prison to deal with drug offenders. Topping this list is Louisiana, which in 1986 incarcerated 4 per 100,000 state residents for drug offenses. In 1996, Louisiana had catapulted to second place in incarceration rates for drug offenders with 107 per 100,000—a 2890% increase. Likewise, Georgia imprisoned 3 drug offenders per 100,000 citizens in 1986, the lowest in the nation. By 1996, Georgia was admitting 65 per 100,000 to state prisons—a 2079% increase.

West Virginia (–5%) and Hawaii (–10%) are the only two states showing a drop in drug admission rates; all other states report an increase.

Drug Commitments Outstrip All Others

The growth of drug commitments has disproportionately contributed to the overall growth of prison populations in the US. From 1980 to 1997, the number of offenders committed to state prison nearly doubled (+82%), the number of non-violent offenders tripled (+207%) while the number of drug offenders increased 11-fold (+1040%). In 1988, for the first time, the number of drug offenders being committed to prison exceeded the number of violent offenders being sent to prison, and has exceeded it every year since.

> *"The growth of drug commitments has disproportionately contributed to the overall growth of prison populations in the US."*

Thirty states increased the percent of new admissions to prison from 1986 to 1996. Seven states reported lower admissions for drug offenses in 1996 than in 1986. . . .

The numbers above describe a nearly unilateral increase in the use of prison as an attempt, to deal with the drug issue in the United States. They tell only part of the story. The following data clearly show the brunt of the war on drugs being shouldered by the African American community. While many more whites use drugs than blacks in America, prison space for drug offenses is increasingly reserved for African Americans.

The overall rate of admission to prison for drug offenses was 63 per 100,000 in 1996. When dichotomized by race, however, the rates reveal vast disparities. Whites were sent to prison for drug offenses at a much lower rate (20 per 100,000) than were African Americans (279 per 100,000), in 1996. That means blacks are incarcerated for a drug offense at a rate 14 times that of whites, while survey data reveals that five times as many whites use drugs as blacks.

Both whites and blacks were admitted to prison at higher rates in 1996 than 1986. But for blacks the increase was much more dramatic. Whites experienced a 115% increase in the rate of drug admissions, from 9 to 20. Meanwhile the black rate of 49 per 100,000 in 1986 skyrocketed by 465% to 279 per 100,000 in 1996. Put another way, while the white drug commitment rate doubled from 1986 to 1996, the black rate quintupled. Despite the doubling of the white drug commitment rate between 1986 and 1996, the black rate of commitment to prison for drug offenses in 1986 was still 2 1/2 times the 1996 white rate.

The "Punishing 90's"

In 1986 the gap between the percent of new admissions for blacks and whites that were the result of drug convictions was small and in some states the percentage for whites exceeded that of blacks. During the "Punishing 90's," however, the percent of blacks entering prison for drug offenses outstripped that of whites, in some states more than two to one.

State level data reveal an even starker image of the change in white and black rates of incarceration. Earlier we reported that Hawaii and West Virginia experienced a decrease in their overall drug incarceration rates. However, we find that in these states the decrease is fully attributable to a white decrease in incarceration. The percent change in the rate of incarceration for whites in West Virginia was -38%, for Hawaii it was -58%. Blacks in each state did not fair so well with increases of 172% in West Virginia and 87% in Hawaii.

Five other states also reduced the drug incarceration rates for whites between 1986 and 1996. Like Hawaii and West Virginia, however, blacks in those states weathered a dramatic increase. For example, in South Carolina, Texas, and North Carolina, while the white commitment rate for drug offenses was declining by 32%, 27%, and 21%, respectively, the comparable black rate was exploding by 270%, 216%, and 501%, respectively.

In no state did the rate of increase for whites outpace that for blacks. In most states the black percentage change far exceeds that of whites. The states with the largest percent increases for blacks are Louisiana (10,102%), Georgia (5,499%), Arkansas (5,033%), Iowa (4,284%) and Tennessee (1,473%). Each of these states began with a low rate of incarceration of blacks (and whites) for drug offenses in 1986. The next eleven years were spent catching up with and passing other states in the race to incarcerate black drug users. . . .

Next we asked how prison policies regarding drug offenders affected America's young adults.

America has certainly gotten tougher on its youth. In 1986, nearly at the height of the drug war, 31 out of every 100,000 youth were admitted to state prisons for drug offenses. In 1996, 122 youth per 100,000 were entering prison on drug convictions. This represents a 291% increase in the rate at which young people were incarcerated because of drug involvement.

Hawaii was the only state to show a decrease in the rate of youth incarceration for drug offenses (-10%).

> *"The . . . data clearly show the brunt of the war on drugs being shouldered by the African American community."*

Georgia youth experienced the largest increase (6,322%) followed by Louisiana (6,197%), Iowa (1,736%), Tennessee (1,432%) and Arkansas (1,250%).

Again we examined how this significant increase was being played out across racial lines. These findings are even more disturbing than those that looked at all ages. Nationally, the percent increase in the rate of incarceration for drug offenses between 1986 and 1996 was 539% for young blacks compared to 90% for whites. In 1986 young blacks were incarcerated at a rate of 80 per 100,000; young whites were incarcerated at a rate of 16. In 1996 the young white rate of incarceration had doubled to 30 but the young black rate had grown nearly six and one-half times to 511 per 100,000.

At the state level, we were not surprised to find great discrepancy in the rates at which white and black youth are admitted to prison or in the disparate levels of change in admission rates over time. In six states, the rate of prison admission of white youth for drug offenses decreased—black youth did not share the same experience. . . .

Minimal Connection Between Incarceration Rates and Drug Usage

It is, of course, important to ask how drug incarceration rates might be influencing drug use. After all, some support such high rates of incarceration by claiming that they are having a salutary impact on drug use. A thorough analysis of this question is extremely difficult given the paucity of data on state-by-state drug use. At the present time, since the Substance Abuse and Mental Health Services Administration (SAMHSA) data is not reported on a state-by-state basis, no annual state-by-state data is available to properly analyze changes over time in state drug use.

However, in 1993, SAMHSA produced a three-year average of 1991–1993 estimates of state-by-state drug use in 26 states which was reported in the recent Human Rights Watch report. Of those, 23 corresponded to states whose incarceration data are available through the National Corrections Reporting Program [NCRP]—the program we have used for our state-by-state drug incarceration analysis. . . .

Using the NCRP admissions data for [1991 to 1993], we computed the average rate of drug admission to prison in the twenty-three corresponding states.

We wanted to know if this available data could give us a clue as to any association between rates of incarceration and the percent of people using drugs. . . . In other words, for those states with data available, the connection between drug commitment rates to prison and the percent of those using drugs is associated—states with higher rates of drug incarceration have higher rates of drug use. . . .

Are high rates of incarceration in 1991 associated with lower drug use in subsequent years? Again, the correlation between admission rates to prison and drug use rates is positive. . . . High rates of incarceration in 1991 are associated with high drug use rates in 1991–1993. Indeed, despite the massive increase in drug admissions to prison for young people during the 1990s, a recent Center for Disease Control study found that drug use among high school children increased during the 1990s, with twice as many kids reporting [they] have used cocaine.

Mandatory Sentences Are Not Justifiable

As with other examinations of the impact of the drug war on incarceration rates, the Justice Policy Institute has found that the imprisonment of drug offenders has grown at an alarming rate over the past two decades, even when compared to the generally explosive growth of incarceration in the US during that time. While the number of persons imprisoned in state institutions for violent offenses nearly doubled from 1980 to 1997, the number of nonviolent offenders has tripled and the number of persons imprisoned for drug offenses has increased eleven-fold.

Nearly one in four persons imprisoned in the United States is imprisoned for a drug offense. The number of persons behind bars for drug offenses is roughly the same as the entire prison and jail population in 1980. There are 100,000 more persons imprisoned in America for drug offenses than *all* prisoners in the European Union, even though the EU has 100 million more citizens than

> *"High rates of incarceration in 1991 are associated with high drug use rates in 1991–1993."*

the US. The cost of incarcerating over 458,000 prisoners for drug offenses now exceeds $9 billion annually.

This punitive and costly approach has fallen most heavily on young, black males. Even though surveys continue to show similar drug usage rates for young blacks and whites, prison commitments for young black males has increased six-fold while prison commitments for young whites has doubled. In 6 states, drug commitment rates for young whites actually declined while comparable black rates experienced two- to eight-fold increases.

Finally, we utilized data from 23 very diverse states around the country for which we had both drug use data and rates of drug offender admissions to prison. We found a significant, positive correlation between the two, suggesting that, if anything, states with *higher* rates of drug incarceration experience *higher*, not lower, rates of drug use.

This is not the first study to question the effectiveness of incarceration as a means to reduce substance abuse. According to 1997 research by the RAND Corporation, spending additional funds to provide treatment for heavy cocaine users would reduce drug consumption by nearly four times as much as spending the same amount on law enforcement, and more than seven times as much as spending the same amount on longer sentences. Additionally, RAND estimated that treatment reduced drug-related crime as much as 15 times more than mandatory sentences. According to RAND:

> *Mandatory minimum sentences are not justifiable on the basis of cost-effectiveness at reducing cocaine consumption, cocaine expenditures, or drug related-crime. Mandatory minimums reduce cocaine consumption less per million taxpayer dollars spent than does spending the same amount on enforcement under the previous sentencing regime. And either type of incarceration approach reduces drug consumption less than does putting heavy users through treatment programs, per million dollars spent.*

A More Rational Approach

While there remains plenty of bad news to report about the overreliance on incarceration as a solution to America's drug dilemma, there are beginning to be some rays of hope in creating a more rational and effective response to our nation's drug problem. Faced with data like these and the costs and human tragedies they reflect, states around the country have begun to experiment with ways to address substance abuse without breaking the bank and deteriorating the human condition through unnecessary imprisonment. . . .

The country is going through a period of unprecedented prosperity, but not all of America's citizens are sharing in that prosperity. A population approximately the size of the District of Columbia is currently incarcerated for drug offenses, many of whom are nonviolent, many of whom could be addressed more effectively through diversion into treatment rather than costly and debilitating incarceration. As states like New York and California have led the nation's move toward incarcerating drug offenders, perhaps those states can lead the nation in a more reasonable, effective, and humane approach to combating substance abuse and its concomitant problems.

Drug Policies Should Focus on Harm Reduction

by Robert Maccoun and Peter Reuter

About the authors: *Robert Maccoun is a psychologist and professor of public policy and law at the University of California, Berkeley. Peter Reuter is an economist and professor of public policy and criminology at the University of Maryland, College Park.*

What would actually happen if drugs were legalized in America? For the last decade advocates of such a course, though politically weak, have dominated the intellectual debate for the simple reason that their criticism of existing policy holds a great deal of truth. The most conspicuous harms associated with drugs nowadays—violent crime, public disorder, government corruption, and diseases related to injection with dirty needles—are caused in large part by the country's prohibition policies.

But it's quite a leap from this critique to the conclusion that the best way to eliminate harms is to eliminate prohibition; the story is far more complicated. A decade of study presented in our book, *Drug War Heresies: Learning from Other Vices, Times, and Places* has convinced us that legalization of cocaine, marijuana, and heroin would lead to large reductions in drug-related crime and mortality, but also to large increases in drug use and addiction. Poor urban minority communities, which have been devastated by drug violence and drug imprisonments, might benefit substantially, but the larger body of middle-class Americans would likely be moderately worse off. It's impossible to persuasively quantify any of these effects, but in the face of this certainty (about the directions of change) and uncertainty (about magnitudes), it's much less clear than legalization advocates generally acknowledge just what American drug policy should be.

Regulation of Vices Is Not the Answer

The usual assumption is that sales of cocaine, marijuana, and heroin would be carefully regulated if made legal. But the U.S. experience with regulating other dangerous vices is not encouraging. State and federal governments have ended up allowing gambling, smoking, and drinking to be heavily promoted in the marketplace, notwithstanding the abundant evidence that they cause great harm to many people.

Take gambling: In one generation the nation has shifted from an almost universal prohibition to the near universal availability of lotteries and casinos (and dizzying gambling promotion by government itself). A recent New York State lottery ad proclaimed, "We won't stop until everyone's a millionaire." In California the come-on is, "Everybody gets lucky sooner or later, so don't take any chances."

> *"Current American policies . . . remain ineffective, unnecessarily harsh, and the source of considerable social damage."*

The legalization of gambling has brought great gains quite apart from the pleasure many people derive from fantasies of sudden wealth. Money that previously went to criminals and corrupt police has been diverted to public coffers. Still, the policy has also generated serious costs, from the moral debasement of state government to the expansion of problem gambling and, probably, white-collar crimes committed to cover gambling losses. About three million adults and adolescents now gamble so much that it causes real harm to themselves and others, up from about 1.1 million in 1975. As for lotteries, the poor spend a much higher share of their income on them than anyone else, making this method of financing public programs appallingly regressive. Households with incomes of less than $10,000 spent an average of $600 (on average more than 6 percent of their total incomes) on lottery tickets in 1997, the last year for which survey data are available. Compare this with households whose incomes exceed $100,000; they spent an average of $300 (less than one-third of 1 percent).

Tobacco is a different story. A continuing and aggressive public-health campaign has cut overall smoking rates in half in a generation. Few today doubt that cigarettes are hazardous (although smokers tend to think they're less hazardous for themselves than for other people), and the combination of civil restrictions on where a person can smoke, health-insurance incentives, and pressure from physicians has made smoking a stigmatized behavior in many communities and subcultures.

Nonetheless, it's striking that a generation after the nation became aware of smoking's dangers, the tobacco industry manages to retain and promote a mass legal market for a deadly product. Indeed, the proportion of young people taking up smoking has stayed about the same over the last 20 years. The tobacco industry, meanwhile, remains a power in politics at every level of government. It fought off one set of advertising restrictions by establishing the Freedom to Advertise Coalition, which included the American Association of Advertising Agencies, the Outdoor Advertising Association of America, and the Association of National Advertisers. The industry's position was also supported by magazine and newspaper publishers and by the American Civil Liberties Union, which announced its strong opposition to cigarette advertising restrictions on First Amendment grounds. To defeat large increases in federal tobacco taxation, the tobacco industry allied itself with groups fighting against tax increases generally. It has very successfully broadened its political base by making strategic donations to nonprofit groups. To date it has also succeeded in staving off regulation by the U.S. Food and Drug Administration.

Alcohol regulation has historically been more restrictive than tobacco control. In 1933 the country rejected Prohibition but with less than a ringing endorsement of easy access to liquor. When Prohibition was repealed, 15 states initially established state liquor monopolies; only nine states allowed retail sale of alcohol without food. In some states patrons could only be served at tables; standing at a bar was believed to encourage overindulgence. Sunday sales were widely forbidden.

Since World War II, however, all such restrictions, except those governing the minimum legal drinking age, have eroded and restrictions on the promotion of alcohol were squarely halted by the Supreme Court's 1996 decision in *44 Liquormart, Inc., v. State of Rhode Island.* By now even federal liquor taxes are, by international and historical standards, very modest.

In the case of alcohol, it was apparently not the repeal of Prohibition that increased drinking: Consumption rates in the mid-1930s were well below those before Prohibition. But as restrictions on the liquor industry

> *"Redistributing the damage away from the poor is desirable and might even justify some worsening of the overall problem."*

were eased after World War II and aggressive advertising began, consumption rates climbed to a 1975 peak of 2.7 gallons of pure alcohol per capita from about 1.6 gallons in 1940. Lately, programs aimed at reducing drunken driving, particularly among youths, have had a substantial impact on road fatalities but not on drinking itself. And alcohol consumption still leads to 100,000 deaths annually.

Regulating Hard Drugs Would Be Difficult

It may be possible to design a regulatory scheme for drugs that in theory would avoid the harms of prohibition as well as the dangers of open commercialization. But experience suggests that we'll have considerable trouble maintaining it. If we're unable to effectively restrain the promotion of alcohol and tobacco, each of which levies a terrible burden on society, it's particularly unlikely that the United States will do any better with marijuana, a drug less harmful than either of these (though not without hazards or addictive qualities).

Would regulation of hard drugs fare better? Those who now oppose legalization often cite the United States's experience during the time when cocaine, heroin, and other opiates were legally available. But we have found that the lessons of history are not so obvious. For example, before it was prohibited in 1914, use of cocaine was only about one-fifth as common as it is now and led to much less violent crime, according to new research by Joseph Spillane, reported in his *Cocaine: From Medical Marvel to Modern Menace in the United States, 1884–1920*. A point for the legalizers? Perhaps, but criminalizing the drug did result in sharp reductions in use

> **"We do not have to choose between two extremes—an all-out war on drugs or a libertarian free market."**

for two generations, until the explosion of users in our own times.

Less equivocal is the effect, once again, of commercialization. By the 1890s respectable doctors and pharmacists had stopped prescribing and dispensing cocaine, having seen that it generated addiction and violence in patients. The pharmaceutical industry, however, did not give up so quickly. As late as 1892, Parke-Davis, the most prominent of cocaine industry firms, published a reference book with 240 pages on coca and cocaine of which only three contained negative reports—and these ignored much of what was widely known by then about the drug's dangers. Cocaine manufacturers continued to promote their product extensively, soliciting some of the earliest celebrity endorsements in the advertising business. Sigmund Freud himself was persuaded to tout the quality and purity of Parke-Davis cocaine.

The result: As medical use stopped, recreational use grew, especially among the poor. A *Pharmaceutical Era* report from 1904 reflects the public concern at the time: "The cocaine habit is steadily growing in Newark among the boys who pool in the upstairs pool and billiard rooms. . . . Scores of young men have recently lost ambition and employment by the use of the drug in this manner and . . . several deaths have recently been caused by the habit." There was little hesitation about prohibiting cocaine in the Harrison Narcotics Act of 1914.

Our mixed findings about other vices and other times do not bolster the case for legalization. Nor do they endorse current American policies, which remain ineffective, unnecessarily harsh, and the source of considerable social damage. What we have learned from other places, however, suggests that these two strategies are not the only choices. Not only is it possible to implement prohibition more sensibly, many other Western countries have already done so.

The Dutch Approach

The Dutch decision to allow the sale of small amounts of marijuana and hashish in specially regulated coffee shops provides the best available evidence about the advantages and limitations of such an approach. Dutch law unequivocally prohibits possession of any form of cannabis, the plant from which both marijuana and hashish are derived; international treaties signed by the country require that. Yet in 1976, the Dutch adopted a formal written policy of nonenforcement for violations involving possession or sale of up to 30 grams. Since 1995 that's been changed to five grams, but either is a sizeable quantity given that few Dutch users, according to research done at the University of Amsterdam, consume more than 10 grams a month. The Dutch implemented this system of quasi-legal commercial availability in order to prevent excessive punishment of casual users, and to weaken the link between soft- and hard-drug markets by allowing marijuana users to avoid contact with illegal sellers.

At first, cannabis use under this system remained stable—at rates well below those in the United States. But between 1980 and 1988, the number of coffee shops selling cannabis in Amsterdam increased tenfold. They spread to more prominent and accessible locations in the central city and began to promote the drug more openly, even though they were not allowed to advertise in conventional ways. By the mid-1990s somewhere between 1,200 and 1,500 coffee shops (about one for every 12,000 inhabitants) were selling cannabis products in the Netherlands, and use had exploded. Whereas 15 percent of 18-to-20-year-olds reported having used marijuana in 1984, the figure had more than doubled to 33 percent by 1992—during a period when rates were flat or declining in most other Western nations. And it has not dropped since.

Still, this rate of use in the Netherlands is somewhat lower than in the United States and in the middle of the range for Western Europe. One can be impressed by the speed with which marijuana use spread after the coffee shops started selling it widely—or by the plateau of use at rates lower than those in the United States, notwithstanding America's roughly 700,000 annual arrests for marijuana possession in the 1990s.

> *"It's possible to realize most of the benefits of prohibition without inflicting the harms caused by the punitive U.S. system."*

The Dutch data suggest that, by itself, removing criminal penalties against users has little effect on cannabis consumption. Experience elsewhere reinforces that conclusion. Decriminalization of marijuana possession in 12 U.S. states during the 1970s, and in two Australian states more recently, was not associated with any discernible increase in use. That's probably because merely removing the penalties for use, without permitting commercial promotion of the drug, does not make it significantly more available than under prohibition. In that sense decriminalization offers only modest risks. But it also offers fairly modest gains, leaving black markets intact and failing to address the crime and health problems aggravated by prohibition.

Other European Policies

The other major European innovation comes from conservative Switzerland. In January 1994, Switzerland opened a number of heroin-maintenance clinics in a three-year national trial of a treatment alternative for addicts not helped by available methadone-maintenance programs. The average age among addicts admitted to the trial was about 33, with 12 years of injecting heroin and eight prior treatment episodes. Addicts could choose the heroin dose they needed and could inject up to three times daily, 365 days of the year, a regimen intended to remove any incentive for black market purchases.

By the end of the trial more than 800 patients had received heroin on a regular basis, apparently without leakage into the illicit market. Seventy percent were still in treatment a year and a half later, a much higher retention rate than for most methadone programs; and Swiss researchers believe that a substantial fraction of the 30 percent who dropped out of heroin maintenance went on to other kinds of treatment. No overdose deaths were reported among participants while they stayed in the program, and their behavior exposed them to less risk of AIDS. Crime was much reduced, according to both the addicts' own reports and the government's arrest records. Those in the trial group holding jobs they described as "permanent" rose to 32 percent from 14 percent; unemployment among them fell to 20 percent from 44 percent.

Due to a weak research design, it's not clear from the Swiss trial if the improvement in patients was due to heroin maintenance or to the psychological and social services that addicts also received. Still, no one has made a claim that the heroin problem in the trial communities worsened as a result of allowing heroin maintenance. In 1997 the Swiss government approved a large-scale expansion of the program, although other countries continue to criticize it because Swiss participants receive an average daily dose of 500 to 600 milligrams of pure heroin, a massive amount by the standards of U.S. street addicts.

The Best Policy for the United States

Choosing the best policy for our own country is not a simple matter of adding up benefits and harms. For one thing, even if the average harm caused to society by an incident of cocaine or heroin use were much reduced (as it very likely would be with full legalization, for instance), that might not result in an overall improvement. The total harm to society is average harm multiplied by the total quantity of drugs consumed. With any policy that results in many more users—and perhaps heavier use among the most seriously addicted—total harm might rise even as average harm fell.

> *"It would be . . . rational . . . to seek . . . to reduce the harmful consequences of drug use when it occurs."*

Moreover, there are many different kinds of damage: How does one weigh the increased addiction certain to result from legalization against the reduced crime and corruption that would also be generated? How does one balance reductions in violence against potential increases in accidents and other behavioral risks of drug use? Money is hardly a satisfactory measure.

Another complication is that the advantages and disadvantages of different approaches will be unevenly distributed in society. Any substantial reduction in illegal drug markets will help urban minority communities, where drug sales now cause so much crime and disorder. And that's likely to be true even if the levels of drug use and addiction were to increase in those communities. For the middle class, however, the benefits of eliminating the black market may look very small in comparison to the increased risk of drug involvement, particularly among adolescents. For liberals such as ourselves, redistributing the damage away from the poor is desirable and might even justify some worsening of the overall problem, but not everyone will agree with that.

To further confuse the public debate, one size will not fit all. There is, for instance, a strong case to be made for not only eliminating the penalties for marijuana possession but also allowing people to cultivate the plant for their own use—the approach currently taken in the state of South Australia. The downside risks (increases in marijuana use and respiratory illness) seem modest while the gains look very attractive: the elimination of 700,000 marijuana possession arrests in the United States annually and the possibility of weakening the link between soft- and hard-drug markets without launching Dutch-style commercial promotion. But in the case of heroin, the desirability of some sort of prescription approach, on the model of the Swiss heroin-maintenance regimen, is much harder to gauge. (Further evidence will soon be available from a pilot heroin-maintenance program in the Netherlands, which may be helpful.) And with cocaine, it seems that any policy that permits easier access is likely to produce sizeable increases in use.

What's clear, however, is that we do not have to choose between the two extremes—an all-out war on drugs or a libertarian free market—usually presented in the American debate. More moderate alternatives are possible. The policies of the Netherlands, Switzerland, and, increasingly, the United Kingdom and Germany, demonstrate that it's possible to reap most of the benefits of prohibition without inflicting the harms caused by the punitive U.S. system. The American failure to see this is largely traceable to the popular notion that the only defensible goal for drug policy is reducing the number of users (preferably to zero). It would be equally rational, however, to seek also to reduce the harmful consequences of drug use when it occurs. To this end we could aim at reducing the quantity of drugs consumed by those who won't quit taking them, a tack familiar from the American approach to controlling the use of alcohol. And we could undertake harm reduction with efforts based on the model of American product-safety regulation, which focuses as much on reducing the consequences of accidents as on reducing the number of them.

Working out similar strategies for drug control would not be easy nor would the results be without risk. But they would likely be far more humane than either of the options usually put before us.

Liberalizing Drug Policies Would Increase Crime and Violence

by James R. McDonough

About the author: *James R. McDonough is the director of the Florida Office of Drug Control.*

An oft-repeated mantra of both the liberal left and the far right is that antidrug laws do greater harm to society than illicit drugs. To defend this claim, they cite high rates of incarceration in the United States compared with more drug-tolerant societies. In this bumper-sticker vernacular, the drug war in the United States has created an "incarceration nation."

But is it true? Certainly rates of incarceration in the United States are up (and crime is down). Do harsh antidrug laws drive up the numbers? Are the laws causing more harm than the drugs themselves? These are questions worth exploring, especially if their presumptive outcome is to change policy by, say, decriminalizing drug use.

It is, after all, an end to the "drug war" that both the left and the right say they want. For example, William F. Buckley Jr. devoted the Feb. 26, 1996, issue of his conservative journal, *National Review*, to "the war on drugs," announcing that it was lost and bemoaning the overcrowding in state prisons, "notwithstanding that the national increase in prison space is threefold since we decided to wage hard war on drugs." James Gray, a California judge who speaks often on behalf of drug-decriminalization movements, devoted a major section of his book, *Why Our Drug Laws Have Failed and What We Can Do About It*, to what he calls the "prison-industrial complex." Ethan Nadelmann, executive director of the Drug Policy Alliance and perhaps the most unabashed of the "incarceration-nation" drumbeaters, says in his Web article, "Eroding Hope for a Kinder, Gentler Drug Policy," that he believes "criminal-justice measures to control drug use are mostly ineffective, counterproductive and unethical" and that administration "policies are really about punishing people for the sin of drug use." Nadelmann goes on to attack the drug-court system as well, which offers treatment in lieu of incarceration, as too coercive since it uses the threat of the criminal-justice system as an inducement to stay the course on treatment.

False Assertions Win Converts for Decriminalizers

In essence, the advocates of decriminalization of illegal drug use assert that incarceration rates are increasing because of bad drug laws resulting from an inane drug war, most of whose victims otherwise are well-behaved citizens who happen to use illegal drugs. But that infraction alone, they say, has led directly to their arrest, prosecution and imprisonment, thereby attacking the public purse by fostering growth of the prison population.

Almost constant repetition of such assertions, unanswered by voices challenging their validity, has resulted in the decriminalizers gaining many converts. This in turn has begotten yet stronger assertions: the drug war is racist (because the prison population is overrepresentative of minorities); major illegal drugs are benign (ecstasy is "therapeutic," "medical" marijuana is a "wonder" drug, etc.); policies are polarized as "either-or" options ("treatment not criminalization") instead of a search for balance between demand reduction and other law-enforcement programs; harm reduction (read: needle distribution, heroin-shooting "clinics," "safe drug-use" brochures, etc.) becomes the only "responsible" public policy on drugs.

But the central assertion, that drug laws are driving high prison populations, begins to break down upon closer scrutiny. Consider these numbers from the U.S. Bureau of Justice Statistics compilation, *Felony Sentences in State Courts, 2000.* Across the United States, state courts convicted about 924,700 adults of a felony in 2000. About one-third of these (34.6 percent) were drug offenders. Of the total number of convicted felons for all charges, about one-third (32 percent) went straight to probation. Some of these were rearrested for subsequent violations, as were other probationers from past years. In the end, 1,195,714 offenders entered state correctional facilities in 2000 for all categories of felonies. Of that number, 21 percent were drug offenders. Seventy-nine percent were imprisoned for other crimes.

Therefore, about one-fifth of those entering state prisons in 2000 were there for drug offenses. But drug offenses comprise a category consisting

> *"The notion that harsh drug laws are to blame for filling prisons to the bursting point ... appears to be dubious."*

of several different charges, of which possession is but one. Also included are trafficking, delivery and manufacturing. Of those incarcerated for drug offenses only about one-fourth (27 percent) were convicted of possession. One-fourth of one-fifth is 5 percent. Of that small amount, 13 percent were incarcerated for marijuana possession, meaning that in the end less than 1 percent (0.73 percent to be exact) of all those incarcerated in state-level facilities were there for marijuana possession. The data are similar in state after state. At the high end, the rates stay under 2 percent. Alabama's rate, for example, was 1.72 percent. At the low end, it falls under one-tenth of 1 percent. Maryland's rate, for example, was 0.08 percent. The rate among federal prisoners is 0.27 percent.

If we consider cocaine possession, the rates of incarceration also remain low 2.75 percent for state inmates, 0.34 percent for federal. The data, in short, present a far different picture from the one projected by drug critics such as Nadelmann, who decries the wanton imprisonment of people whose offense is only the "sin of drug use."

Drug Laws Are Not Harmful

But what of those who are behind bars for possession? Are they not otherwise productive and contributing citizens whose only offense was smoking a joint? If Florida's data are reflective of the other states and there is no reason why they should not be the answer is no. In early 2003, Florida had a total of 88 inmates in state prison for possession of marijuana out of an overall population of 75,236 (0.12 percent). And of those 88, 40 (45 percent) had been in prison before. Of the remaining 48 who were in prison for the first time, 43 (90 percent) had prior probation sentences and the probation of all but four of them had been revoked at least once. Similar profiles appear for those in Florida prisons for cocaine possession (3.2 percent of the prison population in early 2003). They typically have extensive arrest histories for offenses ranging from burglary and prostitution to violent crimes such as armed robbery, sexual battery and aggravated assault. The overwhelming majority (70.2 percent) had been in prison before. Of those who had not been imprisoned previously, 90 percent had prior probation sentences and the supervision of 96 percent had been revoked at least once.

> *"The proposition that drug laws do more harm than illegal drugs themselves falls into disarray."*

The notion that harsh drug laws are to blame for filling prisons to the bursting point, therefore, appears to be dubious. Simultaneously, the proposition that drug laws do more harm than illegal drugs themselves falls into disarray even if we restrict our examination to the realm of drugs and crime, overlooking the extensive damage drug use causes to public health, family cohesion, the workplace and the community.

Law-enforcement officers routinely report that the majority (i.e., between 60 and 80 percent) of crime stems from a relationship to substance abuse, a view that the bulk of crimes are committed by people who are high, seeking ways to obtain money to get high or both. These observations are supported by the data. The national Arrests and Drug Abuse Monitoring (ADAM) program reports on drugs present in arrestees at the time of their arrest in various urban areas around the country. In 2000, more than 70 percent of people arrested in Atlanta had drugs in their system; 80 percent in New York City; 75 percent in Chicago; and so on. For all cities measured, the median was 64.2 percent. The results are equally disturbing for cocaine use alone, according to Department of Justice statistics for 2000. In Atlanta, 49 percent of those arrested

> *"Looking only at crime and drugs, it is apparent that drugs drive crime."*

tested positive for cocaine; in New York City, 49 percent; in Chicago, 37 percent. Moreover, more than one-fifth of all arrestees reviewed in 35 cities around the nation had more than one drug in their bodies at the time of their arrest, according to the National Household Survey on Drug Abuse.

If the correlation between drug use and criminality is high for adults, the correlation between drug use and misbehavior among youth is equally high. For children ages 12 to 17, delinquency and marijuana use show a proportional relationship. The greater the frequency of marijuana use, the greater the incidents of cutting class, stealing, physically attacking others and destroying other peoples' property.

A youth who smoked marijuana six times in the last year was twice as likely physically to attack someone else than one who didn't smoke marijuana at all. A child who smoked marijuana six times a month in the last year was five times as likely to assault another than a child who did not smoke marijuana. Both delinquent and aggressive antisocial behavior were linked to marijuana use: the more marijuana, the worse the behavior.

Strict Drug Laws Are Necessary

Even more tragic is the suffering caused children by substance abuse within their families. A survey of state child-welfare agencies by the National Committee to Prevent Child Abuse found substance abuse to be one of the top two problems exhibited by 81 percent of families reported for child maltreatment. Additional research found that chemical dependence is present in one-half of the families involved in the child-welfare system. In a report entitled No Safe Haven: Children of Substance-Abusing Parents, the National Center on Addiction and Substance Abuse at Columbia University estimates that substance abuse causes or contributes to seven of 10 cases of child maltreatment and puts the federal, state and local bill for dealing with it at $10 billion.

Are the drug laws, therefore, the root of a burgeoning prison population? And are the drug laws themselves a greater evil than the drugs themselves? The answer to the first question is a clear no. When we restricted our review to incarcerated felons, we found only about one-fifth of them were in prison for crimes related to drug laws. And even the miniscule proportion that were behind bars for possession seemed to have serious criminal records that indicate criminal behavior well beyond the possession charge for which they may have plea-bargained, and it is noteworthy that 95 percent of all convicted felons in state courts in 2000 pleaded guilty, according to the Bureau of Justice Statistics.

The answer to the second question also is no. Looking only at crime and drugs, it is apparent that drugs drive crime. While it is true that no traffickers, dealers or manufacturers of drugs would be arrested if all drugs were legal, the same could be said of drunk drivers if drunken driving were legalized. Indeed, we could bring prison population down to zero if there were no laws at all. But we do have laws, and for good reason. When we look beyond the crime driven by drugs and factor in the lost human potential, the family tragedies, massive health costs, business losses and neighborhood blights instigated by drug use, it is clear that the greater harm is in the drugs themselves, not in the laws that curtail their use.

Parents Should Oppose Drug Liberalization

by Drug Watch International

About the author: *Drug Watch International is a drug information network and advocacy organization that promotes the creation of drug-free cultures in the world and opposes the legalization of drugs.*

Criminal justice, transportation, and emergency-room studies conclude overwhelmingly that violent episodes, accidents, crime, and other anti-social behaviors among adolescents are often drug related. In the face of widespread drug use among children, Drug Watch International believes that preventing drug use should be the goal of every parent. Parents need to become more informed not only about youth drug use but also about the agenda and strategies of those who would legitimize, legalize, and sell drugs to our children. Well-informed parents can successfully stand against drugs and vigorously counter pro-drug propaganda with facts and caring intervention in the lives of youth. The time has come for parents everywhere to give their full attention to the disintegrating adolescent world.

Prevention science has tended to focus on the problems of dysfunctional families and has had less to say about how the average family can avoid youth drug use. We know from many studies that parents who state strong opposition to youth drug and alcohol use, and who monitor youth activities to enforce anti-drug rules, decrease the chance of drug use among their children. What there studies don't explain is how the cultural environment has become so toxic, poisoned by the promotion of drugs to youth.

Drug use in the 1960s and 1970s spawned a number of groups of tokers (marijuana smokers) and acid heads (LSD users) who have poured their time and resources into legitimizing and legalizing psychoactive drugs, primarily so that they could use these substances with impunity and social approval. Over the years, the groups that have been in the forefront of the international effort to legalize drugs are the National Organization for the Reform of Marijuana Laws (NORML), the Drug Policy Foundation, and The Lindesmith Center.

Harm Reduction Is Another Name for Legalization

When their failed policy of out-and-out recreational use of drugs did not gain public approval, pro-legalizers adopted their current plan, which is called "harm reduction," a euphemism for the liberalization of drug policy. Harm reduction is intended to soften attitudes toward the personal use, production, and sales of dangerous mind-altering drugs. It is legalization by the back door. In February 1979, Keith Stroup, then out-going director of NORML, told students at a U.S. university that NORML was trying to get marijuana reclassified medically, particularly for chemotherapy patients. [Stroup said,] "We'll be using the issue as a red herring to give marijuana a good name."

Substantial funding from multi-millionaire Richard Dennis, international billionaire George Soros, and other wealthy sympathizers has enabled organizations such as The Lindesmith Center, headed by Ethan Nadelmann, and the Drug Policy Foundation to mount expensive marketing campaigns designed to sell pro-drug propaganda to an uninformed and naive public. A major part of these funds has been used to change the image and mask the agenda of the pro-legalization movement. Slick advertising and polished speakers representing the legalizers convey a plethora of messages designed to make drug legalization sound logical, reasonable, and inevitable, even though it is none of these.

A recent study reveals that roughly one fifth of popular songs contain references to illicit drugs, and illicit drugs appear in 22 percent of movies. The entertainment industry reflects an obsession with drugs. Many believe these drug messages increase youth drug use, because in many cases drug use is celebrated. Both radio and television have aired programs written to influence public opinion in favor of illicit drug use. Magazines and newspapers have given all too much credibility to pro-drug propaganda. Pro-drug advocates have been advisors to federal governments regarding drug policy. Former U.S. Surgeon General Joycelyn Elders is but one of a number of influential public officials who have made statements in favor of some form of drug legalization.

The harm reductionists rationalize their position by telling themselves and a trusting public that there is a crying need for medicinal marijuana, "industrial" marijuana hemp, needle giveaways, and drug law reform, despite the lack of scientific research to support these notions.

Marijuana Is Not Medicine

Few parents realize that THC, the main psychoactive ingredient in marijuana (the drug that produces marijuana's "high"), is already available in pill form by prescription under the brand name Marinol. However, Marinol has far more negative side effects than other available medicines and is usually the medicine of last choice by physicians. Marijuana is a weed containing more than 450 different compounds; marijuana should not be confused with THC. Smoking toxic, carcinogen-laden marijuana cigarettes has repeatedly been rejected as medicine, most recently in the 1999 Institute of Medicine Report.

Harm reductionists tout "industrial" marijuana hemp as nature's answer to rope, paper, clothing, and good skin care; they allege it will save the family farm and the rain forests. These claims are false and rival the hype of 19th-century snake-oil salesmen. Leaders of the pro-drug movement have stated that "the way to legalize marijuana is to sell marijuana legally," believing that if they can get marijuana hemp products in stores, legalization of marijuana will soon follow.

Needle Exchange Programs (needle giveaways, known as NEPs) are another strategy to facilitate drug use by giving clean needles to injecting drug users, thus endangering the user as well as society. Advocates of NEPs falsely claim that free needles are necessary to curb the spread of AIDS. However, there is no valid scientific evidence that providing needles has resulted in the lowering of HIV/AIDS rates. There is, in fact, mounting evidence that NEPs significantly increase the risk of both hepatitis B and C. Drug trafficking, drug abuse, crime, and public squalor in the areas where NEPs are located magnify the underlying destructive activity of intravenous drug use.

> *"The cultural environment has become so toxic, poisoned by the promotion of drugs to youth."*

Harm reductionists claim that non-violent first time drug offenders are arrested and locked up indefinitely. However, a study of 22,000 people in the New York prison system gives a different picture. Eighty-seven percent were traffickers, in for selling drugs, in many cases by the ton. The vast majority of the remaining 13 percent were arrested for dealing drugs, but their lawyers plea-bargained their convictions down to possession.

Strongest Messages Must Come from Parents

Today's parents live in a time when society turns its head, and drug peddlers and drug sympathizers openly market drugs and drug-theme movies, music, clothing, jewelry, and posters to children. Parents are the primary influence on their children and must be proactive by giving a strong, unequivocal "No Drug Use" message to their children and grandchildren. In their own families and through local, state, and national parent networks, parents can, and should:

1. Be prepared to counter the drug culture's claims and expose its true agenda when their children parrot the legalizers' arguments. A visit to Drug Watch International's Web site can give insight as to why marijuana is not harmless, why smoked marijuana should not be legalized as medicine, why hemp is unnecessary, why needle exchange doesn't work, and why decriminalization spreads drug use.

2. Avoid denial and be vigilant. Understand that ALL children are at risk. Since 1992, drug use among U.S. 12–17 year-olds has doubled. A recent study reveals that drug use is the No. 1 concern of youth in the United States. Should it not also be the primary concern of parents? Study the harm done by specific drugs, and learn the signs of use. Realize that local libraries and the Internet do not differentiate between accurate and inaccurate, outdated, or contrived pro-drug information.

3. Send a clear no-use zero-tolerance message to their children, and discuss the pitfalls of drug use with them. If a child comes home drunk or stoned, parents must impose a serious consequence. Grounding and loss of telephone privileges make an impression on adolescents. If it happens more than once, drug testing and counseling should be considered.

4. Make their children accountable for money given to them. Parents have unwittingly supported their children's drug habits by not paying attention to where the money they give their children is going.

5. Monitor and screen their children's friends, music, television, movie, and Internet activity. Many movies, songs, and celebrities celebrate drug use and other anti-social behaviors. Know what their children are being exposed to. Watch for clothing and jewelry with drug symbols.

6. Be proactive in their community. Join the local prevention council or, if there isn't one, start one. Through it, create a newsletter for parents alerting them to drug culture issues. Organize wholesome activities for young people. Become familiar with drug education in local schools, and be sure their children are getting a clear no-use message at school.

7. Become an advocate at all governmental levels. If anyone proposes pro-marijuana legislation or attempts to decriminalize drugs, contact elected officials and urge them to defeat the bill. Write or call legislators, and urge them to be advocates for a serious effort to stop drug trafficking and to increase funding for prevention efforts. Encourage like-minded parents to join in this effort.

8. Vote. And get friends to vote for candidates willing to [take] a stand against illicit drugs.

> *"When . . . out-and-out recreational use of drugs did not gain . . . approval, pro-legalizers adopted . . . 'harm reduction,' a euphemism for the liberalization of drug policy."*

The drug culture's messages about marijuana and other drug use are flawed, and its products imperil our youth. Drugs and the drug-culture propaganda are seductive, but parents who learn the facts and commit themselves to protecting their children can be effective in keeping drugs out of their communities, schools, and homes. From 1980 to 1992, drug use was cut in half in the United States by a well-orchestrated national campaign to reduce demand, reaching from national leaders to private citizens, and especially encompassing parents. A similar approach can be successful again.

Drugs Should Not Be Legalized

by Dan P. Alsobrooks

About the author: *Dan P. Alsobrooks is a district attorney for the Twenty-Third Judicial District in Tennessee and president of the National District Attorneys Association in Virginia.*

Prosecutors know through experience that the majority of crimes in communities are drug-related. This is an indisputable fact, backed by incontrovertible evidence, including prosecutors' bulging caseloads. Those who seek to decriminalize drug use ignore the facts and the evidence, relying on myths to mislead the public and advance their cause.

The crimes related to substance abuse range far beyond drug possession. They run the gamut from environmental pollution to murder. Crimes include gang wars to control drug markets; methamphetamine manufacturing sites that are a biohazard; and deaths caused by drug-impaired drivers. The list goes on.

Propositions, proposals and legislation to legalize or decriminalize controlled substances are springing up around the country. The drug legalization movement is well-funded and highly adept at manipulating the media. Unless law enforcement speaks out more forcefully, our communities will find themselves facing an onslaught of violence and death directly attributable to the use of dangerous and poisonous drugs that have previously been controlled. We face a well-financed opposition with a well-organized political machine that can outspend us state by state and referendum by referendum. Operating under umbrella groups, the opposition uses a legislative strategy akin to the death of a thousand cuts. Those who want to legalize drugs advance their position, issue by issue, winning by incremental victories, while law enforcement officials often regard such victories as isolated losses.

For example, in one state, a legalization referendum misleads voters to believe that the issue is alleviating suffering for cancer patients. In another state, the issue is disguised as a legislative mandate to decriminalize certain types of drug use and provide treatment programs. And in a third state, legalization efforts are an attempt to limit asset forfeiture. Each such manipulation chips away at the foundation of law enforcement's efforts to fight substance abuse throughout the nation. With each such victory, those who would undermine law enforcement grow stronger and our communities become less safe.

Legalization Efforts Are Disguised

More than 100 of these so-called and cleverly disguised drug policy "reforms" have been enacted in 40 states since 1996 and 41 were enacted in 2001 alone. There have been some successful efforts to reject some so-called reforms, most notably in Massachusetts and Oregon, but they remain in the minority. Those who would legalize drugs boast of their success in Nevada, where last year [2001], marijuana was decriminalized and where this year, the issue on the ballot was actual legalization. Their propaganda machine exulted that "voters in Florida, Michigan and Ohio will likely vote on sweeping 'treatment instead of incarceration' initiatives in November. The initiatives are similar to measures voters approved in Arizona (1996) and California (2002)."

More ominously, those who support the drug legalization effort brag that the American people are significantly changing their opinions on drug abuse and the criminal justice system and that this "shift in public opinion" will lead to a groundswell of support for their cause. On one of the proponents' Web sites, they boldly claim, "States are reining in the excesses of the war on drugs regardless of what the federal government is doing. Since most drug arrests occur at the state level, state reforms are having a huge impact on the lives of millions of Americans. At the rate states are reforming their drug laws, the federal government may very soon find itself alone in supporting punitive and antiquated drug policies."

A major aspect of the public relations effort to bring about the state-by-state change rests on the continual repetition of myths. This, plus the American public's lack of understanding of the real dangers of substance abuse, provides those who support legalization with a sometimes-winning media campaign. Americans appear to be in serious denial about the problems associated with drugs: It is "someone else's child"; "something that will never hurt me"; or "someone else's life that will be jeopardized, not mine." Unless law enforcement officials counter such myths and convince America that these substances

> *"Those who seek to decriminalize drug use ignore the facts and the evidence, relying on myths to mislead the public."*

are not harmless, that the criminal justice system does not ruin people's lives, but rather, dangerous and addictive drugs do, they will continue to lose the fight and the legalization lobby's prophecies will come true.

One of the most popular myths regarding drugs is that jails are filled with people who are guilty only of possession for personal use. Law enforcement officials know that this is not true. The fact is that most individuals who are found in simple possession of drugs are placed in diversion and treatment programs and that this is not a new trend. Prosecutors and the courts have long recognized that prison cells should be reserved for the worst offenders and for those who refuse to rehabilitate and reform their dangerous conduct. Unfortunately, part of the basis for this myth is a practice of some prosecutors that should be explained or changed. Too often, offenders are sent to prison as the result of a plea agreement under which a charge of selling drugs is reduced to simple possession. Additionally, offenders may be incarcerated for possession with intent to distribute a controlled substance—a very different offense than possession for personal use. Further, many offenders who have been provided with rehabilitation opportunities and probation violate the conditions of their release and leave the courts no option but to incarcerate them.

> *"The use of illegal drugs is not victimless."*

Drug Abuse Is Not a Victimless Crime

According to a study published by the New York State Department of Corrections, of the 22,000 people in jail in New York for drug crimes, 87 percent were incarcerated for selling drugs or intent to sell drugs. Of the 12 percent incarcerated for possession, 76 percent were arrested for selling drugs and pleaded down their charges to possession. Additionally, the study found that most convicted first-time drug offenders end up on probation or in drug treatment rather than in jail. Statistics from Florida are similar. According to the Florida Department of Law Enforcement, of the 1,555 inmates in prison for drug possession on July 31, 2001, none were first-time offenders.

Each state has a similar story to tell and research must be conducted and data obtained that reflect the actual basis for incarceration. Likewise, prosecutors must understand that by pleading down cases, they are, in some instances, providing ammunition to their opponents. They need to tell their many success stories—of their drug courts, their diversion and treatment programs, and their efforts at all stages in the criminal justice system to provide substance abuse treatment. Prosecutors also must inform the public that without the threat of incarceration, habitual and addicted drug offenders will not enter or complete rehabilitation programs. This is very much in accord with former President Teddy Roosevelt's axiom of speaking softly but carrying a big stick—here, prosecutors' "stick" to ensure diversion program participation is the fear of going to jail.

Another myth, popular with a culture that has advertising campaigns flouting the need to follow societal rules, is that drug abuse is a victimless crime. The use of illegal drugs is not victimless. Regretfully, nearly every family has been hurt by addiction, It has consequences that touch the lives of children and adults nationwide. The victims of drug abuse range from those physically harmed by drug-induced crimes to taxpayers footing the bill for drug treatment. In other words, every citizen is a victim, either directly or indirectly.

Drugs are illegal because they are harmful, both to immediate users and to others who become victimized by the effects of drugs on users. In 1999, there were 19,102 deaths from drug-induced causes (legal and illegal drugs). During that year, there were 168,763 cocaine-related emergency room episodes alone. The following year, the Substance Abuse and Mental Health Administration's Drug Abuse Warning Network reported that there were 601,563 drug-related episodes in hospital emergency rooms nationwide. Who is paying the bills for these cases? The numbers speak for themselves. Between 1992 and 1998, the overall cost of drug abuse to society increased at a rate of 5.9 percent annually. By 1998, victimless crime was costing society $143.4 billion each year for health-related expenses alone. This, however, does not include the emotional costs to those actually victimized by substance abuse: the battered spouses, victims of impaired drivers and victims of assault and rape. These costs are beyond calculation.

Drug Use Impacts Crime Rates

A third myth used to support legalization is that drug use does not impact crime rates. One must wonder whether the people who say this have ever spoken to the victim of an assailant high on drugs; to the parents of a child killed by an impaired driver; or to a nurse who sees babies born to drug-addicted mothers every day. It is well-known that crimes result from a variety of factors and often cannot be attributed solely to drug abuse. The connection between drug use and crime is difficult to quantify due to exaggeration or minimization by the offender, lack of prompt testing and inaccuracy of victims' descriptions of whether the offender used drugs. However, many of the criminal acts seen every day have their origins in drug use. The American public must be convinced of this.

The need to obtain money to feed a habit, the rage empowered by drugs, the protection or disruption of the drug marketplace—each has its role in the crime cycles surrounding drug use. There is an indisputable correlation between drug use and crime, and it is obvious that the combination of increased availability of drugs and a decrease in the stigma for drug use will result in an increase in crime. Although the number of drug-related homicides has decreased in recent years, murders related to narcotics rank as the fourth most documented murder circumstance of 24 possible categories. In 2000, the Uniform Crime Reporting Program of the FBI reported that 4.4 percent of the

> *"Many of the criminal acts seen every day have their origins in drug use."*

12,943 homicides in which circumstances were known were narcotic-related. In 1998, 36 percent of convicted jail inmates were under the influence of drugs at the time of the offense. Drugs affect the user's judgment and behavior. In 1997, illicit drug users were 16 times more likely to be arrested for larceny or theft,

> *"Decriminalizing drugs sends the dangerous message that drug abuse is not harmful."*

14 times more likely to be arrested for driving under the influence and more than nine times more likely to be arrested on assault charges.

During that same year, 29.4 percent of state and federal prison inmates reported being under the influence of drugs at the time they committed murder, 27.8 percent reported being under the influence of drugs at the time they committed robbery and 13.8 percent reported being under the influence at the time they committed assault. How much more proof is needed? Against these statistics, arguments that legalization will not impact crime rates do not hold up.

A final myth being advanced by legalization supporters is that decriminalization will not increase drug use. This is a fatalistic kind of a *"que sera, sera"* argument: "whatever will be, will be." Decriminalizing drugs sends the dangerous message that drug abuse is not harmful. This, an obvious lie, ignores the fact that drug abuse claims the lives of 14,000 Americans annually and costs taxpayers nearly $70 billion. In conveying this message, society would be tacitly approving the use of drugs. If drugs were legalized and market forces prevailed, what, for example, would stop the marijuana industry from sponsoring commercials for children to see during Super Bowl halftime?

According to the 2001 Monitoring the Future Study, 73.3 percent of high school seniors had used alcohol within the past 12 months. During the same period, 37 percent had used marijuana. Arguably, the difference is attributed to the fact that alcohol is more readily available because it is legal for adults to purchase and consume. Conversely, the private industrial sector has repeatedly demonstrated that a tough, enforced drug policy sharply reduces sick days, on-the-job accidents and workers' compensation claims. Drugs, even legally used, are not harmless; nor are they cost-free to society.

The War on Drugs Is Not Lost

America's drug policy is not, as the critics contend, a dismal failure and a wasted effort. The statistics prove otherwise. The problem has been law enforcement's failure to effectively report its successes, warn of the true risks of substance abuse and to fully involve an educated community.

Overall drug use is down 50 percent since the late 1970s, which translates into 9.3 million fewer people using illegal drugs. Cocaine use has decreased 75 percent during the past 15 years, which means that 4 million fewer people are using cocaine on a regular basis. Less than 5 percent of the population use illegal drugs of any kind. Moreover, in the past, legalization and decriminalization reforms have failed, leading to increased drug use and the accompanying increases in social problems, health costs and economic repercussions. The use of drugs has decreased markedly since it reached the high point in the late 1970s, but it is not low enough. Too many Americans use drugs and too many other Americans are becoming victims of those who use drugs.

Even more dangerous is the complacency among prosecutors. If they, and others in law enforcement, do not sustain their efforts to tell the American people the truth about substance abuse, society as a whole will suffer and statistics on drug-related crime will continue to rise, fall and rise again as each generation relearns the mistakes of the previous generation. Law enforcement officers are sworn to protect the public and they need to be consistent and successful in their efforts to educate and warn society of the dangers of drug abuse. To date, there has not been success in these efforts. For the sake of the nation's future, success must be realized.

Media Advocacy for Drug Legalization Is Harmful

by the Northwest Center for Health and Safety

About the author: *The Northwest Center for Health and Safety is the educational and informational arm of Drug Watch Oregon, an antidrug advocacy organization.*

In 1964 the Surgeon General, Dr. Luther L. Terry, issued a report stating that cigarette smoking was the primary cause of lung cancer. The 1971 book *Cigarette Country*, written by Susan Wagner and published by Praeger Publishers, documented how the tobacco industry and the media worked together to discredit the surgeon general's report and keep the public in the dark. This same phenomenon is going on today with illicit drugs, particularly with marijuana and ecstasy, the two drugs favored by the media. The following includes excerpts from Ms. Wagner's book as well as from documents obtained from [the] American Lung Association, and Jeanette McDougal of Drug Watch International.

In 1968 free lance writer Stanley Frank wrote an article for *True Magazine* entitled "To Smoke or Not to Smoke—that is Still the Question," which concluded that the "hazards of cigarette smoking may not be so real as we have been led to believe" and that "Statistics alone link cigarettes with lung cancer, a correlation that is not accepted as scientific proof of the cause and effect." He stated further that ". . . there is absolutely no proof that smoking causes human cancer."

A few months later another article "Cigarette Cancer Link Is Bunk" echoing the exact same refrain, appeared in the *National Inquirer.* This article carried the byline Charles Golden. In 1968 a curious senator, Warren Magnuson, asked the new Surgeon General, William H. Stewart to take a look at the two articles. It was discovered that Frank "worked for a public relations firm that had been on retainer to the Tobacco Institute since 1963." Alerted to a possible conspiracy, writer Ronald Kessler of the *Wall Street Journal* looked into the matter and found that at least 600,000 copies of the *True* article had been sent out by a To-

Northwest Center for Health and Safety, "Tobacco, Marijuana, Ecstasy and the Media," www.drugand healthinfo.org, March 2003. Copyright © 2003 by the Northwest Center for Health and Safety. Reproduced by permission.

bacco Institute PR firm to influential individuals throughout the country, and further, that writer Stanley Frank had authored both articles.

True Editor Linked to Tobacco Firm

The Federal Trade Commission [FTC] found that *True* Editor, Douglas Kennedy, a self-professed heavy smoker who believed that a link between smoking and lung cancer was just propaganda, had worked with a tobacco company PR firm to promote the tobacco industry's view regarding smoking. The FTC inquiry further found that a tobacco company attorney had supplied Stanley Frank with "the materials used in writing the *True* article." In a communication to the attorney, the PR firm contact wrote "many thanks for your help in development of this meaningful and impressive story for 'our side.'" One of the four *True* editors who reviewed the article thought it was "completely biased . . . and damn misleading." He further stated "What's wrong here is that our writer didn't go out like a good reporter and do his legwork and his homework. The result is the purest trash—dated, biased and without present justification."

Surgeon General Stewart stated that "According to the Public Health Service, the *True* article conformed to a pattern of attack on former Surgeon General Terry and his advisory committee on smoking and health." Dr. Terry had stated several years earlier that such attacks "are repetitious and cleverly manipulated in a continuing program to shake public confidence in the [Surgeon General's 1964 tobacco] Report."

This was despite the fact that ". . . the most common type of lung cancer—bronchogenic or squamous-cell carcinoma—occurs almost entirely among cigarette smokers and rarely in those who have never smoked."

What we see here is a complicity of the media in writing articles supporting a political agenda rather than doing the labor-intensive investigative reporting necessary to provide an unbiased and factual story.

The most glaring example of this today, and an exact parallel, are the articles being written by John Cloud of *Time* Magazine. Last February [2003] Cloud was one of the plenary presenters at a San Francisco conference promoting Ecstasy. The "State of Ecstasy" conference was co-hosted by the [George] Soros-funded Lindesmith Center, directed since its inception by pro-drug proponent Ethan Nadelmann, and the San Francisco Medical Society. Cloud stated, "The last thing I want to say is, getting back to the media for one second, the best thing to do, I think, is to, is

> *"The only 'opinions'. . . consider[ed] valid are those put forth by those who believe . . . that drugs should be legalized."*

for organizations like this to be more active as Ethan [Nadelmann] is. He calls me every couple of months about pitching stories, and about pitching them in a way that recognizes reporters' strengths and weaknesses." One can only imagine what "strengths" refers to, but their "weaknesses" undoubtedly includes having an affinity for drugs, abject laziness, and a preference for fiction.

Cloud has recently written another article for *Time* Magazine titled "This Bud's Not for You," protesting the Drug Enforcement Administration's [DEA] position against the use of hemp oil in food products. Cannabis hemp is the only variety of hemp—and there are numerous different plants in this category including Manila Hemp, Mexican Hemp, Mauritius Hemp, New Zealand hemp, India hemp, sisal, flax and kenaf—that is smoked for its hallucinogenic properties. And it is the only one that it is illegal to grow. The bias in this article, coupled with Cloud's ecstasy conference statement, leave little doubt that he went back to the same spigot for this story.

Only One Perspective Recognized

In his State of Ecstasy talk, Cloud grouses, "The third mistake is, and this is the worst mistake, is to quote law enforcers on science questions [laughter and clapping from audience]. That happens a lot and again, I hate . . . I'm not . . . I'm harping on this because . . . not because they're competition. I mean, *U.S. News and World Report* is a great magazine and Chitra Ragavan who wrote that story, and who has done some great work for NPR [National Public Radio] before, but, you know, she quotes someone saying a DEA . . . a local DEA official . . . saying 'It could be worse than cocaine.' Well, you know, I guess it could be worse than cocaine. Anything could be. But, you know, it's a sort of scare tactic quote that she shouldn't have put in her article, basically."

The only "opinions" that Cloud considers valid are those put forth by those who believe drug use is a personal choice, and that drugs should be legalized. He does not recognize the perspective of the legions of those working in prevention, many who have lost children to drugs. And he has summarily dismissed law enforcement information as "scare tactics. This is not journalism. At best it is tabloidism. Is he writing at the behest of the Soros-funded legalization machine? Someone needs to investigate Cloud the way that tobacco shill Stanley Frank and anti-D.A.R.E. [Drug Abuse Resistance Education] shill Steven Glass, were investigated, and let the public see what crawled out from under the rock.

The extent of Glass's deliberate and deceitful attacks on D.A.R.E. were suppressed by newspapers from coast to coast. However, in a letter published in the *Washington Times* on September 14, 2000, Joyce Nalepka of Drug Free Kids—America's Challenge, revealed what many of us have suspected but had not seen documented. She wrote: "In a review of his [Steven Glass's] work, the *New Republic* discovered that at least 27 of his 41 published articles were entirely or partially made up. This was described by *Vanity Fair* magazine as 'a breathtaking web of deception that emerged as the most sustained fraud in modern journalism.'"

The settlement of the suit brought by D.A.R.E. against Glass and the *New Republic*, included a substantial monetary settlement and required that Glass write a letter of apology. Nalepka quoted from the apology letter in which Glass wrote: "As the articles reflect, I communicated frequently with people and organizations whom I knew to support, and who (in some cases) told me they supported, legalization of illegal drugs and were anti-DARE. In preparing the articles, I gave credence to what I heard from the anti-DARE people and did not credit the information DARE supplied me . . . most of which I discounted and was not ever published in the articles. . . . I further acknowledge that the March 1997 article in the *New Republic*, which contains many of the same fabrications as are in my March 1998 article for *Rolling Stone*, played a significant role in attracting the interest of *Rolling Stone* and its editors." (Obviously the editors of *Rolling Stone* were looking for articles to support the pro-drug bias often seen in their magazine.) "In editing the *Rolling Stone* article, I referred *Rolling Stone*'s fact-checkers to my prior articles in the *New Republic*, or to sources cited therein."

The last statement above reflects the old axiom that a lie repeated often enough will be believed, especially when it is repeated by the media, and it shows how important it is to actually read the references being used to verify that the information contained in the reference is factual, unbiased and is as implied.

The Tobacco-Marijuana Link

And finally, some illumination on the tobacco company–marijuana connection story that has been alluded to and whispered about since the 1970's. The one that claims that the tobacco companies have been waiting with bated breath for marijuana to be legalized so that they could be first in line to benefit from this potential cash cow, and that they had already registered trademarks for marijuana cigarettes.

A memo provided by the tobacco document information service of the American Lung Association of Colorado, and Tobacco Documents Online, references a 1976 report prepared for the Brown and Williamson Tobacco Corp. by Forecasting International, Ltd. An excerpt from page 57 of this eye-opening 1976 document reads:

> The use of marijuana today by 13 million Americans is socially the equivalent of the use of alcohol by some 100 million Americans. It is the recreational drug; the choice of a significant minority of the population. The trend in liberalization of drug laws reflects the overall change in our value system. It also has important implications for the tobacco industry in terms of an alternative product line. "(The tobacco companies) have the land to grow it, the machines to roll it and package it [and] the distribution to market it." In fact, some firms have registered trademarks, which are taken directly from marijuana street jargon. These tradenames are used currently on little known legal products, but could be switched if and when marijuana is legalized. Estimates indicate that the market in legalized marijuana might be as high as $10 billion annually. . . .

And a very tiny article in the October 23, 1998 *Orlando Sentinel* reports that a memo written in 1972 by a Phillip Morris scientist and made a part of a Mississippi lawsuit against the tobacco industry ". . . suggested Kool cigarettes were considered the best 'after marijuana' smoke to maintain a 'high.'"

Of interest at this juncture is the continuing link between big tobacco and those advocating for reintroduction of cannabis hemp. Gale Glenn, a cannabis hemp activist with the Kentucky Growers Collective, is the wife of Dr. James F. Glenn, who, until 1999, was Chairman of the now "resoundingly denounced" and defunct Council for Tobacco Research, a group funded by the tobacco industry. It should be remembered that almost all of the marijuana smoked during the 1960's and 1970's was the variety known as "ditchweed" because it often grew in ditches adjacent to rural roads in some states. It was, in fact, cannabis hemp that escaped to the wilds from the early years of the 1900's when it was being grown for rope instead of dope.

Marijuana Potency Increases

In 1976, when Forecasting International prepared the report for Brown and Williamson, the potency of marijuana/ditchweed rarely exceeded 1.5% THC, the main psychoactive compound found [in] marijuana. But those days are long gone and some of today's hybrid varieties have even passed the 30% mark.

When Jimmy Carter became president in 1977, he appointed as his Drug Advisor, Dr. Peter G. Bourne. Bourne embraced a permissive drug policy that encouraged "responsible" use of illicit substances. During this period drug use and hedonism flourished, with wife swapping clubs and "bath houses" common in most urban areas and our troops in Viet Nam out of their minds on heroin, hash, and marijuana. Bourne was ultimately dismissed from office for smoking marijuana [and] snorting cocaine, but by this time America was reeling. A backlash from parents who had lost children or who had seen their children's lives destroyed by drug use, gave rise to the more restrictive drug policy of the Reagan administration and by 1990, drug use in the U.S. had been cut by 50%. This astounding progress was abruptly curtailed under the Clinton administration when those favoring a liberal drug policy began to flood back into the White House and into government agencies. These new legalizers referred to themselves as Drug Policy Reformers and Harm Reductionists, and drug prevention was no longer a priority, in fact it became a target for ridicule by the media. As could be anticipated, drug use began to spiral upward once more.

> *"Permissive drug policy leads to escalation of the use of psychoactive and addictive substances."*

The bottom line is that permissive drug policy leads to escalation of the use of psychoactive and addictive substances, a behavior that leads to, causes, or exacerbates every social and criminal problem known to man. The media, with its steady drumbeat of pro-drug propaganda, must accept responsibility for its complicity in leading not just the U.S., but the rest of the world, down that now slimy, slippery slope into the turmoil of a society rife with drug addiction and crime.

Mandatory Sentencing Is Necessary in the War on Drugs

by David E. Risley

About the author: *David E. Risley is an assistant U.S. attorney in the Central District of Illinois.*

The purpose of mandatory minimum sentences is to prevent the judicial trivialization of serious drug crimes. They do that well, to which some object.

Because the federal sentencing system is the model most often cited, it will be used for illustration throughout the following discussion.

Before the advent of mandatory minimum sentences in serious drug cases, federal judges had unbridled discretion to impose whatever sentences they deemed appropriate, in their personal view, up to the statutory maximum. Because individual judges differ widely in their personal views about crime and sentencing the sentences they imposed for similar offenses by similar defendants varied widely. What some judges treated as serious offenses, and punished accordingly, others minimized with much more lenient sentences.

Ironically, more lenient sentences became particularly prevalent in areas with high volumes of major drug crime, such as large metropolitan and drug importation centers. Perhaps the sheer volume of cases in such areas led to a certain degree of desensitization. When serious crime becomes routine, there is human tendency to treat it routinely, and sentences often drop accordingly. In some areas across the country, that phenomenon can even be seen with crimes such as murder.

While the ideal is that sentences be perfectly personalized by wise, prudent, and consistent judges to fit every individual defendant and crime, the reality is that judges are human, and their wide human differences and perspectives lead to widely different sentences, if given completely unbridled discretion.

Such wide disparity in sentencing is inherently unfair, at least to those who receive stiff sentences for crimes for which others are punished only lightly. But such inconsistency was welcomed by drug dealers, since it meant they could hope for a light sentence for serious drug crimes. That, of course, created a much bigger problem.

Remove the Hope of Leniency

Drug dealers are risk takers by nature. Lack of certainty of serious sentences for serious crimes encourages, rather than deters, such risk takers to elevate their level of criminal activity in the hope that, if caught, they will be lucky enough to draw a lenient judge and receive a lenient sentence. The only possible deterrence for people who are willing to take extreme risks is to remove their cause for hope for leniency.

Some counter that drug dealers are undeterrable by criminal sanctions because they sell drugs to support their own addictions, and so should be treated for their addictions rather than imprisoned. While there may be some merit to that argument for many low-level street dealers, it is generally untrue of their suppliers, and even many other street dealers. Most dealers and distributors at any substantial level do not use drugs themselves, or do so only infrequently. They are exploiters and predators, and users are their captive prey. Drug dealing is a business. As in any other business, drug addicts are unreliable and untrustworthy, especially around drugs, and so make poor business partners. Because drug dealers usually run their operations as high-risk businesses, they necessarily weigh those risks carefully, and so are deterrable when the risks become too high. Many dealers who used to carry firearms, for example, now avoid doing so when they are selling drugs due to the high mandatory federal penalties when guns and drugs are mixed.

However, drug dealers seldom view the risks as too high when they see reason to hope for a light sentence. Congress, however, can, and did, step in to take away that hope. By establishing mandatory minimum sentences for serious drug offenses, Congress sent a clear message to drug dealers: no matter who the judge is, serious crime will get you serious time.

To those who do not view crimes subject to mandatory minimum sentences as serious, including drug dealers and their support systems, that message is objectionable. To most, it is welcome. Mandatory minimum sentences put steel in the spine of our criminal justice system.

> *"The purpose of mandatory minimum sentences is to prevent the judicial trivialization of serious drug crimes."*

The natural question which follows is, what level of dealing must defendants reach before being subject to mandatory minimum sentences, and what are those sentences? The answer varies with the type of drug and whether the defendant is a repeat offender.

Chapter 2

Two Levels of Mandatory Minimums

In the federal system, there are two levels of mandatory minimums, with each level doubling for defendants with prior convictions. The first tier requires a minimum sentence of imprisonment for five years (10 with a prior felony drug conviction), and the second tier requires a minimum of 10 years (20 with one prior felony drug conviction, and mandatory life with two such prior convictions). Of that, defendants can receive a reduction in the time they serve in prison of only 54 days per year as a reward for "good behavior," which means they must actually serve about 85% of their sentences.

For a prior drug offense to be considered a felony, it must be punishable by more than one year. In the federal system and most states, a drug offense is rarely classified as a felony unless it involves distribution of the drugs involved, or an intent to do so. For most practical purposes, therefore, a prior felony conviction for a drug such as marijuana can be read to mean a prior conviction for distribution. And, since most small distribution cases are reduced to misdemeanor simple possession (personal use) charges as part of plea bargains, especially for first-time offenders, a prior felony drug conviction for a drug such as marijuana usually means the prior conviction either involved a substantial amount of the drug or a repeat offender undeserving of another such break.

> *"By establishing mandatory minimum sentences for serious drug offenses, Congress sent a clear message . . . serious crime will get you serious time."*

In the case of marijuana, those who oppose mandatory minimum sentencing on so-called "humanitarian" grounds seldom mention that, to be eligible for even a five-year minimum sentence, a defendant must be convicted of an offense involving at least 100 kilograms (220 pounds) of marijuana, or, in the case of a marijuana growing operation, at least 100 plants. Such defendants are not low-level offenders.

With marijuana available at the Mexican border in Texas for wholesale prices between $600 to $1100 per pound, and selling in most areas at a retail price of between $1300 to $2000 per pound, and with any reasonably healthy cultivated marijuana plant producing at least one and sometimes two pounds of finished products, eligibility for even the lowest mandatory minimum sentence requires conviction of an offense involving between $132,000 to $440,000 worth of marijuana, or plants capable of producing marijuana worth a bulk retail price of between $130,000 to $400,000.

To be eligible for the next, 10-year tier of minimum sentence, a defendant must be convicted of an offense involving 1000 kilograms (1.1 tons) of marijuana or 1000 marijuana plants. Even at a low wholesale price of $600 per pound, such offenses involve marijuana worth at least $1.3 million.

It would be difficult to describe any offense involving between $130,000 to $440,000 worth of drugs as undeserving of even a five-year prison sentence.

Yet, those who oppose mandatory minimum sentences for marijuana and other drug offenses do just that, usually by attempting to convey the false impression the criminals they are attempting to protect are only low-level offenders.

In examining the deterrent potential of such mandatory minimum sentences, one must consider that the profit potential for marijuana offenses is relatively high, and the penalties relatively low, which makes marijuana an attractive drug in which to deal, as evidenced by its widespread availability. To illustrate, if a dealer bought 200 pounds of marijuana in Texas for $900 per pound for a total of $180,000, transported it to the Midwest and sold it for as low as $1400 per pound, for a total of $280,000 with minimal overhead, the profit for just one such trip would be $100,000. When the street-level price of between $125 to $300 per ounce is considered, or the lower acquisition costs if the marijuana is grown by the dealer himself, the profit potential for such a venture can be huge, and yet still not involve enough drugs to trigger even the lowest mandatory minimum penalty. Since the chance of getting caught for any single trip of that sort is relatively low, the prospect of a quick $100,000 profit lures plenty of eager dealers, even with the risk of spending close to five years in prison.

> *"Those who oppose mandatory minimum sentences . . . convey the false impression [that] the criminals they are attempting to protect are only low-level offenders."*

Of course, if drug dealers are undeterrable, as the actions of many demonstrate they are, the only realistic options left are to either give up and allow them to ply their predatory trade unhindered (the legalization "solution"), or incapacitate them with even longer sentences. The debate, it would seem, should be about whether the mandatory minimum penalties for marijuana offenses are currently too lenient, not too harsh. The next question is whether the more recent advent of the federal sentencing guidelines, which also limit judicial sentencing discretion, made mandatory minimum penalties obsolete. The answer is definitely no. As a practical matter, only through mandatory minimum sentences can Congress maintain sentencing benchmarks for serious drug crimes that cannot be completely circumvented by the commission that establishes, and sometimes quietly alters, those guidelines. One of the best illustrations is that of the sentencing guidelines for marijuana growers, who have achieved favorable treatment under the sentencing guidelines, but fortunately not under Congress' statutory mandatory minimum sentences.

United States Sentencing Commission

To appreciate the significance of that illustration, one must understand a little about the sentencing guideline system, and its relationship to mandatory minimum sentences. As part of the Sentencing Reform Act of 1984, Congress mandated the formation of the United States Sentencing Commission as an independent agency in the judicial branch composed of seven voting members, appointed by the President with the advice and consent of the Senate, at least three of whom must be federal judges, not more than four of whom may be from the same political party, serving staggered six-year terms. That Commission was charged with the formidable task of establishing binding sentencing guidelines to dramatically narrow judges' sentencing discretion, in order to provide reasonable uniformity in sentencing throughout the country, while at the same time taking into reasonable account the myriad of differences between the hundreds of federal crimes and limitless array of individual defendants.

The result of that enormous undertaking was the adoption, effective November 1987, of the United States Sentencing Guidelines. Using its provisions, contained in a book one inch thick, courts determine the seriousness of the offense and the extent of the defendant's past criminal history, and use that information to determine on a chart the relatively narrow sentencing range within which they have sentencing discretion. In drug cases, the seriousness of the offense (offense level) is determined mostly on the basis of the amount of drugs for which a defendant is accountable, with adjustments for factors such as role in the offense, whether a firearm was involved, and whether the defendant accepted responsibility for his or her actions through a candid guilty plea.

As part of its broad delegation of authority, Congress provided that changes promulgated by the Commission to the Sentencing Guidelines automatically become law unless Congress, within a 180-day waiting period, affirmatively acts to reject them. By that means Congress avoided a great deal of detailed work, but also created the possibility that changes to the Sentencing Guidelines to which they would object if carefully considered would become law if no one raises a sufficient alarm.

> *"The debate . . . should be about whether the mandatory minimum penalties . . . are currently too lenient, not too harsh."*

Because the Commission has only seven voting members, a change of only one member can result in the reversal of a previous 4-3 vote, sometimes with great consequences. Congress is ill-equipped to deal with the intricacies of the impact of many amendments to the Sentencing Guidelines, and is sometimes preoccupied with other, more pressing or "hot button" issues. Therefore, the only realistic check on the delegation of authority to the Commission to make changes in drug sentences is the trump card of mandatory minimums.

Mandatory Minimums Are Beyond the Commission's Control

That is true because defendants receive the higher of whatever sentence is called for by the statutory mandatory minimums or the Sentencing Guidelines. If the Commission promulgates a change to the Sentencing Guidelines that calls for lower sentences than required by the statutory mandatory minimums, the mandatory minimums trump the Sentencing Guidelines. In other words, the mandatory minimums are mandatory, and are beyond the control of the Commission.

With that background, the vital importance of mandatory minimum sentences as at least a partial check over the Commission in drug sentences is dramatically illustrated by the changes the Commission made regarding sentences for marijuana growers. The mandatory minimum sentences for marijuana growers imposed by Congress, which kick in at 100 plants, equate one marijuana plant with one kilogram (2.2 pounds) of marijuana. Until November 1995, the Sentencing Guidelines used that same equivalency in calculating the offense level in cases involving 50 or more plants, but for cases involving

> *"Only through mandatory minimum sentences can Congress maintain sentencing benchmarks for serious drug crimes."*

less than 50 plants considered one plant as the equivalent of only 100 grams (3.5 ounces). That 10:1 ratio between the amount of marijuana which plants were considered to represent was a major logical inconsistency, since marijuana plants do not produce significantly more or less marijuana just because they happen to be in the company of more or less than 49 other marijuana plants.

The Commission solved that inconsistency in early 1995 by promulgating an amendment to the Sentencing Guidelines which, instead of eliminating the unrealistically low 100 gram equivalency for smaller cases, eliminated the one kilogram equivalency for larger cases. Congress did nothing, so, as of November 1995, the Sentencing Guidelines treat all marijuana plants as if they were only capable of producing 3.5 ounces of marijuana.

In explanation, the Commission stated:

> In actuality, a marihuana plant does not produce a yield of one kilogram of marihuana. The one plant = 100 grams of marihuana equivalency used by the Commission for offenses involving fewer than 50 marihuana plants was selected as a reasonable approximation of the actual average yield of marihuana plants taking into account (1) studies reporting the actual yield of marihuana plants (37.5 to 412 grams depending on growing conditions); (2) that all plants regardless of size are counted for guideline purposes while, in actuality, not all plants will produce useable marihuana (*e.g.*, some plants may die of disease before maturity, and when plants are grown outdoors some plants may be consumed by animals); and (3) that male plants, which are counted for guideline purposes, are frequently culled because they do not produce the same quality marihuana as do female plants. To enhance fairness and consistency, this amendment adopts the equivalency of 100 grams per marihuana plant for all guideline determinations.

Contrary to those claims, no self-respecting commercial marijuana grower would ever admit his plants produce no more than 412 grams (14.5 ounces) of marijuana, much less that they average only 100 grams. Based upon long experience with actual marijuana growing operations, it is widely recognized in law enforcement circles that cultivated marijuana plants typically produce about one pound of marijuana (453 grams), and sometimes two pounds (907 grams). While it is true that some growers cull out the male plants in order to produce the potent form of marijuana known as sinsemilla, derived from the unpollinated female plant, not all growers do so. And, the observations of the Commission completely ignore the fact that a marijuana plant is a renewable resource— the seeds from one plant can be used to grow several more plants. It is unrealistic, therefore, to treat one plant as representing only that amount of marijuana it can produce itself, and to require courts to assume all marijuana growers standing before them are incapable of producing more than 100 grams of marijuana per plant.

Stair Step Effect

Fortunately, Congress was more realistic in establishing its mandatory minimum sentences. And, for cases involving 100 or more plants, those mandatory minimums trump the Sentencing Guidelines. The result, however, is still a boon to commercial marijuana growers who are informed enough to keep the number of plants in their operations under 100, or under 1000. That is because the interaction between the lenient Sentencing Guidelines and the stricter mandatory minimums produces a stair step effect on sentences at the 100 and 1000 plant marks.

If a marijuana grower is caught raising 99 marijuana plants, no mandatory minimum sentence is triggered. Under the Sentencing Guidelines, those plants would be treated as the equivalent of 9.9 kilograms of marijuana ($28,370 worth, using a conservative price of $1300 per pound), which, for an offender caught for the first time, would result in an unadjusted sentencing guideline range of only 15 to 21 months. With the normal adjustment to reward a candid guilty plea, that guideline range would drop to 10 to 16 months.

> *"We can be grateful those mandatory minimum sentences preserve at least some deterrent impact in federal sentences."*

In contrast, if that same grower raised just one more plant, for a total of 100, the first tier of mandatory minimum sentences would be triggered, and the court would be required to impose a sentence of five years. The jump from a maximum sentence of 20 months for 99 plants up to five years for 100 plants is due solely to the overriding effect of the mandatory minimum sentence.

Not until that same grower was caught with 800 to 999 plants, treated as the equivalent of 80 to 99.9 kilograms of marijuana (at least $229,275 worth), would his unadjusted sentencing guideline range reach the 51 to 63 month mark, and even then a candid guilty plea would drop it to 37 to 46 months. Consequently, the five year mandatory minimum would probably still control the sentence. But, if the grower was caught with just one more plant, raising the total to 1000, the second tier of mandatory minimum sentences would be triggered, requiring a sentence of 10 years. Again, the jump from a maximum sentence of 63 months for 999 plants up to 10 years for 1000 plants is due solely to Congress' mandatory minimum sentence scheme.

The Sensible View of Congress

Without those mandatory minimum sentences, the Commission's view that marijuana plants should only be treated as the equivalent of 100 grams of marijuana would be controlling, which marijuana growers would doubtless applaud. Only because of the mandatory minimums does the more sensible view of Congress that each marijuana plant should be treated as the equivalent of one kilogram of marijuana impact growing operations involving 100 or more plants.

At a time when indoor marijuana growing operations are increasing in both number and the quality of their product, we can be grateful those mandatory minimum sentences preserve at least some deterrent impact in federal sentences, even if currently inadequate.

Ultimately, whether the effect of those mandatory minimum sentences is good or bad depends upon how seriously one views marijuana use. If a person believes a sentence of five years is too harsh for growing 100 marijuana plants capable of producing at least $28,600 and more likely $130,000 worth of marijuana, or distributing 220 pounds, of marijuana worth a wholesale price of at least $132,000 and retail price of at least $286,000, the mandatory minimum sentences for marijuana should be abolished. If, however, a five year sentence for such crimes seems reasonable, or even lenient, the mandatory minimums should be retained, and perhaps toughened.

There is no doubt about on which side of that question the marijuana growers, dealers, users, and their supporters stand. There is also little room to doubt on which side those who take marijuana crimes seriously should stand.

Drug Policies Should Not Be Based on Harm Reduction

by Joe Santamaria

About the author: *Joe Santamaria was foundation chairman of the Addiction Research Institute and the director of community medicine at St. Vincent's Hospital in Melbourne, Australia, from 1970 to 1988.*

The principle of "harm minimisation" has underpinned the national drug offensive since 1985. In the review document The National Drug Strategic Plan 1993–97, produced by the [Australian] National Drug Strategy Committee, harm minimisation is described as follows:

> Harm Minimization is an approach that aims to reduce the adverse health, social and economic consequences of alcohol and other drugs by minimising or limiting the harms and hazards of drug use for both the community and the individual without necessarily eliminating use.

The concept of harm minimisation or harm reduction focuses on the choices of the individual drug user and the belief that the greatest harm is caused by the criminalisation of those who use drugs prohibited by law. The catchcry that underscores this policy is that prohibition has failed and the drug user has become the victim of criminal syndicates, corrupt officials and a misguided drug policy (for example [psychiatrist] John Marks has written: "None of the drugs are a serious risk to health: the risks come about entirely from the dirty, secret, criminal circumstances in which, under prohibition, drugs of unknown strength and composition are consumed").

The illegal drugs become expensive to obtain and the drug user has to resort to crime or prostitution to obtain the money required to exercise a free choice or to meet the physiological demands of addiction or to numb the pain of social or emotional distress. It is also claimed that all societies have used psychoactive substances, which illustrates the universal demand.

Normalisation of Drug Use

According to the harm minimisation concept, such substances should be readily available through reputable channels of supply, conforming to quality controls imposed by government. This constitutes normalisation of such drug use. It is postulated that the criminal syndicates will not be able to compete with the legal channels of supply that will guarantee the strength and purity of the product. The money used for law enforcement should be directed to treatment programs (often based on maintenance of drug use) and the community will be taught how to use the drugs "responsibly and safely" (whatever that means) so that the number of casualties can be reduced to a minimum. Those who exhibit problems due to such drug use will be managed by a variety of programs such as drug

> *"The deliberate long-term maintenance of the addicted and cognitively impaired ... amounts to state-sponsored assistance to maintain a life in bondage."*

maintenance, supervised injecting facilities and needle and syringe distribution centres. Extensive social services will complement the work in the field until the disease reaches its burnt-out stage many years down the track, if the addicted person lives that long.

What constitutes a casualty becomes a moot point if a person is constantly maintained in an addicted state and with continuing cognitive impairment. The argument that only by maintaining the addiction can you manage such persons is highly debatable, given the experience of recovered addicts and reputable therapeutic communities. The deliberate long-term maintenance of the addicted and cognitively impaired state amounts to state-sponsored assistance to maintain a life in bondage. Moreover, the recently published studies by the New South Wales Bureau of Crime Statistics and Research throw great doubts on the claim that "the war against drugs is lost".

The simplistic model of harm minimisation fails to appreciate certain scientific and historical evidence:

1. All psychoactive drugs have significant neurological and pharmacological effects that vary with each category of drug used. All affect the cognitive functions of the brain and the control of behaviour and skilled performance.

2. All have the potential for inducing tolerance and addiction.

3. All have the potential to cause physical and psychiatric complications.

4. There is a direct relationship between availability of a drug, social approval of its use and the incidence (the number of new cases in a given period of time) and prevalence (the number of cases in a community at a point of time) of its use in the community.

5. There is a direct relationship between the prevalence of drug use and the number of chronic and heavy users.

6. There is a large population at risk of using such drugs on a repetitive and chronic basis.

7. There are other harmful effects which affect families and the wider society to a degree much greater than the advocates of this model are prepared to admit.

8. Most of the complications are not commensurable and their weighting is often determined by ideological preferences.

9. It is a mistake to believe that the harm minimisation policy, as promoted in most parts of the world, is simply about the management of the individual drug addict. At the root of the policy is an ideological agenda based on the primacy of personal autonomy or freedom of choice within a human society. This primacy overrides the common good which is the basis of public health policy.

Responsible Use

A Swiss psychologist and pharmacist, Dr F. Haller, presented this analysis of the situation in Switzerland in a paper given at an international conference in Italy in October 1996:

> Harm minimisation is a theory which maintains that society must learn to accept all levels of addictive and psychoactive drug consumption by adults and adolescents and that "responsible use" of these drugs must be taught in order to reduce harm. "Harm reduction" ignores the physiological and psychological effects of drug use. The implementation of harm reduction policies in Europe has resulted in a dramatic increase in the number of drug users in Great Britain, the Netherlands and Switzerland.

She concluded with the comment:

> One of the most important persons responsible for this model is the former Zurich city councillor for social affairs, Mrs Lieberherr. She declared two years ago: "My long term goal . . . is legalisation . . . Do you know how long I have been working for legalisation now? For years, I have co-operated with other cities, in Germany, in Italy. I have even managed to establish strong contacts in the United States . . . And we all stand for drug legalisation."

Harm Reduction Is Just the Start

Dr Haller described the subtle technique of moving to achieve that end, by promoting in the first instance the concept of "harm reduction".

The outcome is inevitable. Promote the package of harm reduction or harm minimisation and the population of users will continue to expand. Drug use then becomes a widely practised form of behaviour and to treat the problem by law enforcement becomes difficult and costly. So the proposed solution is to normalise the use of such drugs and to teach people how to use them "responsibly and safely". But the outcomes of this policy are catastrophic.

Haller makes the point that the leading promoters of harm minimisation ignore the physiological and psychological effects of drug use. These effects are related to cognitive impairment, the tunnel vision of the addicted state, the impact on learning, on the growth and maturation of the personality, and on the dynamics of social relationships. In an exchange on a proposed drug policy which appeared in the *Health Promotion Journal of Australia* for August 2000, I wrote:

> [Alex] Wodak simply ignores the mountain of scientific research on the pharmacodynamics and pharmacological effects of cannabis, its increased potency, its impact on families and its addictive properties. . . . The introduction of sanctions against the use of opium and cannabis was based on the experience of other countries with high prevalence rates: China and opium and Egypt and cannabis. High prevalence rates always raise community concerns because of the depersonalising effects of such substances. These effects are more clearly recognised within families than by counsellors, who mistake the addicted and intoxicated person for the same one known to family members before the drugs were used.

Early this year [2002] the famous English neuroscientist Susan Greenfield voiced similar concerns about the impact of psychoactive drugs on the brain and their serious effect on the "personalisation" of brain circuits.

The fact is that the promoters of the harm minimisation strategy are dismissive of the neuroscientific evidence, which does not support the normalisation of use of such drugs. They have failed to understand the importance of drug dependence and cognitive impairment on the ability of drug addicts to recover from their state of bondage. They persist in refusing to recognise that the drug-addicted state is a grave personal harm and they do not acknowledge that the prevalence of drug abuse is a serious social harm that their so-called preventive measures have exacerbated.

Problems of the Severely Addicted Person

Many workers in the field of drug abuse are deeply disturbed by the problems involved in helping the severely addicted person. They assert that:

1. There is a marked tendency for such heavily addicted persons to be marginalised and not to receive medical and social help.

2. Possibly a majority of such addicts avoid the existing services for a variety of reasons.

3. They are at high risk of dying from overdoses or medical complications, or of being socially abandoned.

4. They are at risk of contracting AIDS or hepatitis C.

5. They are reluctant to enter an abstinence program.

Such workers also believe that the use of penalties for drug use is either disproportionate or discriminatory, especially for the young immature person at the early stages of drug experience. They have succumbed to a flawed policy based on the persuasive slogans of harm minimisation for drug users.

However, their proposals lead to outcomes that conflict with the principles of public health that need to be applied to conditions that have reached epidemic proportions. Most countries recognise that the widespread use of mind-altering drugs constitutes a major health and social problem. Those responsible for a nation's drug policy work in a complex and highly volatile field of public health.

Drug abuse is now a public health issue because it has developed into a major epidemic of addicted persons at various levels of incapacity, and a larger body of persons either beginning to experiment with such drugs or doing so on a casual or regular basis. It is compounded by the operations of the street markets where dealers easily trade their products without consideration for the health or functioning of their customers or the concerns of the wider society.

It is important to understand the principles of public health, for they include the dimension of the numbers involved and the concept of prevention. There are three levels of prevention—primary, secondary and tertiary:

Primary prevention: applying measures to prevent a disorder from occurring, such as tetanus vaccination or health education.

Secondary prevention: instituting measures to diagnose and treat a disorder in its early stages of development and then preventing any further relapse or recurrence.

Tertiary prevention: management of a case at a later stage—to apply measures to slow down progression or to reduce the number of relapses.

The Significance of Primary Prevention

Many field workers make a fundamental mistake in some of their proposals, for they lack a global vision and fail to understand the significance of primary prevention. They are operating at the level of secondary or tertiary prevention, or early and late intervention of individual chronic drug users. At the level of primary prevention, the issue is different. The object of primary prevention is to reduce the number of drug users—that is, the incidence and prevalence of drug use. That is a cardinal objective of any public health policy. If you do not control the number of drug users, the problem will escalate and expand.

You cannot contain an epidemic if you do not adopt measures to reduce the numbers. The road toll is a classic example. Several factors have contributed to the current serious problem—drinking and driving, high speed, unlicensed drivers, poor road conditions and so on. There has been a public awareness campaign on television and other sources of public communication—a form of public education.

> *"'The implementation of harm reduction policies in Europe has resulted in a dramatic increase in the number of drug users.'"*

But it has also been backed by sanctions and costly deterrent processes—such as high police visibility, widely dispersed across the state, breathalyser units, speed cameras and intersection cameras. Deterrence means penalties and they are not light penalties, as befits the concept of a painful learning experience. They are justified not simply on the basis of protecting the other road users from harm but also to protect the individual against his own indiscretions because he has become a threat both to himself and to the common good.

It is a feature of human nature to act negligently at times, to make a calculated choice to behave in a risky manner and to believe (wrongly) that one is hurting nobody else, especially family members. The sharp intrusion of disincentives, including the negative image of being anti-social (such as now applies to smokers), is salutary for the health and smooth functioning of the whole community.

The same applies to illicit drug use or dangerous levels of consumption

> *"Promote the package of harm reduction . . . and the population of users will continue to expand."*

of alcohol or legal mood-altering drugs. The last thing the community needs is for a message to be sent that the use of mind-altering drugs should be normalised and all that is needed is for people to learn how to use them responsibly. For they are mind-altering drugs which in the first instance act upon the cognitive functions and on behaviour and skilled performance.

Public health is based on the concept of the common good. Society does have a duty to protect its members, especially its more vulnerable members, as well as a duty to distribute, in an equitable manner, the money available for social and medical services derived by taxation from the community. Society has a moral obligation to assist the casualties of human activities but it also has a duty to introduce measures to limit the number of casualties, if necessary by limiting some human choices.

Common Good Versus Personal Autonomy

The perception that the taking of mind-altering drugs is of no consequence to the rest of society is an illusion. In the last twenty-five years, the concept of the common good has been attacked by the proponents of personal autonomy and by the pervasive demands of individualism. However, it is worth noting that [John] Locke, an early libertarian philosopher, maintained that there were social constraints on personal autonomy. Locke observed that complete personal liberty existed only in the state of nature, of the individual person living as a lone being. But because such an existence proved to be inadequate, man entered into civil society and consented to limit his liberty in conformity with a common good. The contemporary English philosopher John Finnis comments that the common good is a set of conditions which enable the members of a community to attain certain agreed values such as life, health, well-being, security and justice.

The concept of primary prevention in the field of public health is built on transmitting knowledge and information, on incentives and disincentives, on teaching social and emotional skills and the imparting of that subtle but profound form of education which is described as normative. The harm minimisation package, as currently purveyed, fails to minimise the number of drug users and uses general statements without giving specific answers to vitally important questions about the details of their proposals.

The term "harm minimisation" (or harm reduction) has a persuasive ring, and constitutes an attractive slogan to capture the support of the public in general, the media, health professionals and politicians in particular. It is when one sees the fine print and the messages and the programs put in place to implement such a policy that its flawed nature emerges.

In Victoria, children in state care at the Berry Street Welfare Centre were allowed to inhale dangerous substances using a plastic bag ("chroming"). This resulted in a public outcry in January, directed against the hapless Minister for Community Services. This "monitored" use of inhalants by the young has been backed by officers of other drug treatment centres and policy advisers. Everything is justified if it can be claimed that it conforms to "best practice" of harm minimisation. It is not surprising that even well intentioned but naive government ministers can be deluded by the rhetoric of the harm minimisation proponents.

Chapter 3

Should Marijuana Laws Be Relaxed?

Chapter Preface

Cannabis sativa is industrial hemp if its THC (the chemical that makes users high) level is less than 1 percent and it is grown for fiber and seed oil. However, it is marijuana if its THC level is between 5 and 20 percent and it is used for medicinal or recreational purposes. While uses, cultivation practices, processing, and distribution of the end products are vastly different, industrial hemp and marijuana are both illegal according to the federal government. The Drug Enforcement Administration (DEA) insists that the terms "hemp" and "marijuana" do not appear in any federal law; only *Cannabis sativa*—the plant's Latin genus/species name—is used. Thus, as far as federal drug laws are concerned, industrial hemp and marijuana are the same.

Farmers in several states who have become interested in growing hemp for its industrial and agricultural potential have run into this federal road block. Major tobacco-producing states, such as Kentucky, which have seen tobacco revenues fall in recent years, are looking to hemp as a possible replacement crop. In fact, seven states—Kentucky, Arkansas, California, Illinois, Maryland, Minnesota, and New Mexico—have passed laws authorizing studies of industrial hemp. Montana and North Dakota have legalized hemp, and Hawaii is test planting the crop. Legislation to legalize or study the potential of hemp is pending in several other states. At the urging of farmers, legislators in Hawaii asked President George W. Bush to support their interest in hemp as a cultivated crop. In 2001 they wrote in a letter to the president, "Industrial hemp is a state agricultural issue, not a drug issue."

The DEA, however, does not share that point of view. In 1997 then–drug czar Barry McCaffrey wrote in a letter to Paul Patton, governor of Kentucky, "Hemp and marijuana are the same plant; the seedlings are the same, and in many instances the mature plants look the same." One of the DEA's concerns is that hemp fields could be used to hide marijuana plants thus confusing federal and local authorities and hindering drug enforcement. Hemp growers, however, contend that cultivation practices make it easy to tell the difference between the two varieties of *Cannabis*.

Legitimate farmers who want to grow the industrial hemp variety of *Cannabis sativa* as a legal crop with significant agricultural potential are prohibited from doing so under current drug laws. Those states that have legalized industrial hemp risk federal sanction. Hemp advocates argue that there is no scientific reason to prohibit the safe, profitable crop. However, until federal *Cannabis* laws are changed or the federal government is willing to defer to the states in this area, industrial hemp cannot be legally grown in the United States. Authors in the following chapters explore other debates concerning marijuana laws.

Marijuana Laws Should Be Relaxed

by William F. Buckley Jr.

About the author: *Conservative writer William F. Buckley Jr. is editor-at-large for the* National Review, *and an advocate of marijuana legalization.*

Conservatives pride themselves on resisting change, which is as it should be. But intelligent deference to tradition and stability can evolve into intellectual sloth and moral fanaticism, as when conservatives simply decline to look up from dogma because the effort to raise their heads and reconsider is too great.

The laws concerning marijuana aren't exactly indefensible, because practically nothing is, and the thunderers who tell us to stay the course can always find one man or woman who, having taken marijuana, moved on to severe mental disorder.

But that argument, to quote myself, is on the order of saying that every rapist began by masturbating.

General rules based on individual victims are unwise.

And although there is a perfectly respectable case against using marijuana, the penalties imposed on those who reject that case, or who give way to weakness of resolution, are very difficult to defend.

If all our laws were paradigmatic, imagine what we would do to anyone caught lighting a cigarette, or drinking a beer. Or—exulting in life in the paradigm—committing adultery.

Send them all to Guantanamo [Bay, Cuba, detention camp for terrorists]?

Legal practices should be informed by realities.

These are enlightening in the matter of marijuana.

Politicians Are Afraid to Change the Laws

There are approximately 700,000 marijuana-related arrests made very year. Most of these—87 percent—involve nothing more than mere possession of small amounts of marijuana.

This exercise in scrupulosity costs us $10 billion to $15 billion per year in direct expenditures alone.

Most transgressors caught using marijuana aren't packed away to jail, but some are, and in Alabama, if you are convicted three times of marijuana possession, they'll lock you up for 15 years to life. Professor Ethan Nadelmann, of the Drug Policy Alliance, writing in *National Review*, estimates at 100,000 the number of Americans currently behind bars for one or another marijuana offense.

What we face is the politician's fear of endorsing any change in existing marijuana laws. You can imagine what a call for reform in those laws would do to an upward[ly] mobile political figure.

Gary Johnson, as governor of New Mexico, came out in favor of legalization—and went on to private life. George Shultz, former secretary of state, long ago called for legalization, but he was not running for office, and

> *"What we face is the politician's fear of endorsing any change in existing marijuana laws."*

at his age, and with his distinctions, he is immune to slurred charges of indifference to the fate of children and humankind.

But Kurt Schmoke, as mayor of Baltimore, did it, and survived a re-election challenge.

But the stodgy inertia most politicians feel is up against a creeping reality. It is that marijuana for medical relief is a movement that is attracting voters who are pretty assertive on the subject.

Every state ballot initiative to legalize medical marijuana has been approved, often by wide margins.

Of course we have here collisions of federal and state authority.

Federal authority technically supervenes state laws, but federal authority in the matter is being challenged on grounds of medical self-government. It simply isn't so that there are substitutes equally efficacious. Richard Brookhiser, the widely respected author and editor, has written on the subject for the *New York Observer.* He had a bout of cancer and found relief from chemotherapy only in marijuana—which he consumed, and discarded after the affliction was gone.

The court has told federal enforcers that they are not to impose their way between doctors and their patients. . . . Critics of reform do make a pretty plausible case when they say that whatever is said about using marijuana only for medical relief masks what the advocates are really after, which is legal marijuana for whoever wants it.

That would be different from the situation today.

Legalization Would Not Increase Usage

Today we have illegal marijuana for whoever wants it. An estimated 100 million Americans have smoked marijuana at least once, the great majority abandoning its use after a few highs.

But to stop using it does not close off its availability. A Boston commentator observed years ago that it is easier for an 18-year-old to get marijuana in Cambridge than to get beer. Vendors who sell beer to minors can forfeit their valuable licenses.

It requires less effort for the college student to find marijuana than for a sailor to find a brothel. Still, there is the danger of arrest (as 700,000 people a year will tell you), of possible imprisonment, of blemish on one's record.

The obverse of this is increased cynicism about the law.

We're not going to find someone running for president who advocates reform of those laws. What is required is a genuine republican groundswell. It is happening, but ever so gradually.

Two of every five Americans, according to a 2003 Zogby poll cited by Dr. Nadelmann, believe "the government should treat marijuana more or less the same way it treats alcohol: It should regulate it, control it, tax it, and make it illegal only for children." Such reforms would hugely increase the use of the drug? Why? It is de facto legal in the Netherlands, and the percentage of users there is the same as here. The Dutch do odd things, but here they teach us a lesson.

Marijuana Should Be Decriminalized

by Stuart Taylor Jr.

About the author: *Stuart Taylor Jr. is a senior writer and columnist for* National Journal *and a contributing editor at* Newsweek.

The Supreme Court delivered a timely reminder of the social costs of our "war on drugs" with its May 14 [2001] decision rejecting a medical-necessity exception to the federal law criminalizing marijuana. Meanwhile, President [George W.] Bush has moved toward abandoning his own best instincts and repeating his predecessors' mistakes by endlessly escalating a $20 billion-a-year "war" that—as most Americans now understand—we have lost.

In the face of overwhelming evidence that tens of thousands of patients suffering from cancer, AIDS, and other serious illnesses can greatly alleviate their pain, and even extend their lives, by smoking marijuana, the Court held that Congress had allowed no room for a medical exception to the law making it a crime to distribute marijuana or even to possess it for personal use. This means that a doctor could be sent to prison for giving—perhaps even for recommending—marijuana to a terminal cancer patient whose pain and nausea cannot otherwise be relieved. The cancer patient could be sent to prison, too, although such prosecutions seem unlikely, in part because most jurors would simply refuse to convict.

The Justices were correct. Congress specified in 1970 that marijuana had no "currently accepted medical use"—at least, none that Congress was prepared to accept. In cases brought by the federal government, this congressional ban overrides the laws of California and the eight other states that have exempted medical marijuana from their own state anti-drug statutes. The Supreme Court neither agreed nor disagreed with Congress, but rather deferred to an enactment that it had no power to reverse—an enactment that inflicts needless suffering and ought to be revised by Congress.

The most obvious proof that marijuana alleviates some patients' pain is that so many of them say so. When a patient racked by agonizing pain says, "I feel much better after smoking marijuana," who is Congress to say otherwise? For those who need expert assurances, plenty exist. "A small but significant number of seriously ill patients who suffer from cancer, HIV/AIDS, multiple sclerosis, epilepsy, or other conditions do not benefit from, or cannot tolerate, the leading or conventional therapies," the American Public Health Association and others said in an amicus brief. "Some . . . have found cannabis to be effective at alleviating symptoms of their condition or side effects of their treatment. . . . [It] can mean the difference between life and death or relative health and severe harm." Marijuana is also safer, less

> *"President [George W.] Bush has moved toward . . . escalating a $20 billion-a-year 'war' that . . . we have lost."*

addictive, less subject to abuse, and less likely to have had side effects than many legal pain relievers and prescription medications. The U.S. Institute of Medicine (a National Academy of Sciences affiliate), the California Medical Association, and Britain's House of Lords have all given guarded approval to carefully monitored marijuana smoking as a therapy for certain patients.

Indeed, no serious analyst could doubt that marijuana alleviates some patients' sufferings. Serious drug warriors' real concern is that "state initiatives promoting 'medical marijuana' are little more than thinly veiled legalization efforts," as William J. Bennett, the first President Bush's drug czar, said in a May 15 [2001] *Wall Street Journal* op-ed. There is some truth to this. Many medical marijuana champions do have such an agenda: Some exaggerate the medical benefits, and the 1996 ballot referendum in which California's voters became the first to approve marijuana for medical use was so loosely drafted as to leave room for recreational users to concoct bogus medical excuses.

But most advocates of a less-punitive approach to drug policy are unpersuaded (at least so far) by the advocates of legalization—a group that includes such prominent conservatives as Milton Friedman, George Shultz, and William F. Buckley Jr. And Congress could easily legalize marijuana only for patients with certain severe illnesses without vitiating the criminal sanctions for all other sellers and users. Why do hard-line drug warriors fight even that idea? Apparently out of fear that it would muddy the message they want to send to people like my teenagers. The message, in Bennett's words, is that "drug use is dangerous and immoral."

Much as I respect Bennett, I take that personally. I smoked some marijuana myself in the late 1960s and early 1970s, when it was hard to go to a party without being offered a puff of the stuff. (Unlike President Bill Clinton, I inhaled.) Most of my peers seemed to smoke more than I did. They also seemed less dangerous when smoking than when drinking.

Were we all immoral? Were our parents or grandparents immoral when they drank bootlegged liquor during Prohibition? Is having too many beers immoral? Was President [George W.] Bush immoral when he did whatever it was that he did when he was "young and irresponsible"? When he drank too much? When he drove drunk?

Like Bennett, I hope that my teenagers will shun illegal drugs. But I don't tell them that marijuana would be immoral or dangerous to their health, because I don't believe that. The danger, I tell them, is that using any illegal drug could leave them with criminal records or land them in jail.

Bush and some of his advisers have said some vaguely encouraging things about drug policy. "Maybe long minimum sentences for the first-time users may not be the best way to occupy jail space and/or heal people from their disease," Bush mused on January 18 [2001]. But on May 10 he named as his drug czar former Bennett deputy John P. Walters, who immediately stressed that he wants "to escalate the drug war." Like Attorney General John D. Ashcroft, he has pushed the cruel and futile policy of imprisoning small-time participants in drug deals—many or most of them nonviolent—by the hundreds of thousands. Walters has also displayed a special relish for sending the military into Latin America to help friendly regimes chase cocaine growers and suppliers— notwithstanding such collateral damage as the April 20 [2001] deaths of an American missionary and her daughter in a small plane that a Peruvian fighter mistakenly shot down.

"Tens of thousand of patients suffering from cancer, AIDS, and other serious illnesses can greatly alleviate their pain . . . by smoking marijuana."

Walters revealed his mind-set in 1996, when he assailed the Clinton Administration's emphasis on drug treatment for hard-core addicts as "the latest manifestation of the liberals' commitment to a 'therapeutic state' in which government serves as the agent of personal rehabilitation." In fact, treatment programs have proven more effective on a dollar-for-dollar basis than criminal sanctions—although many addicts cannot get access to treatment unless they first get themselves arrested.

In his *Wall Street Journal* op-ed, Bennett argued that the Reagan and (first) Bush Administrations had been winning the war on drugs until the Clinton Administration took over with a policy of "benign neglect." He stressed that between 1979 and 1992, "the rate of illegal drug use dropped by more than half, while marijuana use decreased by two-thirds." Then, Bennett noted, the rate began to climb again, especially among teens.

But critics counter that such surveys of drug use are inherently volatile and unreliable. "In 1979, almost anybody would tell a surveyor that they smoked marijuana," says Ethan A. Nadelmann, head of the Lindesmith Center-Drug Policy Foundation; by 1992, drug use had become legally risky and socially stigmatized. And Bennett's depiction of President Clinton as soft on drugs does not withstand scrutiny. While Clinton Administration officials softened the "war" rhetoric by speaking of drug abuse as a "cancer" and slashed the budget of the drug czar's office, they protected their political backsides by increasing overall spending on drug enforcement and interdiction. They also outdid even Republicans in supporting savagely severe mandatory minimum prison sentences for (among others) minor, first-time, nonviolent drug offenders.

More fundamental, the surveys cited by Bennett are a less-valid window into the costs and benefits of the drug war than some other facts: the nearly 500,000 drug offenders now behind bars—many of them first-timers nailed for mere possession—which is a tenfold increase since 1980; the death toll from HIV infections and drug overdoses that could have been prevented by public health measures such as needle-exchange programs, which Bennett and Walters condemn; the crack epidemic that ravaged inner cities from the mid-1980s into the early 1990s; the undiminished hard-core abuse of cocaine, heroin, and other hard drugs, which have fallen steadily in price since 1980, and to which some users have turned as the price of marijuana—bulkier, smellier, harder to smuggle—has gone up; the gang warfare; the police corruption; the racial profiling; the invasions of privacy.

These and other harms inflicted on America by the drug war—especially in black neighborhoods, where families have been decimated by drug-related incarceration—dwarf the importance of the fluctuations in pot smoking among middle-class teenagers that so interest Bennett. Ninety-nine percent of them will never be serious drug abusers.

[Former president Richard] Nixon went to China. Bush should go to a commonsense drug policy that might actually work. It's not too late.

Marijuana Should Be Legalized for Medical Purposes

by the National Organization for the Reform of Marijuana Laws

About the author: The National Organization for the Reform of Marijuana Laws (NORML) seeks to move public opinion sufficiently to achieve the repeal of marijuana prohibition so that the responsible use of cannabis by adults is no longer subject to penalty.

> Federal authorities should rescind their prohibition of the medical use of marijuana for seriously ill patients and allow physicians to decide which patients to treat. The government should change marijuana's status from that of a Schedule I drug . . . to that of a Schedule II drug . . . and regulate it accordingly.
> —*The New England Journal of Medicine, January 30, 1997*

Marijuana prohibition applies to everyone, including the sick and dying. Of all the negative consequences of prohibition, none is as tragic as the denial of medicinal cannabis to the tens of thousands of patients who could benefit from its therapeutic use.

Evidence Supporting Marijuana's Medical Value

Written references to the use of marijuana as a medicine date back nearly 5,000 years. Western medicine embraced marijuana's medical properties in the mid-1800s, and by the beginning of the 20th century, physicians had published more than 100 papers in the Western medical literature recommending its use for a variety of disorders. Cannabis remained in the United States pharmacopoeia until 1941, removed only after Congress passed the Marihuana Tax Act which severely hampered physicians from prescribing it. The American Medical Association (AMA) was one of the most vocal organizations to testify against the ban, arguing that it would deprive patients of a past, present and future medicine.

Modern research suggests that cannabis is a valuable aid in the treatment of a wide range of clinical applications. These include pain relief—particularly of neuropathic pain (pain from nerve damage)—nausea, spasticity, glaucoma, and movement disorders. Marijuana is also a powerful appetite stimulant, specifically for patients suffering from HIV, the AIDS wasting syndrome, or dementia. Emerging research suggests that marijuana's medicinal properties may protect the body against some types of malignant tumors and are neuroprotective.

"Of all the negative consequences of prohibition, none is as tragic as the denial of medicinal cannabis to . . . patients who could benefit from its therapeutic use."

Currently, more than 60 U.S. and international health organizations— including the American Public Health Association, Health Canada and the Federation of American Scientists—support granting patients immediate legal access to medicinal marijuana under a physician's supervision. Several others, including the American Cancer Society and the American Medical Association support the facilitation of wide-scale, clinical research trials so that physicians may better assess cannabis' medical potential. In addition, a 1991 Harvard study found that 44 percent of oncologists had previously advised marijuana therapy to their patients. Fifty percent responded they would do so if marijuana was legal. A more recent national survey performed by researchers at Providence Rhode Island Hospital found that nearly half of physicians with opinions supported legalizing medical marijuana.

Government Commissions Back Legalization

Virtually every government-appointed commission to investigate marijuana's medical potential has issued favorable findings. These include the U.S. Institute of Medicine in 1982, the Australian National Task Force on Cannabis in 1994, and the U.S. National Institutes of Health Workshop on Medical Marijuana in 1997.

More recently, Britain's House of Lords' Science and Technology Committee found in 1998 that the available evidence supported the legal use of medical cannabis. MPs [Members of Parliament] determined: "The government should allow doctors to prescribe cannabis for medical use. . . . Cannabis can be effective in some patients to relieve symptoms of multiple sclerosis, and against certain forms of pain. . . . This evidence is enough to justify a change in the law." The Committee reaffirmed their support in a March 2001 follow-up report criticizing Parliament for failing to legalize the drug.

U.S. investigators reached a similar conclusion in 1999. After conducting a nearly two-year review of the medical literature, investigators at the National

Academy of Sciences, Institute of Medicine [IOM] affirmed: "Scientific data indicate the potential therapeutic value of cannabinoid drugs . . . for pain relief, control of nausea and vomiting, and appetite stimulation. . . . Except for the harms associated with smoking, the adverse effects of marijuana use are within the range tolerated for other medications." Nevertheless, the authors noted cannabis inhalation "would be advantageous" in the treatment of some diseases, and that marijuana's short-term medical benefits outweigh any smoking-related harms for some patients. Predictably, federal authorities failed to act upon the IOM's recommendations, and instead have elected to continue their long-standing policy of denying marijuana's medical value.

NORML first raised this issue in 1972 in an administrative petition filed with the Drug Enforcement Administration (DEA). NORML's petition called on the federal government to reclassify marijuana under the Controlled Substances Act as a Schedule II drug so that physicians could legally prescribe it. Federal authorities initially refused to accept the petition until mandated to do so by the US Court of Appeals in 1974, and then refused to properly process it until again ordered by the Court in 1982.

Fourteen years after NORML's initial petition in 1986, the DEA finally held public hearings on the issue before an administrative law judge. Two years later, Judge Francis Young ruled that the therapeutic use of marijuana was recognized by a respected

> *"Marijuana has been accepted as capable of relieving distress of great numbers of very ill people . . . with safety under medical supervision."*

minority of the medical community, and that it met the standards of other legal medications. Young found: "Marijuana has been accepted as capable of relieving distress of great numbers of very ill people, and doing so with safety under medical supervision. It would be unreasonable, arbitrary and capricious for DEA to continue to stand between those sufferers and the benefits of this substance in light of the evidence in this record." Young recommended, "The Administrator transfer marijuana from Schedule I to Schedule II, to make it available as a legal medicine."

DEA Administrator John Lawn rejected Young's determination, choosing instead to invoke a differing set of criteria than those used by Judge Young. The Court of Appeals allowed Lawn's reversal to stand, effectively continuing the federal ban on the medical use of marijuana by seriously ill patients. It is urgent that state legislatures and the federal government act to correct this injustice.

Public Support for Medical Marijuana

Since 1996, voters in eight states—Alaska, Arizona, California, Colorado, Maine, Nevada, Oregon and Washington—have adopted initiatives exempting patients who use marijuana under a physician's supervision from state criminal penalties. In 1999, the Hawaii legislature ratified a similar law. These laws do not legalize marijuana or alter criminal penalties regarding the possession or cultivation of marijuana for recreational use. They merely provide a narrow exemption from state prosecution for defined patients who possess and use marijuana with their doctor's recommendation. Available evidence indicates that these laws are functioning as voters intended, and that reported abuses are minimal.

As the votes in these states suggest, the American public clearly distinguishes between the medical use and the recreational use of marijuana, and a majority support legalizing medical use for seriously ill patients. A March 2001 Pew Research Center poll reported that 73 percent of Americans support making marijuana legally available for doctors to prescribe, as did a 1999 Gallup poll. Similar support has been indicated in every other state and nationwide poll that has been conducted on the issue since 1995. Arguably, few other public policy issues share the unequivocal support of the American public as this one.

The Supreme Court ruled on May 14, 2001 that federal law makes no exceptions for growing or distributing marijuana by third party organizations (so-called "cannabis buyers' cooperatives"), even if the goal is to help seriously ill patients using marijuana as a medicine. Nevertheless, the Court's decision fails to infringe upon the rights of individual patients to use medical cannabis under state law, or the ability of legislators to pass laws exempting such patients from criminal penalties. This fact was affirmed by Justices Stevens, Ginsburg and Souter, who wrote in a concurring opinion: "By passing Proposition 215, California voters have decided that seriously ill patients and their primary caregivers should be exempt from prosecution under state laws for cultivating and possessing marijuana. . . . This case does not call on the Court to deprive all such patients of the benefit of the necessity defense to federal prosecution when the case does not involve any such patients."

NORML filed an amicus curiae (friend of the court) brief in this case, and hoped the Court would protect California's patient-support efforts from federal prosecution. The sad result of this decision is that tens of thousands of seriously ill patients who use marijuana to relieve their pain and suffering no longer have a safe and secure source for their medical marijuana. NORML calls on our elected officials to correct this injustice and is currently lobbying Congress to legalize marijuana as a medicine.

Available Evidence Does Not Prove That Marijuana Is a Gateway Drug

by Andrew R. Morral, Daniel F. McCaffrey, and Susan M. Paddock

About the authors: *Andrew R. Morral, Daniel F. McCaffrey, and Susan M. Paddock are research scientists at the RAND Drug Policy Research Center, a research and policy institution.*

Alcohol, tobacco and marijuana are widely regarded as 'gateway' drugs. Although the gateway concept admits a number of definitions, one in particular predominates in drug policy discussions: use of gateway drugs causes youths to have an increased risk of progressing to other, more serious drugs. For instance, in debates on marijuana decriminalization or the medicinal use of marijuana, policy makers frequently suggest that use of marijuana increases youths' risk of initiating more dangerous drugs such as cocaine and heroin. Although marijuana is the least prevalent of the three principal gateway drugs, it is currently the focus of extensive policy reassessment in the United States, Canada, Western Europe and Australia. Using a simulation model, we demonstrate that the primary evidence supporting the marijuana gateway effect can be explained completely by the order in which youths first have the opportunity to use marijuana and other drugs, and by assuming a non-specific liability to use drugs, without any assumption that use of marijuana contributes to the risk of initiating use of hard drugs. We argue that although marijuana gateway effects may truly exist, available evidence does not favor the marijuana gateway effect over the alternative hypothesis that marijuana and hard drug initiation are correlated because both are influenced by individuals' heterogenous liabilities to try drugs.

The popular concern that marijuana use increases the risk of progressing to other, more serious drugs is a long-standing one, and has influenced US drug

Andrew R. Morral, Daniel F. McCaffrey, and Susan M. Paddock, "Reassessing the Marijuana Gateway Effect," *Addiction*, vol. 97, December 2002. Copyright © 2002 by the Society for the Study of Addiction to Alcohol and Other Drugs. Reproduced by permission of Blackwell Publishers.

policy since at least the 1950s. Some social scientists have also suggested that marijuana gateway effects probably account for several phenomena observed in adolescent drug use initiation patterns. Three such phenomena represent the primary evidence for a marijuana gateway effect. The first concerns the *relative risk* of hard drug initiation for adolescent marijuana users vs. non-users. In general, marijuana users in many countries appear to have a significantly elevated risk for drug use progression. Indeed, one US study found their risk to be 85 times those of non-users of marijuana. Another form of relative risk that is occasionally cited in support of the gateway effect is that younger marijuana initiates have a higher risk of initiating hard drug use than older marijuana initiates. This relative risk differs from the first only insofar as it finds that risk of hard drug initiation is conditioned on a characteristic of the user (age), rather than on marijuana use alone. Therefore, it does not provide strong evidence supporting a gateway effect.

> *"Available evidence does not favor the marijuana gateway effect."*

The second observation routinely cited in support of the marijuana gateway effect concerns the remarkably invariant *ordering* in adolescents' initiation of different drug classes. Adolescents rarely initiate hard drug use before marijuana. For instance, in a longitudinal sample of 1265 New Zealand youths between the ages of 15 and 21, [researchers] found only three cases reporting use of hard drugs before marijuana. This figure is dramatically lower than the roughly 124 such cases that would be expected from annual incidence rates if use of marijuana and hard drugs were independent.

The third phenomenon used to support claims of a marijuana gateway effect concerns the strong relationship between the frequency of marijuana consumption and the risk of hard drug initiation: as the frequency of marijuana use increases, so too does the risk of initiating hard drug use. [D.M.] Fergusson & [L.J.] Horwood, for instance, developed a proportional hazards model suggesting that youths reporting 50 or more uses of cannabis in the past year had hazards of progression to hard drugs that were more than 140 times greater than those for youths reporting no use of cannabis. Findings like this suggest an even stronger form of the marijuana gateway effect declined earlier: not only does marijuana use increase youths' risk of hard drug initiation, but every instance of marijuana use adds to that risk. For convenience, we refer to this phenomenon as marijuana's apparent *dose-response effect* on hard drug initiation.

Insufficient Proof

The three phenomena of relative risk, ordering in drug use initiation and dose-response are not sufficient to prove that use of marijuana, rather than some associated factor, increases the risk of hard drug initiation. Indeed, a frequently cited alternative explanation is that a common factor, which we might refer to generically as a propensity for drug use, could influence use of both marijuana and hard drugs, thereby causing initiation of these drugs to be correlated. For instance, if high drug use propensities elevate individuals' risk for use of both marijuana and hard drugs, this could explain why marijuana users have a higher relative risk of hard drug initiation in comparison with non-users.

This 'common-factor' model does not immediately account for the ordering and dose-response phenomena. To make sense of these observations, proponents of the common-factor approach suggest that ordering in drug use initiation results from the order in which opportunities to use marijuana and hard drugs are presented to young people. Those with the highest propensities to use drugs are likely to use the first one offered to them, and that happens to be marijuana in most cases. Moreover, if a high drug use propensity is associated with greater frequencies of drug use, the common-factor theory can also account for the dose-response phenomenon: marijuana use frequency is associated with risk of hard drug initiation because both are controlled by drug use propensity.

The common-factor model is appealing in part because it takes account of what is a substantial scientific literature demonstrating the existence of genetic, familial and environmental characteristics associated with a generalised risk of using both marijuana and hard drugs. For instance, several studies examining drug use among monozygotic [identical] and dizygotic [fraternal] twins in the USA demonstrate genetic and family environment contributions to the likelihood of any drug use and any drug use initiation. Similarly, community drug use or drug availability may contribute to individuals' risk of using drugs.

The Common-Factor Explanation

Although the common-factor model is plausible, previous research has not demonstrated that propensities to use drugs and environmental factors such as drug use opportunities could, in fact, account for the strong relative risk, ordering and dose-response phenomena observed among adolescents. Indeed, two lines of research provide some evidence that the common-factor model cannot account for drug use initiation without assuming a marijuana gateway effect.

Firstly, several studies examine the association between marijuana use and the risk of hard drug initiation after controlling for a large number of risk factors, such as delinquency and peer drug use. By the logic of this approach, any residual marijuana effect on hard drug initiation that remains

> *"Those with the highest propensities to use drugs are likely to use the first one offered to them, and that happens to be marijuana."*

after controlling for these candidate common factors lends credence to the suggestion that marijuana use *per se* increases the risk of hard drug initiation. However, if the selected covariates are less good proxies for the propensity to use drugs than is marijuana use itself, these findings are perfectly consistent with a strict common-factor model. Because this approach does not observe all or even most individual risk factors, it provides little persuasive evidence against a common-factor explanation. . . .

A second approach to contrasting the gateway and common-factor models of drug use initiation use instrumental variables in an effort to account for both observed and unobserved person-level risk of initiation. Two of these studies suggest that common factors alone cannot explain observed gateway phenomena. The third provides qualified evidence that observed marijuana gateway phenomena are not attributable to a gateway effect, but instead derive from individuals' predispositions to use both marijuana and hard

> *"Marijuana use . . . is associated with risk of hard drug initiation because both are controlled by drug use propensity."*

drugs. However, none of these studies take into account the observation that opportunities to use marijuana precede those for hard drugs, and may themselves be associated with propensity to use drugs through, for instance, drug-seeking behavior. This is a critical omission, since proponents of the common-factor model have consistently cited the ordering in drug use opportunities as an essential part of the explanation of ordering in drug use initiation. Indeed, in a series of analyses on US and Panamanian data, [J.L.] Anthony, [M.L.] Van Etten and colleagues have shown that gender, race and neighborhood differences observed in rates of drug use initiation are attributable, to a large extent, to differences in the rates at which groups are exposed to drug use opportunities. Thus, econometric models have not tested the common-factor model adequately.

In this report we describe a Monte Carlo model of drug use initiation with parameters selected to match the drug use experiences of the population of US residents under the age of 22. The model describes the joint distribution of four events: the ages of first opportunity to use marijuana and hard drugs, and the ages of first use of marijuana and hard drugs. Each of these events depends on a common factor—drug use propensity—but conditional on this factor, the ages of first opportunity to use and first use of marijuana are independent of opportunity to use and use of hard drugs. Thus, the model is designed to exclude any causal gateway effect. Random draws from the modeled joint distribution are used to examine the relative risk, ordering and dose-response phenomena that might be expected by chance in the US if model assumptions are accurate. . . .

A Plausible Alternative to the Gateway Effect

The model and analyses . . . do not disprove the gateway effect. Instead, they demonstrate that each of the phenomena that appear to support such an effect are, in fact, equally consistent with a plausible alternative that accounts for the known general liability to use drugs and the known differences in when youths receive their first opportunities to use drugs.

Something like a marijuana gateway effect probably does exist, if only because marijuana purchases bring users into contact with a black market that also increases access to hard drugs. However, this observation does not refute [our] analysis . . . since there are at least two ways that gateway effects could exist without undermining a model of drug use initiation that fails to include them. Firstly, it is possible that any true marijuana gateway effects can explain only a tiny fraction of individuals' risk of hard drug use in comparison with the risk attributable to their propensities to use drugs, and is therefore a negligible factor in our model. A second possibility is that marijuana use could increase the risk of hard drug use for some youths, while decreasing the risk for others. As such, true marijuana gateway effects may be counterbalanced in the population by negative marijuana gateway effects, with the net effect of marijuana use on hard drug use being insignificant. Negative gateway effects could occur if, for instance, marijuana sated some youths' desires to experiment with illicit drug use, or if unsatisfying (or penalised) marijuana use experiences discouraged drug use progression among some youths.

The purported marijuana gateway effect is frequently invoked by policy makers as among the primary reasons to resist efforts to relax marijuana policies, such as permitting the medicinal use of marijuana. Whereas social scientists often acknowledge that relative risk, ordering in drug use initiation and dose-response phenomena do not prove the existence of a marijuana gateway effect, they too have frequently drawn policy conclusions that pre-suppose such an effect. For instance, many have concluded that by postponing youths' marijuana initiation, prevention efforts will reduce the likelihood of hard drug use and abuse. Our model demonstrates how the observed correlations in the use of marijuana and hard drugs may be entirely due to individuals' propensity to use drugs and their opportunities to use them. As such, marijuana policies would have little effect on hard drug use, except insofar as they affected either an individuals' propensity to use any drugs (as might be the case with drug use prevention programs) or they resulted in hard drugs becoming less available or available later in youths' lives.

Because our model provides a straightforward, parsimonious and plausible explanation for each of the phenomena used to support claims of a marijuana gateway effect, we believe the validity of that effect must remain uncertain until new evidence is available directly comparing it with the alternative common-factor model.

The Federal Government Should Respect State Medical Marijuana Laws

by Seth Zuckerman

About the author: *Seth Zuckerman is a contributor to Writers on the Range, a syndicated column service of* High Country News *in Paonia, Colorado.*

Like the Democrats in the U.S. Senate, marijuana advocates suffered a setback at the polls last month [November 2002]. By a margin of 2 to 1, Nevada voters trounced a much-publicized proposal to legalize cannabis for personal use.

But the Bush administration would be ill-served to mistake this landslide for an endorsement of its zero-tolerance marijuana policy, any more than a net gain of two seats in the Senate puts a nationwide stamp of approval on conservative doctrine.

In fact, a chasm is opening between the federal government and the states over the medical use of cannabis. States have begun to make the distinction between medical and recreational uses of the plant, even when Washington can't seem to tell the difference.

Eight states—all but one of them in the West—have approved cannabis for medical purposes. Nine out of ten Westerners live in states with medical marijuana legislation, and all but Hawaii's were passed by popular vote. But federal law recognizes no such exception. Since John Ashcroft took over the Department of Justice, Washington has been forcing the issue with increasing vigor.

Federal Crackdown

The conflict has come to a head most dramatically in California, where federal drug teams have cracked down on at least 12 clubs that distribute cannabis to patients. [From August to December 2002] U.S. agents have raided the homes of state-sanctioned cannabis users in Washington and Oregon as well.

It is no longer just woolly-headed stoners who want to relax the absolute pro-hibition on pot. According to a 2002 *Time/CNN* poll, 80 percent of Americans asked approve of using marijuana for medical purposes. Editorial boards in such conservative bastions as Orange County, Calif., have asked federal drug officials to call off the dogs. And af-ter a high-profile federal bust on the California coast, a cannabis club dis-tributed its medical marijuana to pa-tients in front of city hall, at the invi-tation of Santa Cruz officials.

> *"A chasm is opening between the federal government and the states over the medical use of cannabis."*

Medical-marijuana statutes have led officials to set norms for the acceptable use of cannabis. Throughout much of California, county sheriffs and district attorneys have spelled out how much marijuana a patient may raise and possess. In states such as Oregon, Nevada and Colorado, the state maintains a registry of patients authorized to take cannabis, and medical users have even gone to court to recover pot seized from them by local police.

Marijuana advocates display their own set of confusions. They mistook the widespread support of medicinal use for a bandwagon that would put cannabis on a par with alcohol. But once pollsters got beyond the issue of medical use, they found greater resistance. Only 34 percent of those questioned in [the afore-mentioned] *Time/CNN* poll backed recreational use of marijuana—a sentiment reflected in the Nevada measure's defeat. Whether that's good public policy, it is the current state of public opinion.

The blindness of cannibis promoters is a mirror image of the federal insis-tence that all use of marijuana must be eradicated. Fortunately, Western cus-toms of common sense and practicality have cultivated a more nuanced ap-proach to the drug, reflected in our medical-marijuana laws.

States' Rights

If the [George W.] Bush administration continues to insist on a zero-tolerance policy, it pits itself against the poster children of medical marijuana—those cancer sufferers and AIDS patients who rely on marijuana to curb their nausea and increase their appetite. An obvious way out is to leave the matter to the states to sort out what is and is not legitimate medical use; to decide when a recreational user is trying to hide behind a medical exemption.

One reason the Justice Department's position seems so absurd is that it pre-tends drug law is a matter of moral absolutes. But bans on mind-altering sub-stances aren't written in stone; they're more accurately a matter of political choice and social convention. When my parents were growing up, the FBI hounded bootleggers who supplied liquor in defiance of Prohibition. Marijuana smokers had nothing to fear. By the beginning of the Second World War, the sit-uation was reversed.

In prosecuting medical cannabis users, the federal government is showing its disdain for state choices. Like Attorney General Ashcroft's attack on Oregon's assisted-suicide law, the federal crusade against medical marijuana reflects the paternalistic, father-knows-best side of the [Bush] administration. With sleeper terrorist cells abroad in the land, surely the Justice Department has more important assignments for its agents.

Marijuana Laws Should Not Be Relaxed

by Don Feder

About the author: *Don Feder is a syndicated columnist for the* Boston Herald. *He is also the author of* Who's Afraid of the Religious Right *and* A Jewish Conservative Looks at Pagan America.

The freedom to take drugs leads to behavior that is anathema to a free society.

Besides being bad social policy, legalization of marijuana is antithetical to true conservatism. The conservative philosophy as it has evolved since the 18th century . . . adds up to more than "do your own thing."

Pot legalization is a libertarian position. Allowing individuals to use narcotics is consistent with the laissez-faire worldview, which holds that people should be free to choose their own path to perdition, so long as they don't drag others down with them. But while conservatism has an individualistic element and is wary of state action, it does not hold personal autonomy to be the highest value. It weighs individual rights against the needs of society.

Unfortunately, several on the right—including William Buckley Jr., economist Milton F. Friedman, *National Review* Editor Richard Lowry, columnist Arianna Huffington—are beating the drums for this fraud masquerading as reform.

Some are libertarians who labor under the illusion that their creed is synonymous with conservatism. Others are hungry for the establishment's approval. Legalization is popular with alumni of the sixties, who've come to dominate our culture.

The Freedom to Take Drugs Is Fatal to Society

Authentic conservatives understand that liberty must be ordered and rights balanced with responsibilities. The exercise of certain rights is fatal to both the social order and the long-term survival of self-government. The freedom to take drugs is foremost among these.

If "to each his own" is the essence of conservatism, then conservatives should also support legalization of prostitution, hardcore pornography and homosexual marriage—the first two reputed to be victimless crimes.

But the expression is a misnomer. Prostitutes spread disease. Pornography provokes sex crimes. Same-sex marriage undermines the institution.

Addicts commit crimes to get drugs. Addiction affects everyone—from family members to victims of auto accidents to the public that's forced to pay for drug-related medical costs.

Some conservatives are comfortable with a pro-pot position because the culture encourages us to think of cannabis as a harmless recreational substance—the stuff of dorm-room parties and yuppie socializing. "It's far less harmful than alcohol, and that's legal," proponents argue. Of course, drinking alcohol is roughly 20 times more common than marijuana use, so you'd expect the harm to be proportionally greater.

In a recent issue of *National Review*, Lowry pronounced the weed "widely used, and for the vast majority of its users nearly harmless and represents a temporary experiment or enthusiasm." I'm not sure what planet he inhabits, but here on Earth marijuana isn't quite the equivalent of a few beers.

In 1997, I attended the annual pot rally on the Boston Common, where 40,000 juveniles congregated to get high and hear harangues from rock-station personalities on marijuana's manifold blessings. Most of the revelers were long-term users. Conservatives such as Lowry should attend one of these bashes to see just how "nearly harmless" and what a passing fad marijuana use can be.

One young lady, who had enough metal in her face to set off an airport alarm, claimed a physician suggested she use pot to slow down her "multifaceted (by which I assume she meant hyperactive) brain." If that was the objective, it was working admirably. Her brain was barely functioning.

Another, Michelle, assured me: "Everybody's doing it [getting high]. Eighty percent of doctors and lawyers—and cops, too." Who says marijuana distorts the user's perception of reality?

Symptomatic of habitual users was George, age 21, who was selling "End the Drug War" buttons. "It helps clear up the eye weakness. It helps you see a little better if you're blind," George informed me. This is hard to dispute. While his eyes were glazed, George definitely wasn't blind. He wasn't educated or motivated, either. A user

> *"[Marijuana] legalization is popular with alumni of the sixties, who've come to dominate our culture."*

since he was 15, George dropped out of school and was living alone and barely supporting himself by delivering flowers. He hadn't spoken to his parents in six years ("They treated me wrong, man"), which, not by chance, coincided with his initiation into the drug culture.

Marijuana Use Alters the Personality

The above is anecdotal. But evidence—mounds of it—exists, for those whose vision isn't impaired. Roughly 100,000 people are in rehab programs for marijuana use. The drug lobby claims most of them were arrested for possession and given the alternative of treatment or imprisonment.

That almost sounds plausible, until one looks at marijuana mentions in emergency-room visits. In 1999, more ER visits were related to marijuana than heroin (38,976 versus 38,237), though less than half that for cocaine, according to the University of Maryland Center for Substance Abuse Research. Of the marijuana cases, 27 percent had unexpected reactions, 18 percent had overdosed (something proponents assure us is impossible) and 14 percent sought detox.

Marijuana use alters personality in unpleasant ways. Based on data collected from 1994 to 1996, the center found a direct correlation between frequency of marijuana use and "delinquent/depressive behaviors." Among those ages 12 to 17 who had been placed on probation in the last year, 1 percent never used the drug, 7 percent used it one to 11 times during the year and 20 percent used it at least weekly.

Of those who had committed an assault in the last six months, 7 percent never smoked pot, 18 percent used it one to four days a month and 26 percent used it one to seven days a week. A child who smoked a joint

> *"Pot makes many long-term users sullen, antisocial, muddled and not likely to apply themselves productively."*

weekly or more often was three times as likely to have thought about suicide in the last six months, and six times more likely to have run away from home, than nonusers.

In 1999, about 60 percent of juveniles arrested in Washington tested positive for marijuana, according to the District of Columbia's Pretrial Services Agency. None of this is coincidental. Pot makes many long-term users sullen, antisocial, muddled and not inclined to apply themselves productively.

Removing legal sanctions from marijuana will result in an upsurge of juvenile experimentation. A May 9 [2001] *Wall Street Journal* editorial noted that, following liberalization of its drug laws in the 1980s, the Netherlands saw a 250 percent increase in adolescent marijuana use.

Marijuana Users Are More Likely to Try Cocaine

The drug lobby sneers at the gateway theory—that pot leads to harder drugs. While many never graduate to more potent substances, research by the Center for Addiction and Substance Abuse at Columbia University showed that 12- to 17-year-olds who smoke marijuana are 85 times more likely to try cocaine.

Legalizers maintain that this is no more relevant than the fact that 100 percent of coke heads drank milk as children. But milk doesn't get you high. Drinking milk does not create a desire for more-intense experiences ("This was fun. I wonder what that would do"). Even with a dollop of chocolate syrup, milk doesn't alter thinking and impair the ability to make rational decisions.

The individual-liberty argument used for marijuana can be applied to every other drug. If X snorts cocaine or mainlines heroin, who is directly harmed other than X? Every narcotic has its enthusiasts who argue that, besides opening up new psychic horizons, the drug is relatively benign.

> *"Removing legal sanctions from marijuana will result in an upsurge of juvenile experimentation."*

Legalization of marijuana will provide a powerful impetus for ending the prohibition on drugs across the board. "Look at the money we've saved on enforcement and the individuals whose lives weren't mined by a drug bust," those who would extend legalization will argue.

Lowry calls this reasonable concern a drug-war Brezhnev doctrine "under which no drug-war excess can ever be turned back—once a harsh drug law is on the books for marijuana possession, there it must remain lest the 'wrong signal' be sent." But signals are sent, often with unintended consequences. Look how far we've come toward normalization of fornication (with its attendant social pathologies) since removing the stigma on cohabitation.

Finally, conservative legalizers argue the marijuana prohibition is futile. The laws largely are ineffective, except for the unlucky few who are caught. Still, users are said to crowd our jails—taking space which should accommodate real criminals.

But when we fought a real drug war in the 1980s and early 1990s, drug use dropped dramatically. In 1979, current users of illicit substances constituted 14 percent of the population. By 1992, the figure was 4 percent. During the Clinton years of benign neglect, it rebounded to 7 percent.

Those arrested for possession of small quantities of pot constitute an insignificant percentage of state-prison inmates—not that a zero-tolerance policy of locking up small-time users for, say, 90 days might not have a salutary effect. In 1998, only 3.3 percent of state-prison inmates in Florida were doing time for drug possession (any drug) alone.

Plea Bargains Are Common

Drug statutes give police leverage to get career criminals off the streets. Often a defendant who's indicted for a string of offenses on which the evidence might not convict him is allowed to plead down to a possession charge. Records may show they were sent to prison for marijuana or cocaine possession, but police and prosecutors could tell a different story.

Like physicians bound by the Hippocratic oath, the motto of conservatives should be: "First, do no harm." Thoughtful conservatives—those who don't float on the cultural currents—have seen the ravages of 50 years of social experimentation, where restraints were loosened and passions unleashed to the detriment of both the individual and society.

There are freedoms the individual must have—among them the right to earn a livelihood and dispose of the greater portion of his income, to raise a family, to defend himself and those he loves. And there is power too potent to be vested in the state—to direct the national economy, to indoctrinate the impressionable, to screen political speech.

The freedom to get high is neither necessary for a meaningful existence nor conducive to a society where genuine rights are respected. Indeed, it's easier to fit a slave collar on a nation of addicts.

Marijuana Should Not Be Legalized for Medical Purposes

by Gregory M. Gassett

About the author: *Gregory M. Gassett is assistant special agent in charge for the Seattle Field Division of the Drug Enforcement Administration (DEA).*

Arguments for the legalization of "medical" marijuana do little to ensure that the facts concerning marijuana are openly discussed and only further confuse the issue for the American public. The truth is that marijuana is a highly addictive drug and has no medical value.

Marijuana is one of the most abused drugs in this country. It is one of the first illegal drugs young people are exposed to and some experiment with. Using marijuana often lowers their inhibition against trying other, less-forgiving drugs such as Ecstasy, cocaine, methamphetamine and heroin. The drug's effects cause memory loss, trouble with problem-solving, loss of motor skills and an increase in heart rate, panic attacks and anxiety. Marijuana weakens the body's immune system, which further complicates any potential recovery from a serious medical condition.

Marijuana trafficked across the United States is up to 25 times more potent than it was in the 1960s, which makes it much more addictive. Drug traffickers in Mexico and Canada flood this country with vast amounts of marijuana, and citizens of this country grow it with little regard for the damage they are causing. The misleading message that young people receive concerning this drug contributes to their decision to use marijuana.

Misleading Information

If adults are misconstruing the facts surrounding marijuana use for their own benefit, how can a 10- or 11-year-old make a decision on the harmful effects of marijuana or other drugs? If elected officials openly violate the law by distributing marijuana, as recently occurred in California, how can they possibly have the best interests of their community and its young people at heart?

The insinuation that smoking marijuana has widespread support and can assist people suffering from AIDS, Lou Gehrig's disease and many other terminal illnesses is misleading. While some people openly support the legalization of marijuana for medical purposes, it is from a misinformed position.

> *"The truth is that marijuana is a highly addictive drug and has no medical value."*

It does not matter that they are elected political figures; a misguided decision is still a bad one, no matter who makes it. Legalizing marijuana through a political process bypasses the safeguards established by the Food and Drug Administration to safely test all drugs.

Others utilize the medical marijuana claim as a ploy to legalize marijuana altogether, and then will work toward the legalization of other dangerous drugs as well. They work to misinform, mislead and weaken your resolve. Operators of "compassion marijuana distribution centers" have attempted to legitimize themselves in California, Oregon, Washington and elsewhere for too long.

Misinformation causes confusion for the public seeking to make a rational decision on this issue. Legalizers often cite a 1999 White House-commissioned study by the Institute of Medicine, which they say concluded that marijuana has medical benefits. This is not true. The study concluded that smoking marijuana is not good medicine. It went on to state that although marijuana delivers the active ingredient tetrahydrocannabinol (THC), smoking marijuana also delivers harmful substances, including most of those found in tobacco smoke.

No medicine prescribed today is ever smoked. Marijuana contains over 400 chemicals, and when smoked it easily introduces cancer-causing chemicals to the body. Does this sound like good medicine? Marijuana contains numerous compounds and could never deliver the precise effect sought by a medical doctor assisting a patient.

The Drug Enforcement Administration (DEA) supports research into the study of all drugs, including THC. As a result of that research, Marinol was developed, and has been available to the public since 1985. The active ingredient in Marinol is synthetic THC, which battles the nausea and other discomforts associated with chemotherapy in cancer patients, and loss of appetite, often associated with AIDS patients. Marinol is an alternative drug approved by the medical community and the Food and Drug Administration.

Marijuana Is Not Harmless

We have all witnessed the horrific consequences of drug abuse in our country over many years, and it is appalling. The DEA, and other law-enforcement agencies, take the legal measures necessary to combat drug traffickers, including those who grow and distribute marijuana, and who often hide behind "medical marijuana" claims that have misinformed and confused the public.

Accepting the notion that marijuana is harmless leads young people to experiment with it, and allows legalizers the path they seek to undermine the successful drug-prevention programs that law enforcement, community leaders and schools have engaged in.

You can make a difference. Speak out against the false claims of legalizers and put this issue to rest. Enough is enough, America, and it's time that you stood your ground and said so.

Medical Marijuana Proponents Seek to Legitimize All Marijuana Use

by John P. Walters

About the author: *John P. Walters is director of the Office of National Drug Control Policy, a position often referred to as "drug czar."*

Last December [2001] the University of Michigan released its annual survey "Monitoring the Future," which measures drug use among American youth. Very little had changed from the previous year's report; most indicators were flat. The report generated little in the way of public comment. Yet what it brought to light was deeply disturbing. Drug use among our nation's teens remains stable, but at near-record levels, with some 49 percent of high school seniors experimenting with marijuana at least once prior to graduation—and 22 percent smoking marijuana at least once a month.

After years of giggling at quaintly outdated marijuana scare stories like the 1936 movie "Reefer Madness," we've become almost conditioned to think that any warnings about the true dangers of marijuana are overblown. But marijuana is far from "harmless"—it is pernicious. Parents are often unaware that today's marijuana is different from that of a generation ago, with potency levels 10 to 20 times stronger than the marijuana with which they were familiar.

Marijuana Impairs Learning

Marijuana directly affects the brain. Researchers have learned that it impairs the ability of young people to concentrate and retain information during their peak learning years, and when their brains are still developing. The THC in marijuana attaches itself to receptors in the hippocampal region of the brain, weakening short-term memory and interfering with the mechanisms that form long-term memory. Do our struggling schools really need another obstacle to student achievement?

Marijuana smoking can hurt more than just grades. According to the Department of Health and Human Services [HHS], every year more than 2,500 admissions to the District of Columbia's overtaxed emergency rooms—some 300 of them for patients under age 18—are linked to marijuana smoking, and the number of marijuana-related emergencies is growing. Each year, for example, marijuana use is linked to tens of thousands of serious traffic accidents.

Research has now established that marijuana is in fact addictive. Of the 4.3 million Americans who meet the diagnostic criteria for needing drug treatment (criteria developed by the American Psychiatric Association, not police departments or prosecutors) two-thirds are dependent on marijuana, according to HHS. These are not occasional pot smokers but people with real problems directly traceable to their use of marijuana, including significant health problems, emotional problems and difficulty in cutting down on use. Sixty percent of teens in drug treatment have a primary marijuana diagnosis.

> *"A cynical campaign is underway . . . to proclaim the virtues of 'medical' marijuana."*

Despite this and other strong scientific evidence of marijuana's destructive effects, a cynical campaign is underway, in the District [of Columbia] and elsewhere, to proclaim the virtues of "medical" marijuana. By now most Americans realize that the push to "normalize" marijuana for medical use is part of the drug legalization agenda. Its chief funders, George Soros, John Sperling and Peter Lewis, have spent millions to help pay for referendums and ballot initiatives in states from Alaska to Maine. Now it appears that a medical marijuana campaign may be on the horizon for the District.

Why? Is the American health care system—the most sophisticated in the world—really being hobbled by a lack of smoked medicines? The University of California's Center for Medicinal Cannabis Research is currently conducting scientific studies to determine the efficacy of marijuana in treating various ailments. Until that research is concluded, however, most of what the public hears from marijuana activists is little more than a compilation of anecdotes. Many questions remain unanswered, but the science is clear on a few things. Example: Marijuana contains hundreds of carcinogens. Moreover, anti-smoking efforts aimed at youth have been remarkably effective by building on a campaign to erode the social acceptability of tobacco. Should we undermine those efforts by promoting smoked marijuana as though it were a medicine?

While medical marijuana initiatives are based on pseudo-science, their effects on the criminal justice system are anything but imaginary. By opening up legal loopholes, existing medical marijuana laws have caused police and prosecutors to stay away from marijuana prosecutions.

Giving marijuana dealers a free pass is a terrible idea. In fact, thanks in part to excellent reporting in *The [Washington] Post*, District residents are increasingly aware that marijuana dealers are dangerous criminals. The recent life-without-parole convictions of leaders of Washington's K Street Crew are only the latest evidence of this.

Marijuana Dealers Are Violent

As reported in *The Post*, the K Street Crew was a vicious group of marijuana dealers whose decade-long reign of terror was brought to an end only this year [in 2002] after a massive prosecution effort by Michael Volkov, chief gang prosecutor for the U.S. attorney's office. The K Street Crew is credited with at least 17 murders including systematic killings of potential witnesses. (It should not be confused with the L Street Crew, a D.C. marijuana gang that killed eight people in the course of doing business.)

Says prosecutor Volkov: "The experience in D.C. shows that marijuana dealers are no less violent than cocaine and heroin traffickers. They have just as much money to lose, just as much turf to lose, and just as many reasons to kill as any drug trafficker."

Skeptics will charge that this kind of violence is just one more reason to legalize marijuana. A review of the nation's history with drug use suggests otherwise: When marijuana is inexpensive, as it would be if legal, use soars—bad news for the . . . schools, streets and emergency rooms.

Marijuana Is a Gateway Drug

by Joseph C. Gfroerer, Li-Tzy Wu, and Michael A. Penne

About the authors: *Joseph C. Gfroerer, Li-Tzy Wu, and Michael A. Penne are researchers for the Substance Abuse and Mental Health Services Administration (SAMHSA).*

Marijuana is the most widely used illicit drug in the United States. According to the 2000 NHSDA [National Household Surveys on Drug Abuse] an estimated 14.0 million Americans were current (past month) marijuana users. This represents 6.3 percent of people aged 12 or older and 76 percent of current illicit drug users. Of all current illicit drug users, approximately 59 percent used only marijuana, 17 percent used marijuana and another illicit drug, and the remaining 24 percent used only an illicit drug other than marijuana in the past month.

The NHSDA and the Monitoring the Future (MTF) [survey] have shown generally similar long-term trends in the prevalence of substance use among youths, regardless of substantial differences in methodology between the two primary surveys of youth substance use. Between 1999 and 2000, both the NHSDA and MTF found no significant changes in lifetime, past year, and current use of marijuana.

The MTF found that marijuana use rose particularly sharply among 8th graders in the 1990s, with annual prevalence tripling between 1991 and 1996 (i.e., from 6 to 18 percent). Starting a year later, marijuana use also rose significantly among 10th and 12th graders. Following the recent peak in 1996–1997, annual marijuana use declined somewhat in recent years.

Most New Marijuana Users Are Under Seventeen

Although the prevalence of marijuana use has been studied widely, relatively few incidence (first use) data are available. In the first published analysis of national incidence trends, [J.] Gfroerer and [M.] Brodsky estimated the number of new users of marijuana and other drugs based on combined data of 1985 to

Joseph C. Gfroerer, Li-Tzy Wu, and Michael A. Penne, "Initiation of Marijuana Use: Trends, Patterns, and Implications," Substance Abuse and Mental Health Services Administration, Office of Applied Studies, July 2002.

1991 NHSDAs. They found that fewer than half a million people per year began using marijuana before 1966 and that new use of marijuana began increasing after 1966, reaching a peak in 1973 and declining thereafter. [R.A.] Johnson, [D.R.] Gerstein, [R.] Ghadialy, [W.] Choi, and [J.] Gfroerer studied the incidence of alcohol, cigarettes and illicit drugs using data from the 1991 to 1993 NHSDAs. Their investigation found declining trends of marijuana initiation at all ages since at least the late 1970s. However, the mean age of marijuana initiates declined throughout most of the measurement period, from older than 19 years in the mid-1960s to younger than 18 years in the late 1980s and early 1990s. In addition, the rates of marijuana initiation at ages 12 to 17 (youths) and 18 to 25 (young adults) in the early 1990s were still much higher than corresponding rates in the early 1960s.

> *"Marijuana has been hypothesized to be a gateway drug for other illicit drug use."*

In recent years, youths aged 12 to 17 have constituted about two thirds of the new marijuana users, with young adults aged 18 to 25 constituting most of the remaining third (OAS, 2001b). Additionally, recent rates of new use among youths in 1996–1998 (averaging 86.4 initiates per 1,000 potential new users) were higher than they had ever been. Nonetheless, rates of new use for both youths and young adults decreased between 1998 and 1999. The average age of marijuana initiation has generally declined since 1965 and remained around 17 years after 1992. . . .

Little research exists on the predictors of marijuana initiation. [M.L.] Van Etten and [J.L.] Anthony examined the initial opportunity to try marijuana and the transition from first opportunity to first marijuana use using data from the 1979 to 1994 NHSDAs. They found that an estimated 51 percent of U.S. residents had an opportunity to try marijuana. One striking finding is that 43 percent of those with an opportunity went on to first use marijuana within 1 year of the first opportunity (i.e., making a rapid transition). The study also found that males were more likely than females to have an opportunity to use marijuana, but were not more likely to eventually use marijuana once an opportunity was presented. Research has also shown that the risk of initiating marijuana use is associated with age and birth cohort. [K.] Chen and [D.B.] Kandel found that the major risk period for initiation into marijuana was mostly over by age 20. [J.C.] Gfroerer and [J.K.] Epstein also found that marijuana initiation was unlikely to occur after age 21. Rates of first marijuana use were higher among younger people and cohorts born after World War II than older people and cohorts born before World War II.

The onset of marijuana use also is influenced by a variety of personal, family, and community risk and protective factors, such as affiliation with drug-using peers, personality dimensions (e.g., unconventionality), and the parent-child bond.

Marijuana Is a Gateway Drug

Marijuana has been hypothesized to be a gateway drug for other illicit drug use. Studies by [D.B.] Kandel and other investigators have identified a developmental sequence of drug involvement among youths. Specifically, the initial use of alcohol and/or cigarettes typically precedes the use of marijuana, which then is followed by the involvement of other illicit drugs. By studying a sample of rural youths, [J.F.] Donnermeyer also found that early use of alcohol predicted early use of marijuana, which in turn was predictive of early use of other illicit drugs. Studies of age at initiation of drug use confirmed that initiation of alcohol or tobacco typically occurred before marijuana initiation.

Not only does early marijuana use signal an increased risk for hard drug use by grade 10, but it also is associated with drug use problems, dependency, and treatment need. Among individuals with a history of marijuana dependence, the age at onset of marijuana dependence was younger in the adolescent-onset individuals compared with the adult-onset individuals, and the time from the first use to the onset of dependence also was shorter in the adolescent-onset individuals. Among middle school students, use of marijuana and other drugs before the age of 12 was found to be associated with engaging in greater numbers of health risk behaviors than among students whose age at onset was 12 years or older or the never users. Early marijuana use is associated with later adolescent problems that limit the acquisition of skills necessary for employment and increased risk of contracting the human immunodeficiency virus (HIV) and using illicit drugs. Gfroerer and Epstein used NHSDA data to examine the impact of marijuana initiation on future drug abuse treatment need and found age at first use of marijuana as the most significant predictor of treatment need in all four age groups.

"Delaying the onset of marijuana initiation could be important in preventing the progression into heavy drug involvement."

The number of new marijuana users may have a significant impact on the future demand for substance abuse treatment as some new users continue into heavier marijuana use or other illicit drug taking. Consequently, delaying the onset of marijuana initiation could be important in preventing the progression into heavy drug involvement and other drug-related health risk behaviors, as well as in decreasing the social burdens of illicit drug use.

Taken together, studies of marijuana initiation provide vital information for focused prevention programs about the periods of heightened initiation risk, specify subgroups vulnerable to initial use, and generate estimates on treatment needs and future demand for substance abuse treatment.

Organizations to Contact

The editors have compiled the following list of organizations concerned with the issues debated in this book. The descriptions are derived from materials provided by the organizations. All have publications or information available for interested readers. The list was compiled on the date of publication of the present volume; the information provided here may change. Be aware that many organizations take several weeks or longer to respond to inquiries, so allow as much time as possible.

American Civil Liberties Union (ACLU)
125 Broad St., 18th Fl., New York, NY 10004-2400
(212) 549-2500
e-mail: aclu@aclu.org • Web site: www.aclu.org

The ACLU is a national organization that works to defend Americans' civil rights guaranteed by the U.S. Constitution. It provides legal defense, research, and education. The ACLU opposes the criminal prohibition of marijuana and the civil liberties violations that result from prohibition. Its publications include ACLU Briefing Paper #19: *Against Drug Prohibition* and *Marijuana Myths and Facts.*

American Council for Drug Education
164 W. Seventy-fourth St., New York, NY 10023
(800) 488-DRUG (3784) • (212) 595-5810 ext. 7860 • fax: (212) 595-2553
e-mail: phoenixhouse@acde.org • Web site: www.acde.org

The American Council for Drug Education informs the public about the harmful effects of abusing drugs and alcohol. It publishes educational materials, reviews, and scientific findings and develops educational media campaigns. The council's pamphlets, monographs, films, and other teaching aids address educators, parents, physicians, and employees.

Canadian Centre on Substance Abuse (CCSA)
75 Albert St., Suite 300, Ottawa, ON K1P 5E7 Canada
(613) 235-4048 • fax: (613) 235-8101
e-mail: info@ccsa.ca • Web site: www.ccsa.ca

CCSA works to minimize the harm associated with the use of alcohol, tobacco, and other drugs. It disseminates information on the nature, extent, and consequences of substance abuse; sponsors public debates on the topic; and supports organizations involved in substance abuse treatment, prevention, and educational programming. The center publishes the newsletter *Action News* six times a year.

Canadian Foundation for Drug Policy (CFDP)
70 MacDonald St., Ottawa, ON K2P 1H6 Canada
(613) 236-1027 • fax: (613) 238-2891
e-mail: eoscapel@cfdp.ca • Web site: www.cfdp.ca

Founded by several of Canada's leading drug policy specialists, CFDP examines the objectives and consequences of Canada's drug laws and policies. When necessary, the foundation recommends alternatives that it believes would make Canada's drug policies more effective and humane. CFDP discusses drug policy issues with the Canadian government, media, and general public. It also disseminates educational materials and maintains a Web site.

Cato Institute
1000 Massachusetts Ave. NW, Washington, DC 20001-5403
(202) 842-0200 • fax: (202) 842-3490
e-mail: cato@cato.org • Web site: www.cato.org

The institute, a public policy research foundation dedicated to limiting the control of government and to protecting individual liberty, strongly favors drug legalization. Its publications include the *Cato Journal*, published three times a year, and the bimonthly *Cato Policy Report.*

Center on Addiction and Substance Abuse (CASA)
633 Third Ave., 19th Fl., New York, NY 10017-6706
(212) 841-5200 • fax: (212) 956-8020
Web site: www.casacolumbia.org

CASA is a private, nonprofit organization that works to educate the public about the hazards of chemical dependency. The organization supports treatment as the best way to reduce chemical dependency. It produces publications describing the harmful effects of alcohol and drug addiction and effective ways to address the problem of substance abuse.

Drug Data Center and Clearinghouse
PO Box 6000, Rockville, MD 20849-6000
(800) 851-3420 • (301) 519-5500
Web site: www.ncjrs.org

The clearinghouse distributes the publications of the U.S. Department of Justice, the Drug Enforcement Administration, and other related federal agencies.

Drug Enforcement Administration (DEA)
700 Army Navy Dr., Arlington, VA 22202
(202) 307-1000
Web site: www.dea.gov

The DEA is the federal agency charged with enforcing the nation's drug laws. The agency concentrates on stopping the smuggling and distribution of narcotics in the United States and abroad. It publishes the *Drug Enforcement Magazine* three times a year.

Drug Policy Alliance
925 Fifteenth St. NW, Washington, DC 20005
(202) 216-0035 • fax: (202) 216-0803
e-mail: dc@drugpolicy.org • Web site: www.dpf.org

The Drug Policy Alliance is a merging of the Lindesmith Center, formerly the leading drug policy reform institute in the United States, and the Drug Policy Foundation, a nonprofit organization that advocated sensible and humane drug policies. These two organizations joined in the year 2000 with the objective of building a national drug policy reform movement. The alliance works to broaden the public debate on drug policy and to promote realistic alternatives to the war on drugs based on science, compassion, public health, and human rights. The Web site includes links to fact sheets, documents, and other Internet sources with information on drug research.

Drug Watch International
PO Box 45218, Omaha, NE 68145-0218
(402) 384-9212
Web site: www.drugwatch.org

Drug Watch International is a drug information network and advocacy organization that promotes the creation of drug-free cultures in the world and opposes the legalization of drugs. The organization upholds a comprehensive approach to drug issues involving prevention, education, intervention/treatment, and law enforcement/interdiction. Drug Watch International provides policy makers, the media, and the public with current information, factual research, and resources aimed at countering drug advocacy propaganda. Publications include *Drug Watch World News*, as well as various articles, position statements, and resolutions published on the Web site.

Heritage Foundation
214 Massachusetts Ave. NE, Washington, DC 20008-2302
(202) 546-4400 • fax: (202) 546-8328
Web site: www.heritage.org

The Heritage Foundation is a conservative public policy research institute that opposes drug legalization and advocates strengthening law enforcement to stop drug abuse. It publishes position papers on a broad range of topics, including drug issues. Its regular publications include the monthly *Policy Review*, the Backgrounder series of occasional papers, and the Heritage Lectures series.

International Narcotic Enforcement Officers Association (INEOA)
112 State St., Suite 1200, Albany, NY 12207
(518) 463-6232
Web site: www.ineoa.org

The INEOA examines national and international narcotics laws and seeks ways to improve those laws and to prevent drug abuse. It also studies law enforcement methods to find the most effective ways to reduce illegal drug use. The association publishes a newsletter and the monthlies *International Drug Report* and *NarcOfficer.*

Libertarian Party
2600 Virginia Ave. NW, Suite B-100, Washington, DC 20037
(202) 333-0008
Web site: www.lp.org

The Libertarian Party is a political party whose goal is to protect individual rights and liberties. It advocates the repeal of all laws prohibiting the production, sale, possession, or use of drugs. The party believes law enforcement should focus on preventing violent crimes against persons and property rather than on prosecuting people who use drugs. It publishes the bimonthly *Libertarian Party News* and periodic *Issues Papers* and distributes a compilation of articles supporting drug legalization.

Marijuana Policy Project
PO Box 77492, Capitol Hill, Washington, DC 20013
(202) 462-5747 • fax: (202) 232-0442
e-mail: mpp@mpp.org • Web site: www.mpp.org

The Marijuana Policy Project develops and promotes policies to minimize the harm associated with marijuana. It is the only organization that is solely concerned with lobbying to reform the marijuana laws on the federal level. The project increases public awareness through speaking engagements, educational seminars, the mass media, and briefing papers.

Multidisciplinary Association for Psychedelic Studies (MAPS)
2105 Robinson Ave., Sarasota, FL 34232
(941) 924-6277 • fax: (941) 924-6265
e-mail: info@maps.org • Web site: www.maps.org

MAPS is a membership-based research and educational organization. It focuses on the development of beneficial, socially sanctioned uses of psychedelic drugs and marijuana. MAPS helps scientific researchers obtain governmental approval for funding on psychedelic research in human volunteers. It publishes the quarterly *MAPS Bulletin* as well as various reports and newsletters.

National Clearinghouse for Alcohol and Drug Information
20 Exchange Pl., Suite 2902, New York, NY 10005
(800) 729-6686 • (301) 269-7797 • fax: (301) 269-7510
e-mail: national@ncadd.org • Web site: www.health.org

The clearinghouse distributes publications of the U.S. Department of Health and Human Services, the National Institute on Drug Abuse, and other federal agencies concerned with alcohol and drug abuse. Brochure titles include *Tips for Teens About Marijuana* and *Tips for Teens About Crack and Cocaine.*

National Council on Alcoholism and Drug Dependence (NCADD)
20 Exchange Pl., Suite 2902, New York, NY 10005
(800) 622-2255 • (212) 269-7797 • fax: (212) 269-7510
e-mail: national@ncadd.org • Web site: www.ncadd.org

The National Council on Alcoholism and Drug Dependence works to educate Americans about alcohol and drug abuse. It provides community-based prevention and education programs as well as information and service referrals. NCADD publishes pamphlets, fact sheets, and other materials that provide statistics on chemical dependency.

National Institute on Drug Abuse (NIDA)
National Institutes of Health
6001 Executive Blvd., Rm. 5213, Bethesda, MD 20892-9561
(301) 443-1124
e-mail: information@lists.nida.nih.gov • Web site: www.nida.nih.gov

NIDA supports and conducts research on drug abuse—including the yearly *Monitoring the Future Survey*—to improve addiction prevention, treatment, and policy efforts. It publishes the bimonthly *NIDA Notes* newsletter, the periodic *NIDA Capsules* fact sheets, and a catalog of research reports and public education materials such as *Marijuana: Facts for Teens.*

National Organization for the Reform of Marijuana Laws (NORML)
1600 K St. NW, Suite 501, Washington, DC 20006-2832
(202) 483-5500 • fax: (202) 483-0057
e-mail: natlnorml@aol.com • Web site: www.norml.org

NORML fights to legalize marijuana and to help those who have been convicted and sentenced for possessing or selling marijuana. In addition to pamphlets and position papers, it publishes the newsletter *Marijuana Highpoints*, the bimonthly *Legislative Bulletin* and *Freedom@NORML*, and the monthly *Potpourri.*

Office of National Drug Control Policy (ONDCP)
Drug Policy Information Clearinghouse
PO Box 6000, Rockville, MD 20849-6000
(800) 666-3332 • (301) 519-5212
Web site: www.whitehousedrugpolicy.gov

The Office of National Drug Control Policy is responsible for formulating the government's national drug strategy and the president's antidrug policy as well as coordinating the federal agencies responsible for stopping drug trafficking. Drug policy studies are available upon request.

Partnership for a Drug-Free America
405 Lexington Ave., Suite 1601, New York, NY 10174
(212) 922-1560 • fax: (212) 922-1570
e-mail: webmail@drugfree.org • Web site: www.drugfreeamerica.org

The Partnership for a Drug-Free America is a nonprofit organization that utilizes media communication to reduce demand for illicit drugs in America. Best known for its national antidrug advertising campaign, the partnership works to "unsell" drugs to children and to prevent drug use among youths. It publishes the annual *Partnership Newsletter* as well as monthly press releases about current events with which the partnership is involved.

RAND Corporation
1700 Main St., PO Box 2138, Santa Monica, CA 90407-2138
(310) 393-0411 • fax: (310) 393-4818
Web site: www.rand.org

The RAND Corporation is a research institution that seeks to improve public policy through research and analysis. RAND's Drug Policy Research Center publishes information on the costs, prevention, and treatment of alcohol and drug abuse as well as on trends in drug-law enforcement. Its extensive list of publications includes the book *Sealing the Borders* by Peter Reuter.

Reason Foundation
3415 S. Sepulveda Blvd., Suite 400, Los Angeles, CA 90034
(310) 391-2245 • fax: (310) 391-4395
e-mail: gpassantino@reason.org • Web site: www.reason.org

This public policy organization researches contemporary social and political problems and promotes a libertarian philosophy and free-market principles. It publishes the monthly *Reason* magazine, which contains articles and editorials critical of the war on drugs and smoking regulation.

Bibliography

Books

Anne Alverque	*Ecstasy: The Danger of False Euphoria.* New York: Rosen Publishing Group, 2000.
Tom Carnwath and Ian Smith	*Heroin Country.* New York: Routledge, 2002.
Ted Glenn Carpenter	*Bad Neighbor Policy: Washington's Futile War on Drugs in Latin America.* New York: Palgrave Macmillan, 2003.
Center for Substance Abuse Prevention	*Marijuana: Weeding Out the Hype!* Rockville, MD: U.S. Department of Health and Human Services, 2002.
Mitchell Earleywine	*Understanding Marijuana: A New Look at the Scientific Evidence.* Oxford, UK: Oxford University Press, 2002.
Larry K. Gaines and Peter B. Kraska	*Drugs, Crime, and Justice: Contemporary Perspectives.* Long Grove, IL: Waveland Press, 2002.
Ted Gottfried	*Should Drugs Be Legalized?* Springfield, MO: 21st Century Press, 2000.
James P. Gray	*Why Our Drug Laws Have Failed and What We Can Do About It: A Judicial Indictment of the War on Drugs.* Philadelphia: Temple University Press, 2001.
Mike Gray	*Busted: Stone Cowboys, Narco-Lords and Washington's War on Drugs.* New York: Nation Books, 2002.
Tara Herivel and Paul Wright	*Prison Nation: The Warehousing of America's Poor.* New York: Routledge, 2003.
Julie Holland	*Ecstasy: The Complete Guide: A Comprehensive Look at the Risks and Benefits.* Rochester, VT: Park Street Press, 2001.
Douglas N. Husak	*Legalize This: The Case for Decriminalizing Drugs.* New York: Verso Books, 2002.
James A. Inciardi	*The War on Drugs III: The Continuing Saga of the Mysteries and Miseries of Intoxication, Addiction, Crime, and Public Policy.* Upper Saddle River, NJ: Pearson Education, 2001.
Karl Jansen	*Ketamine: Dreams and Realities.* Sarasota, FL: Multidisciplinary Association for Psychedelic Studies, 2001.

Bibliography

| Timothy Lynch | *After Prohibition: An Adult Approach to Drug Policies in the 21st Century.* Washington, DC: Cato Institute, 2000. |

Robert J. MacCoun and Peter Reuter — *Drug War Heresies: Learning from Other Vices, Times and Places.* New York: Cambridge University Press, 2001.

Bill Masters — *Drug War Addiction.* Lonedell, MO: Accurate Press, 2001.

Bill Masters — *The New Prohibition: Voices of Dissent Challenge the Drug War.* Lonedell, MO: Accurate Press, 2004.

Joel Miller — *Bad Trip: How the War Against Drugs Is Destroying America.* Nashville: WND Books, 2004.

Jeffrey A. Miron — *Drug War Crimes: The Consequences of Prohibition.* Oakland, CA: Independent Institute, 2004.

Ed Rosenthal and Steve Kobby — *Why Marijuana Should Be Legal.* New York: Thunder's Mouth Press, 2003.

Eric Schlosser — *Reefer Madness: Sex, Drugs, and Cheap Labor in the American Black Market.* Boston: Houghton Mifflin, 2003.

Jacob Sullum — *Saying Yes: In Defense of Drugs.* New York: J.P. Tarcher/Putnam, 2003.

Douglas Valentine — *The Strength of the Wolf: The Secret History of America's War on Drugs.* New York: Verso Books, 2004.

Myra Weatherly — *Ecstasy and Other Designer Drug Dangers.* Berkeley Heights, NJ: Enslow Publishing, 2000.

Scott P. Werther — *Ecstasy and Your Heart: The Incredibly Disgusting Story.* New York: Rosen Publishing Group, 2001.

Periodicals

Christie Aschwanden — "Ecstasy for Agony," *Health*, July/August 2002.

Doug Bandow — "Where's the Compassion?: Forget the War on Drugs Already," *National Review Online*, December 19, 2003. www.national review.com.

Christian Bourge — "Analysis: Drug Policy Ignores Reality," United Press International, June 5, 2003. www.upi.com.

James Bovard and Joyce Nalepka — "Is Now the Right Time to Legalize Marijuana?" *Duluth (Minnesota) News-Tribune*, October 16, 2000. www.duluthnewstribune.com.

David Boyum — "Prohibition and Legalization: Beyond the False Dichotomy," *Social Research*, Fall 2001.

David Boyum and Mark A.R. Kleiman — "Breaking the Drug-Crime Link," *Public Interest*, Summer 2003.

Laural Chesky and Bruce Willey — "Medical Marijuana Madness," *Good Times*, October 10, 2002.

James Cole — "Hemp No Cure for Tobacco Ills," *World Tobacco*, July 2002.

Drug Legalization

Ann Coulter	"Don't Do Drug Legalization," *Jewish World Review*, September 29, 2000.
Catherine Cowan	"Banned in the USA," *State Government News*, April 2002.
Jamie Dettmer	"Mexico's Real War on Drugs," *Insight on the News*, September 10, 2001.
Families Against Mandatory Minimums	"Prison Crisis," May 11, 2004.
Gustavo de Greiff	"A Failed Strategy: The War on Drugs," *Narco News Bulletin*, May 1, 2002. www.narconews.com.
Gary E. Johnson	"The Case for Drug Legalization," *World & I*, February 2000.
John L. Kane	"The War on Drugs: An Impossible Dream," Independent Institute, December 15, 2000. www.independent.org.
Daniel Longest	"Drug Laws Are Necessary and Logical," *Collegiate Times*, September 30, 2000.
Jeffrey A. Miron	"The Economics of Drug Prohibition and Drug Legalization," *Social Research*, Fall 2001.
Salim Muwakkil	"A New Opposition Front in the Drug War," *Chicago Tribune*, January 20, 2003.
Ethan Nadelmann	"Addicted to Failure," *Foreign Policy*, July/August 2003.
Ethan Nadelmann	"No Longer Hope for Progress," *Counselor*, August 2002.
Alan Schlosser	"Asset Seizure Laws: A Civil Liberties Casualty of the War on Drugs," American Civil Liberties Union of Northern California, October 27, 2000. www.aclunc.org.
Jacob Sullum	"Altered Minds: Former Drug Warriors Turn Against Prohibition," *Gwinnett (County, GA) Daily Post*, 2003.
Jennifer Thomas	"Early Marijuana Use Leads to Later Drug Use," January 21, 2003. www.drkoop.com.
Mike Tidwell	"America's Misguided Drug War," *(Sonoma, CA) Coastal Post*, January 2000. www.coastalpost.com.
Ian Vasqez	"Cato Handbook for Congress: The International War on Drugs," Cato Institute, 2003. www.cato.org.

Index

on marijuana use, 44
on marijuana use among youth, 192–93
as gateway drug, 194
National Inquirer (newspaper), 140
National Institutes of Health, on medical effects of marijuana, 62–63
National Organization for the Reform of Marijuana Laws (NORML), 131, 169
petition of, for marijuana reclassification, 171
National Parents' Resource Institute for Drug Education, 48
National Review (magazine), 125, 182
National Rifle Association (NRA), 15
needle-exchange programs, 86
facilitate drug use, 132
prevent HIV spread, 168
Nelson, Jack, 69
Netherlands, drug policies of, 55–56, 121
drug use and, 122
New England Journal of Medicine, 18
New Republic (magazine), 142
New York Observer (newspaper), 163
New York Times (newspaper), 44
Nixon, Richard, 43
Northwest Center for Health and Safety, 140
No Safe Haven: Children of Substance-Abusing Parents (National Center on Addiction and Substance Abuse), 128

Office of National Drug Control Policy, 43, 44, 63
on state/local spending on antidrug efforts by, 59
Omnibus Anti-Drug Abuse Act (1988), 87
Operation Containment, 30
opium
international regulation of, 53
use of, before drug prohibition, 105
Organized Crime Drug Enforcement Task Force (OCDETF), 21, 25–26
Orlando Sentinel (newspaper), 143
Ostrow, Ronald J., 69

Paddock, Susan M., 173
parents, should oppose drug policy liberalization, 130–33
Partnership for a Drug-Free America, 85
Penne, Michael A., 192
Perez de Cuellar, Javier, 50
personal autonomy, vs. common good, 158–59
Pew Research Center, 172
Phoenix House, 48–49, 86
police
are subjected to drug-related hostility, 97–98
corruption among, drug legalization would reduce, 104–105
post-traumatic stress disorder, use of Ecstasy in treatment of, 10
prevention
levels of, 157
sanctions as part of, 157–58
Priority Drug Trafficking Organization (PDTO)

initiative, 20, 25
prisons
blacks in
as percentage of all drug offenders, 73, 111
vs. white drug offenders, 111
population in
for drug-related offenses, 69
vs. other offenses, 111, 128–29
federal, 87
growth in, 109
Prohibition (1920–1933), 52, 58
analogy with war on drugs, 46
fall in murder rates after repeal of, 71
led to use of hard liquor, 103
organized crime and, 60, 102–103
property confiscation, 15–16, 69
laws on, should be modified, 95
see also asset forfeiture

racial profiling, should be eliminated, 79
Ragavan, Chitra, 142
RAND Drug Policy Research Center, 49, 116, 173
Reagan, Ronald, 43
Reagan administration, 144, 167
Reefer Madness (film), 189
referenda. *See* ballot initiatives
research
is stifled by war on drugs, 69
as part of alternative drug policies, 94–95
Reuter, Peter, 47, 118
Risley, David E., 145
Rockefeller, Nelson, 87
Rockefeller drug laws, 87, 88
Rolling Stone (magazine), 143
Rosenbaum, Marsha, 10
Rosenthal, Mitchell S., 86, 90

Santamaria, Joe, 153
Schmoke, Kurt, 60, 64, 163
Schultz, George, 50, 60, 163
Sentencing Project, 110
Sentencing Reform Act (1984), 148
Shalala, Donna, 86
Siragusa, Charles, 53, 54
Soros, George, 85, 86, 131, 141, 190
Souter, David, 172
Southeast Asia, DEA operations in, 28
Sperling, John, 190
Spillane, Joseph, 121
state(s)
drug incarceration rates in, correlation with drug use, 116
federal government should respect marijuana laws of, 178–80
medical marijuana referenda in, 42, 64, 171–72, 187
Clinton administration's response to, 63
disguise legalization efforts, 135–36
prisons
incarceration for drug offenses in, 126–27
for blacks vs. whites, 112–13, 114–15

incarceration rates in, 79
spending on antidrug efforts by, 59
Stevens, John Paul, 172
Stewart, William H., 140, 141
Substance Abuse and Mental Health Services Administration (SAMHSA), 40, 115, 137
Sunday, Billy, 52
Supreme Court
on asset forfeiture, 15
on medical marijuana, 165, 172
Surgeon General's Report (1964), 140, 141
surveys
on marijuana regulation, 164
on medical marijuana, 172
vs. recreational marijuana use, 179
synthetic drugs, 24–25

Taylor, Stuart, Jr., 165
temperance movement, 52
focus on drugs by, 53
Tenth Amendment, 60
Terry, Luther L., 140, 141
THC (tetrahydrocannabinol), 144, 187
effects of, on memory, 189–90
vs. marijuana, as medicine, 132
Time (magazine), 142
tobacco, 119–20
tobacco industry
has stake in marijuana legalization, 143–44
linkage between media and, 140–41
"To Smoke or Not to Smoke—that is Still the Question" (Frank), 140–41
trafficking
DEA investigations of, 27–28
marijuana, patterns of, 23
treatment/prevention programs, 79
vs. incarceration, 90–91
vs. mandatory minimum sentences, in crime reduction, 116
U.S. federal spending on, 83
True Magazine, 140
Twenty-First Amendment, 58, 64

Unitarian Universalist Association, 92
United Nations
drug conventions of, 53
U.S. pressure on drug policies of, 56
United Nations International Drug Control Programme (UNDCP), 39, 56
United States
homicide rates, in Holland vs., 56
incarceration rates in European Union vs., 112
see also government, U.S.

United States and International Drug Control, 1909–1997 (Bewley-Taylor), 53
United States Sentencing Commission, 148–49
United States Sentencing Guidelines (United States Sentencing Commission), 149
U.S. News & World Report (magazine), 142

Vanity Fair (magazine), 142
violence
alcohol-related, 105
liberalization of drug policies would increase, 125–29
con, 97–99
marijuana dealing and, 191

Wagner, Susan, 140
Wall Street Journal (newspaper), 59, 166, 183
Walters, John P., 17, 189
on progress in war on drugs, 41
on treatment programs, 167
war on drugs
effects of, on urban minority communities, 76, 78
has blurred distinction between drug use and drug abuse, 92
has claimed innocent lives, 68
rationale for support of, 42–43
scientific research is hindered by, 69
should focus on
demand reduction, 47–49
supply reduction, 20–36
successes in, 41, 138–39
undesirable police actions in, 45
Washington Post (newspaper), 191
Washington Times (newspaper), 142
Webster, William, 44
Wilson, James Q., 43, 85
Wilson, Pete, 41
Wodak, Alex, 156
World Health Organization (WHO), 57
Wu, Li-Tzy, 192

Young, Francis L., 11, 171
youth
drug use among, 82, 115
is increasing, 133
marijuana use among, 192–94
vs. alcohol use, 138
delinquent behavior and, 128, 183

Zeese, Kevin B., 82, 86
Zuckerman, Seth, 178